The Beam and the Mote

The Beam and the Mote

On Blame, Standing, and Normativity

KASPER LIPPERT-RASMUSSEN

OXFORD
UNIVERSITY PRESS

OXFORD
UNIVERSITY PRESS

Oxford University Press is a department of the University of Oxford. It furthers
the University's objective of excellence in research, scholarship, and education
by publishing worldwide. Oxford is a registered trade mark of Oxford University
Press in the UK and certain other countries.

Published in the United States of America by Oxford University Press
198 Madison Avenue, New York, NY 10016, United States of America.

Library of Congress Cataloging-in-Publication Data
Names: Lippert-Rasmussen, Kasper, 1964– author.
Title: The beam and the mote : on blame, standing, and normativity /
Kasper Lippert-Rasmussen.
Description: New York, NY : Oxford University Press, [2024] |
Includes bibliographical references and index.
Identifiers: LCCN 2023022736 (print) | LCCN 2023022737 (ebook) |
ISBN 9780197544594 (hardback) | ISBN 9780197544617 (epub)
Subjects: LCSH: Blame. | Hypocrisy.
Classification: LCC BJ1535 .F3 L57 2024 (print) | LCC BJ1535 .F3 (ebook) |
DDC 205—dc23/eng/20230717
LC record available at https://lccn.loc.gov/2023022736
LC ebook record available at https://lccn.loc.gov/2023022737

DOI: 10.1093/oso/9780197544594.001.0001

Printed by Integrated Books International, United States of America

Contents

Acknowledgments

A previous version of this book was presented at a Louvain la Neuve-Aarhus online workshop, September 24, 2020. In addition to Andreas Bengtson, Göran Duus-Otterström, Søren Flinch Midtgaard, Tom Parr, and Jens Tyssedal, I thank my assigned commentators—Sara Amighetti, Axel Gosseries, Andrei Poama, and Manuel De Araujo E Sa Valente Rosa—for insightful reflections and criticisms. A later version was presented at a GOODPOL workshop, February 19, 2021. I thank Maria Seim and my assigned commentators Andreas Carlson, Jakob Elster, Hallvard Fossheim, Elinor Mason, and Patrick Todd for very helpful comments. Chapter 6 was presented at a another GOODPOL workshop, September 10, 2020. I thank Ludvig Beckman, Simone Chambers, Jakob Elster, Robert Huseby, and Thea Isaksen for their thoughtful comments. Chapter 7 was presented December 1, 2022, at the Department of Philosophy, Lund University. Thanks to Henrik Andersson, Mattias Gunnemyr, Ingvar Johanson, Shervin Mirzaeighazi, Björn Petersson, Wlodek Rabinowicz, Toni Rønnow-Rasmussen, Daniel Telech, Patrick Todd, and Alexander Velichkov for great critical feedback.

Daniel Statman kindly read the last version of the manuscript, and I am grateful for his many helpful suggestions and constructive criticisms. Kartik Upadhyaya and Colleen Macnamara generously provided incisive written and oral comments on Chapter 5, and the former on a paper that later became part of Chapter 2 as well. Andreas T. Schmidt kindly forwarded penetrating comments on Chapter 6. Didde Boisen Andersen, Søren Flinch Midtgaard, Astrid Fly Oredsson, Marion Godman, Anne-Sofie Greisen Højlund, Jake Lehrle-Fry, Lauritz Munch, Simone Sommer Degn, and Fabio Wolkenstein gave thorough comments on parts of Chapter 7 (and in Astrid's case, also on the introduction).

I owe a special debt to Zofia Stemplowska for a couple of crucial conversations on the topic of standing to blame and forgiveness.

Kate Thulin helped me improve the English.

Parts of Chapter 3 draw on material published in "Why the Moral Equality Account of the Hypocrite's Lack of Standing to Blame Fails," *Analysis* 80.4 (2020): 666–674. Parts of Chapter 5 use material published as "Praising without Standing," *Journal of Ethics* 26 (2022): 229–246. Parts of Chapter 6 overlap with material published as "Forgiving the Mote in your Sister's Eye: On Standingless Forgiveness," *Journal of Ethics and Social Philosophy* 23 (2022): 248–272. I thank these journals for permission to reproduce material from the respective articles.

Finally, I thank the Carlsberg Foundation for a Semper Ardens grant (CF17-0036) and the Danish National Research Foundation (DNRF144) for its generous financial support in relation to my work on this book manuscript. Also, I thank the Oxford Centre for the Study of Social Justice (CSSJ) for hosting me on two occasions (2020 and 2023), where I was working on this book.

Introduction

I.1. Topic and Main Aims

"Thou hypocrite, first cast out the beam out of thine own eye; and then shalt thou see clearly to cast out the mote out of thy brother's eye" (Matthew 7:3–5), says the Bible.[1] The "porridge-pot calls the kettle black-arse," says the nonreligious proverb, making its first known literary appearance in Cervantes's (2008, 736) *Don Quixote*. Both sayings point to the same deep fact about the nature of blame—i.e., that blame is interpersonal in that there is something problematic about one person blaming another when the blamer's faults are similar (the pot is black too) or even greater (one would rather have a mote than have a beam in one's eye).[2] Such blaming is hypocritical and, typically, we see ourselves as entitled to dismiss any hypocritical blame that is directed at us. In fact, we often react quite strongly to being subjected to hypocritical blame.

When we dismiss hypocritical blame, we might not deny that we have done something blameworthy (though, of course, we might). Accordingly, we need not think that we would be entitled to dismiss blame from those who have a better moral record than our blamer. After all, those who dismiss their hypocritical brother's blame in the biblical saying *do* have a mote in their eye. Some think this renders our typical responses to hypocritical blame puzzling. If we have done something blameworthy, should not others—even people worse than us—be in a position to blame us for that?[3] If the kettle is

---

[1] The biblical saying indicates that one problem with the beam is that it blurs one's moral vision. While such blurring no doubt often takes place, this is not my main concern in this book.

[2] Blame and, generally, norms pertaining to standing are also interpersonal in other senses, as will become clear as we proceed, especially in Chapter 7. Initially, we can simply note that blaming is interpersonal in that our response to blame is thought to appropriately depend—at least, also—on a comparison of the blamer and the blame and them only.

[3] In this book, I say nothing about what makes us blameworthy, nor anything about whether anyone ever is blameworthy for anything, e.g., in light of the putative nonexistence of free will. This reflects that its main blame-related topic is not blameworthiness as such but the norms regulating how we hold each other, ourselves included, accountable (on the assumption that we are accountable), where blaming is one way of holding accountable.

The Beam and the Mote. Kasper Lippert-Rasmussen, Oxford University Press. © Oxford University Press 2024.
DOI: 10.1093/oso/9780197544594.003.0001

black, why should the pot not be in a position to say so, regardless of its own constitution? Why should not anyone have the standing to state any truth?

Perhaps anyone does have standing to state any fact.[4] However, this has no bearing on standing to blame because, as I shall argue (Section 1.2.1), to blame is to do more than simply state a fact. In paradigmatic cases, to blame is to demand that the blamee respond in a certain way, e.g., by offering an apology, expressing remorse, or acknowledging a duty to provide reparations (Watson 2004, 229–230, 272–280). To issue such demands requires standing. I will argue that hypocrisy manifests, as our two proverbs above suggest, one way in which one can lack standing. Moreover, as our strong reactions to being subjected to hypocritical blame perhaps indicate, we think hypocritical blame often wrongs the blamee.

While hypocrisy in relation to blame is the issue that has drawn philosophers' attention to issues of standing most effectively, many of the same points that apply to hypocritical blame apply not just to other types of moral blame, e.g., meddlesome blame, but also to types of moral responses other than blaming, e.g., praising or forgiving, and even responses that do not in any straightforward way involve holding others morally accountable, e.g., encouraging, as well. As this list suggests, the issue of standing is not even distinct to moral norms and to holding each other morally accountable, but arises in connection with nonmoral norms as well, e.g., prudential and epistemic norms, and with nonmoral accountability. Hence, a second main aim of this book—in addition to the aim of casting light on standing to blame—is to show that issues of standing generalize in this way, beyond the well-recognized case of hypocritical moral blame and even beyond the scope of moral norms. The book's third main aim is to draw attention to the interpersonal nature of a large part of morality, i.e., second-order moral norms regulating our holding one another accountable in relation to first-order moral norms, and, more generally, of a large part of normativity.[5] Attending to these facts has important implications for how we should understand the distinction between consequentialism and deontology and the two moral theories' relation to common-sense morality, as I will argue.

---

[4] As will become clear later (see Section 5.6 on love letters and aesthetic qualities), I am skeptical of this being so.

[5] "Normative judgements concern oughts: what one ought to do, desire, believe, infer, conclude, think, feel and so on. . . . 'Normativity', as philosophers generally use the term, is what normative properties have in common" (Darwall 2001).

I.2. Structure

To realize these three main aims, and several ancillary ones, Chapter 1 offers a definition of hypocritical blame; of what it is to have standing to blame; and of what it is to dismiss blame as standingless. On my account, to have standing to blame is for the blamer to have either the liberty right against the addressee to blame them, or a claim right against the blamee to a response to their blame. Accordingly, to dismiss someone's blame as standingless is to deny either that the blamer has the liberty right against the addressee to blame them, or to deny that the recipient of blame has a duty to the blamer to respond to the blame. Or, to put the latter point differently: that the blamer has the moral authority to put the blamee under a moral obligation to respond to their blame (Piovarchy 2020, 610–614). As this account indicates, my focus in this book is on what I call communicative blame, as opposed to, say, blame understood as an emotion. Chapter 1 explains this notion of communicative blame and argues that it is important, but also concedes that blame is a multidimensional phenomenon, not all dimensions of which are covered by the notion of communicative blame. Most people find hypocritical blame objectionable—perhaps even morally wrong—not only when it is expressed, but also when it is amount to, say, unexpressed private hypocritical resentment of one's wrongdoer. A complete account of hypocritical blame should say something about hypocritical private blame.[6] However, as indicated, this is not my main topic; but as we go along, I shall note whenever our arguments regarding communicative blame cast significant light on the topic of private blame.

While Chapter 1 sets out the essentials of my definition of hypocritical blame, Chapter 2 addresses several complications that this definition, or for that matter the complexity of hypocritical blame as such, gives rise to. For instance, a blamer can hypocritically bear a grudge against someone without ever publicly expressing the blame. Essentially, this complication, in addition to the others that I discuss in Chapter 2, indicates possible

---

[6] Some might even think that, ideally, we want a unified account of private and communicative hypocritical blame. I agree that providing such an account would be nice. However, I am not sure that we have any a priori reason to expect it to be possible. After all, communicative hypocritical blame can be wrong in ways that private hypocritical blame cannot be; e.g., it is humiliating to be subjected to the former but not the latter, and vice versa; e.g., communicative hypocritical blame need not involve the blamer's (implicit) denial of moral equality. A further reason against the a priori expectation is that some think one cannot act morally impermissibly simply by virtue of one's mental acts (Sher 2021), which suggests that while communicative hypocritical blame can be morally impermissible, private hypocritical blame cannot.

limitations of the discussion in Chapter 1. But it also helps us to see better the contours of the conceptual terrain that my definition of (dismissing) blame (as standingless) covers. Independently of these complications, an account of standingless hypocritical blame should also say something about what it is about hypocrisy that undermines the blamer's standing. To satisfy this desideratum, I defend the claim that the hypocrite's lack of standing to blame is due to a lack of commitment to the norm to which they appeal in their blame. I also criticize the main competing account, i.e., that hypocrites' lack of standing is due to the fact that in blaming hypocritically, they (implicitly) deny or act against the equality of moral standing. A close cousin of this account—though an account of a different matter—reappears in the next chapter.

Chapter 3 builds on the conceptual groundwork provided in Chapters 1 and 2 and asks why hypocritical blame is morally objectionable. Intuitively, while hypocritical blame might be deficient in ways that are not, at least in themselves, immoral, e.g., a hypocritical blamer might be irrational because inconsistent, it also involves moral flaws. The challenge then is to explain what those moral flaws are. Chapter 3 examines eight different accounts of what renders hypocritical blame morally wrongful—if not always all things considered, then always (or at least often) pro tanto. I argue that the most promising account—the moral equality account—holds that wrongful hypocritical blame is wrongful because of how the hypocritical blamer relates to the blamee as if the latter is an inferior. This is the main takeaway point from Chapter 3. This point is particularly important in light of my embrace in Chapter 2 of the commitment account of standing to blame, because when conjoined, these two claims entail that what undermines standing to blame is not what renders standingless blame morally wrongful. This is so even if these properties (i.e., those from which the standinglessness and wrongfulness of hypocritical blame derive) are related in certain intimate ways. Eventually—in Chapter 7—we will see further support for this claim about the gap between what undermines standing and what makes standingless addresses morally wrong.

Chapters 4 to 6 generalize the findings of the first three chapters to other kinds of standingless moral blame and to moral responses other than blame. As in the previous chapters, Chapter 4's focus is blame, but it examines sources for why a blamer lacks standing other than hypocrisy, e.g., because of how the blamer is complicit in what they blame the blamee for or because of meddlesomeness. On that basis, I argue that there is an irreducible plurality of conditions that must be met for having standing to blame. I also submit that neither the commitment account of what undermines standing to blame nor the moral equality account of what makes hypocritical blame morally wrongful apply to all the other sources of lack of standing surveyed in Chapter 4, although both apply to some of them. Just as blame is a complex notion, so is standing to blame.

Chapters 5 and 6 leave blame behind and extend the analytical framework of the previous chapters to two moral responses other than blaming, i.e., praising and forgiving. Like blaming, these responses are important parts of our practice of holding each other morally accountable. While there is a growing literature on standing to blame, the issues of standing to praise and standing to forgive have so far only been mentioned in passing, and these two chapters seek to remedy this situation. Chapter 5 starts by offering an explicative definition of praising, which basically understands praising as the positive complement to blaming. It then shows how praising can be dismissed as hypocritical and standingless on the same grounds as blaming. Surprisingly, it also turns out that standingless praise can be wrongful for the same reason as standingless blame; e.g., the moral equality account of the wrongfulness of hypocritical blame is naturally extended to cover hypocritical praise as well. Hence, from the perspective of standing, blaming and praising are symmetric. Finally, the chapter introduces a neutral counterpart to blaming and praising (in my special, technical sense)—praming—and shows that it too is sensitive to considerations about standing.

Chapter 6 focuses on forgiving. Essentially, to forgive—in the communicative sense of forgiveness that is my concern in this book—is to renounce the liberty right to blame or the claim right to direct a response to one's blame (or, as is typically the case, both). Accordingly, if one has no standing to blame in the first place, one cannot have standing to forgive either. Chapter 6 aims to vindicate this proposition, paying special attention to hypocritical standingless forgiveness. The chapter also shows why the moral equality account (in a suitably revised version) can explain the wrongfulness of hypocritical forgiveness, and that forgiveness can be standingless for the reasons discussed in Chapter 4 in relation to blame. Finally, it introduces a negative complement to forgiving—fromtaking—to extend our conceptual map of ways of holding others morally accountable, and submits that considerations of standing apply even to that response. The main claim of the structurally similar Chapters 5 and 6 is that we should extend the scope of our discussions of standing from their present narrow focus on blame to other ways of holding people morally accountable,[7] i.e., praising and forgiving (and the two closely related acts introduced in these two chapters).[8]

Chapter 7 expands the scope of the theory of standing further and in two different ways. Blaming, praising, and forgiving are all directed at what the targets have done or what they were. Encouraging someone to do something—perhaps by demanding that they do it—however, is future-oriented. It involves holding people accountable, in a broad sense, for what they are going to do. In Chapter 7, I show that such encouragements can be standingless in ways parallel to blaming etc. Chapter 7 then proceeds to argue that issues of standing are not distinct to morality. This is what one should expect given that one can encourage someone to act in a certain way for nonmoral reasons. For that purpose, I then turn to epistemic blame to exhibit how it too can be dismissed when hypocritical; e.g., I cannot hypocritically blame you for being gullible if I believe all sorts of conspiracy theories about the 2020 US election being stolen etc. In fact, epistemic blame can be standingless in most of the same ways in which moral blame can be standingless. Having shown that standing applies outside morality, I return to morality to explore what the morality of standing implies in relation to a basic question in ethical theory, i.e., whether we should embrace a consequentialist or a nonconsequentialist ethical theory. I argue that the former cannot accommodate the morality of standing, but that it is also the case, though less clearly so, that the morality of standing also fails to fit standard characterizations of nonconsequentialist ethical theory. Specifically, I show why the morality of standing cannot be fully analyzed using the notions of moral options and moral constraints. Instead, it points to a third way in which nonconsequentialist ethical theory, and for that matter our common-sense moral commitments, differs from consequentialism, i.e., that it includes as a central part the idea of moral authority. Having moral authority

---

[7] Taxonomically, we can distinguish between first- and second-order ways of holding each other responsible. First-order ways of holding each other responsible come in three species: negative (blame), positive (praise), and neutral (what I coin "praming" in Section 5.7). Second-order ways of holding each other responsible address the fact that a certain first-order relation obtains between the agent and the patient of that relation. One can then draw two different distinctions between indirect ways of holding responsible. First, there are agent-initiated (apologizing—Section 6.10) and patient-initiated (forgiving—most of Chapter 6) ways of holding responsible in a second-order way. Second, there are negative (e.g., refusing to accept an apology or what I coin "fromtaking" in Section 6.8) and positive ways of holding responsible in a second-order way (e.g., accepting an apology).

[8] The subject of standing to hold responsible falls under the more general topic of standing norms, where such norms regulate many illocutionary acts other than acts of holding (morally) responsible. Chapter 7 addresses some such acts. Issues of standing extend beyond what I address in this book; see, for example, O'Brien (2021) on whataboutisms.

implies that, on a number of issues, one can change what other agents are morally permitted to do irrespective of how one affects the goodness of the consequences of what they can do and irrespective of how their exercise of that authority affects one's own interests.[9] I also argue that the morality of standing highlights how the second-order norms that regulate our holding each other accountable are conditional in that what one is permitted to do is conditional on the degree to which one complies with the relevant first-order norms noncompliance with which one holds others accountable. This conditionality casts important light on the recent, growing literature on moral encroachment. More specifically, I argue that stereotype users are not necessarily wronged when others form beliefs about them based on stereotypes and, thus, that the latter might be epistemically justified in doing so. The moral stakes involved, i.e., the risk that they will wrong others by forming beliefs about them based on stereotypes, are not as high as they otherwise would have been.[10] All in all, this book offers testimony on the importance of standing—certainly in relation to moral norms, but also, as Chapter 7 in particular shows, in relation to nonmoral norms and to the interpersonal nature of parts of morality.

I.3. Significance

Some might think that the issue of standing is a minor issue in moral philosophy (and beyond). They might think that even if there is something morally problematic about, say, standingless hypocritical blame, the relevant moral wrong is tiny compared to that of many other wrongful acts discussed in moral philosophy, e.g., unjust wars or the omission to help (or stop harming) the global poor.

Of course, the moral wrong involved in my blaming my siblings for the motes in their eyes despite my own beam-sized faults is a much less serious moral wrong than, say, the moral wrong of starting an unjust war or, more parochially, those personal faults of mine. Additionally, perhaps in a wide range of cases, blaming others hypocritically is morally permissible, perhaps in some cases even morally required, in view of the civilizing effects of

---

[9] This is a further sense (in addition to the one mentioned in footnote 2) in which norms of standing and, thus, moral norms are (also) interpersonal.

[10] This is not to deny that there are powerful, impersonal moral reasons why one should not stereotype stereotypers.

blame—even of the hypocritical sort (Elster 1998, 110). Even though I agree with these claims, (unsurprisingly) I nevertheless think that the topic of standing is important. First, in terms of its practical relevance, the fact that the wrong of an instance of hypocritical blaming is not in the same moral league as the wrong of starting an unjust war should be weighed against the fact that (fortunately) very few people have the option of starting such a war (on their own at any rate), whereas engaging in (or being tempted to engage in) or being subjected to hypocritical blame is part of everyone's everyday moral life. Presumably, other things being equal, the more often we are confronted with a particular moral issue, the more practically important it is.[11]

Second, whether or not people *should* care as much about hypocritical blame as they do, the fact is that people *are* hugely concerned with hypocritical blame—and, for that matter, hypocrisy in general. This is true not only in personal relations, where hypocritically blaming others is one of the most effective ways of alienating them. It is also true in politics, where politicians routinely set off scandals for engaging in standingless blame or other forms of hypocritical address (see the opening example in Chapter 1; Aikin and Talisse 2008).[12]

Third, philosophy is an academic discipline, and while one of the benefits it provides is elucidation of practically important problems, this is not the only good we want from philosophy. Issues can be important in philosophy, including moral philosophy, for many reasons other than that they are practically important; e.g., the issue of, say, the nature of causality is important to a philosophical understanding of the world even if which philosophical accounts of causation are correct makes little or no difference to

[11] It is also important not to compare the wrong of an individual instance of hypocritical blame with the wrong of a set of many, say, instances of failures to address the situation of the global poor. We should instead compare the latter to a policy of, say, hypocritically blaming poor people for their predicament, where that policy involves a similarly large number of instances of hypocritical blame. Even when we do so, however, the moral problem of hunger is surely of a different order than the moral problem of a culture of hypocrisy.

[12] Admittedly, being overly concerned with hypocrisy has its dangers too (Aikin and Talisse 2008; O'Brien 2021, 11). Justified charges of hypocrisy are often used to unjustifiably fail to address the valid points that people raise, albeit in a hypocritical way. Additionally, sometimes people refrain from making valuable interventions in public debates out of warranted fears of being accused of hypocrisy. This is particularly true of privileged people with leftist views, who enjoy the benefits that privileged people typically enjoy but find it indefensible that they, and others like them, should enjoy these benefits. And as Dover (2019, 387; see also 413–414) puts it: "[T]hose who demand that others 'practice what they preach' are indeed often more interested in silencing preachers than in challenging them to improve their behavior"; cf. footnote 1, Chapter 1, on the case of Al Gore. Such bad consequences of being preoccupied with hypocrisy, however, do not cast doubt on a *theory* of standing.

our understanding of which instruments we can use to achieve our aims etc. Hence, even if issues of standing were not practically important, they could still be important to philosophy for other reasons. This is indeed (also) the case. As I have indicated, I shall argue that the issue of standing casts important light on the interpersonal nature of part of morality, indeed on normativity in general.

1

Hypocritical Blame

1.1. Introduction

Jack is a philosopher. He often travels to conferences by plane. Sometimes this involves intercontinental flights. On his vacations, he flies to places like Bali and the Maldives. Jack easily flies more than 30,000 miles every year. Jack has two siblings, Al and Greta.[1] One day he has two phone conversations, first with Al and then an hour later with Greta. During the first conversation, Al starts blaming Jack:

> Jack, you really shouldn't fly that much. We all have a moral duty to do our share to reduce global warming, and you are very far indeed from doing your part. I simply fail to get how you can be so indifferent to what you ought to do. How can attending philosophy conferences or swimming in the Indian Ocean be more important to you than not contributing to flooding and droughts and worse across the world?

Amazingly, Greta makes the same complaint ad verbatim to and about Jack half an hour later when she talks to him. Suppose Jack replies in the exact same way to his siblings:

> Perhaps I fly too much.[2] However, I refuse to be held accountable for doing so by you. If you like, we can discuss our, including my, moral obligations

---

[1] Think of Al Gore and Greta Thunberg. To motivate using "Al" consider the complaint that arose shortly after Al Gore's release of the excellent movie *An Inconvenient Truth* in 2007 that Gore's luxury mansion used roughly "more than 20 times the national average of gas and electricity." A right-wing think tank complained: "As the spokesman of choice for the global warming movement, Al Gore has to be willing to walk the walk, not just talk the talk, when it comes to home energy use," http://news.bbc.co.uk/1/hi/6401489.stm (accessed 26 January 2021; cf. Alterman 2004 on Gulfstream liberals). To see the motivation for using "Greta" consider her carbon-neutral journeys via boat across the Atlantic to participate in climate change summits; see https://www.bbc.com/news/newsbeat-50659 318 (accessed 26 January 2021).

[2] Some philosophers deny that we have individual moral obligations in relation to climate change in view of the fact, inter alia, that of each (normal) individual it is true that whatever they do, it makes no difference to climate change-related harms to others (Sinnott-Armstrong 2010; for an

The Beam and the Mote. Kasper Lippert-Rasmussen, Oxford University Press. © Oxford University Press 2024.
DOI: 10.1093/oso/9780197544594.003.0002

in relation to climate change in general, but I will not address your blaming me for flying too much, e.g., by apologizing or by engaging in collective deliberation with you about what I can do to improve my ways.

If you think like me, you think that the following piece of information is relevant to how we should think about the appropriateness of Jack's replies to his siblings: Al is a very successful politician and in any given year he normally flies at least three times as much as Jack does. Greta, however, is a climate activist, who, in the interest of promoting the cause of fighting climate change, almost always travels by train, and who in countless other ways has accepted significant costs and inconveniences to reduce her carbon footprint. If we share an outlook in the way I have suggested, we agree that Jack's reply to Al might be appropriate, while his reply to Greta is not. This is so even though the content of the blame that Al and Greta direct at Jack is identical. While Greta has the standing to blame Jack for his excessive flying habits, Al has no such standing. More generally, I accept the following claim, which much of this book defends and explores:

The appropriate dismissal claim: if X blames Y hypocritically for ϕ-ing, then the facts that render X's blame hypocritical give Y a reason to dismiss X's blame.[3]

overview of critical responses to this view, see Fragnière 2016). Whether or not skeptics of individual climate change-related duties are right has no bearing on the discussion here. In any case, Jack can dismiss blame from Al on the grounds of Al's own flying habit (see next paragraph). If the skeptics are right, Jack can dismiss blame from Al (and Greta) on the additional ground that what he does is not blameworthy.

[3] One virtue of saying that the reason for dismissing blame is the facts by virtue of which blame is hypocritical, e.g., facts about the blamer's own past faulty behavior, and not the fact that the blamer's blame itself is hypocritical is that the latter way of putting it suggests that the blamee has reason to dismiss the blame in question prior to its being voiced (Fritz and Miller 2019b, 554). Additionally, my focus here is on hypocritical blame, and not on hypocrisy in general. One can act hypocritically in many ways other than through blaming. A vegan who often airs her view on why one ought not to eat meat, though she never blames anyone for eating meat, but secretly eats (nonvegan) cheeseburgers whenever she has the chance to do so without running into someone she knows, is a hypocrite—"she says one thing but does another" (Isserow and Klein 2017, 192; Rossi 2021; Schemmel 2021, 172; Chapters 5, 6, and 7.2)—even if she never engages in hypocritical blame. Many forms of hypocrisy do not involve blame, but, say, not practicing as one preaches for no good excusing or justifying reason, or actions that involve pretending—perhaps even to oneself—to be better than one is (see Crisp and Cowton 1994, 343–344; Dover 2019, 389; Rossi 2021; Smilansky 1994, 73; Statman 1997; Szabados 1979, 241–253). For a fascinating empirical study of factors that affect whether laypersons classify something as hypocritical, see Laurent and Clark (2019).

There are various ways in which one can dismiss blame, and I offer a more precise account thereof in Section 1.3. As a first approximation, we can say that, at the least, dismissing blame is matter of denying any moral obligation to the blamer on the part of the blamee to do the things that one normally does in response to blame from someone with the standing to blame, e.g., admitting faults, apologizing, inviting suggestions for how one should make up for one's wrongdoing, making amends for past wrongdoing, publicly announcing plans for future improvements, etc. (Anonymous, forthcoming, 6). Dismissing blame in this sense is consistent with conceding that one has acted wrongfully and, indeed, is blameworthy for having done so. Jack could concede to Al that he is blameworthy for flying as much as he does while, at the same time, asserting that, unlike Greta, Al is in no position to blame him for that. Indeed, dismissing blame in this sense is also compatible with doing the things that people normally do in response to blame from blamers with standing, e.g., explaining oneself, while notifying the blamer that one does not see oneself as being under a duty owed *to the blamer* to do those things and that one does not see the blamer's criticisms as providing a reason to provide this sort of uptake.

The appropriate dismissal claim is weak in the sense that it does not imply that the object of hypocritical blame has an *all things considered* reason to dismiss the hypocritical blame.[4] Perhaps in some cases I have an all-things-considered reason not to dismiss blame that I also have a pro tanto reason to dismiss on account of hypocrisy on the part of the blamer, e.g., because my accepting blame will cultivate good dispositions in others. Even so, some philosophers reject it, and though I think the claim is eminently plausible, in Section 2.7 I address the reasons that some philosophers have canvassed against it. For the moment, I shall simply rely on the assumption that, like me, readers will find the appropriate dismissal claim sufficiently plausible to find it worthwhile to ask the following two questions, which the present chapter is devoted to answering: What is it to blame hypocritically, and what is it to dismiss blame on the ground that the blamer has no standing to blame?

Section 1.2 offers a definition of hypocritical blame and Section 1.3 one of what it is to have standing to blame and, thus, of what it is to dismiss blame as standingless. Section 1.4 briefly and critically reviews three alternative accounts of what it is (not) to have standing to blame. Section 1.5 concludes.

---

[4] Typically, however, there is no strong reason why one should not dismiss hypocritical blame and, thus, typically there is an overall reason to dismiss hypocritical blame.

The main takeaway point from this chapter is that to dismiss blame on grounds of hypocrisy is to deny either that the blamer has the liberty right to issue the demands for an uptake typically involved in blame or to deny, inter alia, that the blamee has any obligation to their blamer to provide them with an uptake to these demands. This core claim, as well as the chapter in general, sets the stage for the discussion in Chapter 2 of a number of complications and finer details in relation to the account of hypocritical blame and standing to blame offered in the present chapter; for the exploration in Chapter 3 of what makes hypocritical blame pro tanto morally wrongful; and for the discussion in Chapter 4 of ways of not having the standing to blame other than being hypocritical.

1.2. When Is Blame Hypocritical?

To know whether hypocritical blame can be dismissed and, if so, what it is to dismiss hypocritical blame (questions I return to in Sections 1.3 and 1.4), we need to know what hypocritical blame is in the first place.[5] Here is the definition of (paradigmatic) hypocritical blame that I will use in this book and which I explicate in this section and defend and examine below in light of several complications (Sections 1.3–1.5 and Sections 2.2–2.6):

X hypocritically blames$_p$ Y for ϕ-ing if, and only if

(1) X blames$_p$ Y for ϕ-ing (*the blaming condition*);

(2) X believes or should believe that they themself have done something that is both relevantly similar to ϕ-ing and contextually relevant (*the incoherence condition*);

(3) in a way that does not reflect a sheer coincidence, either X does not to a suitable degree or in a suitable way, make themself or accept themself being made the target of blame for their conduct that is relevantly similar to ϕ-ing (*the no-self-blame condition*);[6]

---

[5] My focus here is on defining an act of hypocritical blaming, not on defining a hypocritical blamer, i.e., one whose character is such that they are disposed to engage in hypocritical blame. Obviously, the two endeavors are connected; e.g., the "not reflect a sheer coincidence" qualification might render acts of hypocritical blame conditional on a hypocritical character. But one can blame out of character (Telech and Tierney 2019, 32 n. 19). Accordingly, a nonhypocrite can blame hypocritically. Similarly, a hypocrite can blame nonhypocritically.

[6] Suppose that a blamer has not done something like what they blame their blamee$_1$ for, but that the blamer also believes (on equally good grounds) that a blamee$_2$ has done something like the blamee$_1$. Suppose also that the blamer is not differently related to the two such that it is justified to blame

(4) it is neither (a) the case that X believes there are morally relevant differences between blaming their own conduct relevantly similar to φ-ing, on the one hand, and blaming Y's φ-ing, on the other hand, that justify their blaming Y for φ-ing and not blaming themselves for their own conduct relevantly similar to φ-ing to the relevant degree or in the relevant way, nor (b) the case that X has a belief to this effect but that X has it for reasons that they can or should be able to see are not sufficient reasons (*the no-justification condition*).[7]

This is a definition of paradigmatic hypocritical blame as signaled by the index "ₚ" in "blamesₚ." By "paradigmatic blame" I mean the kind of blame that first and most clearly springs to mind as a case of blame (cf. Fricker 2016, 166), i.e., cases where the blamer blames the wrongdoer to their face for what they have done. There are other kinds of blame, of course, as implied by the no-self-blame condition and for the reasons set out in Sections 2.2–2.4.

Before commenting on each of the conditions in this definition, I want to make three preliminary points. First, returning to the opening example, the definition proposed here accounts nicely for the intuitive difference between Greta's and Al's blaming Jack for his flying habits. When presented with the two cases, I conjecture that most assume that the blaming and no-justification conditions are satisfied in both Greta's and Al's case, but that the incoherence and no-self-blame conditions are satisfied only in Al's case. Thus, on the proposed definition, Al's blame is hypocritical, whereas Greta's is not. Admittedly, in my description of the example I do not stipulate that the incoherence, the no-self-blame, and the no-justification conditions are satisfied in Al's case. But if we add some such stipulation to the effect that one or more of them are not, then we would probably also retract our view

---

one, but not the other, e.g., because their blamee₁ is the blamer's child and their blamee₂ is someone else's child. Some would say that such cases involve comparatively unfair blame, but that they do not constitute hypocritical (and, thus, unfair) blame (Telech and Tierney 2019; see also Fritz and Miller 2018, 132–133; Todd 2019, 370–371). While it is possible for blame of this sort to be unfair without being hypocritical, I believe that some such cases amount to unfair hypocritical blame, e.g., when one exempts those people with whom one sympathizes from blame, while subjecting to blame others with whom one does not sympathize and who have done similar wrongs.

[7] One might reject (4), saying that blame that satisfies Conditions (1)–(3) is hypocritical even though the blamer reasonably believes that it is hypocritical blame that is justified all things considered (for an analogous position regarding unfair blame that is justified overall due to "extraneous" factors, see Telech and Tierney 2019 28 n. 8, 36). However, what is crucial according to (4) is not whether there is an extraneous justifying factor, but whether the blamer *believes* that there is. One might add the requirement that this belief is not motivationally inert regarding the blame.

that Jack can dismiss Al's blame on grounds of hypocrisy. If Al thinks for good reasons that, unlike Jack, he always buys ample greenhouse gas compensation when booking a flight, the incoherence condition is not satisfied and, intuitively, he can reject the accusation of hypocrisy; if Al is perfectly willing to accept blame from Jack, which is suitably more severe than what he imposes on Jack, then the no-self-blame condition is not satisfied—suppose that during the last conversation they had, Jack blamed Al thoroughly for Al's flying habits and Al accepted this blame completely—and nor does Al's blame seem hypocritical;[8] and, finally, if Al has some reasonable justification for thinking that it is morally justified to blame Jack without blaming himself, then the no-justification condition is not satisfied, nor does Al's blame seem hypocritical. None of this is to say that Al's blame might not be objectionable for reasons not having to do with hypocrisy. As we shall see later, my definition fits intuitions about other cases of putatively (non)hypocritical blame well.

My second preliminary point concerns the fact that, strictly speaking, "only if" is unwarranted, since there are ways of hypocritically blaming others that do not satisfy the incoherence condition. Suppose that Tartuffe—the main character in Molière's 1664 play who pretends to be pious and morally virtuous but is manipulative through and through—blames Damis—the son of the patron who generously houses Tartuffe, deceived by Tartuffe's pretense—for what Tartuffe knows is regarded as a blameworthy action (Crisp and Cowton 1994, 343–344; Kittay 1982, 285). However, Tartuffe is not in the least emotionally upset about Damis's blameworthy action and, unlike in the case of Al's blaming Jack, while Tartuffe has not done anything that is relevantly like what Damis has done, Tartuffe publicly blames Damis simply to appear better than he is in the eyes of others. Many would classify this as a case of hypocritical blame. However, this is not of the sort of hypocritical blame I am interested in, since arguably, and setting aside some complications, Damis might not be able to dismiss Tartuffe's blame on the ground that Tartuffe has no standing to blame Damis by virtue of his own faults.[9] Hence, I ignore the challenge to my definition that the present case motivates.

---

[8] Admittedly, it might be the case that Al blames others without any pressure in favor of blaming them, whereas he only engages in self-blaming when under pressure to do so and that this differential pattern of blaming can be seen as hypocritical.

[9] I say more about cases like this one in Section 2.2 on private blaming and in Section 4.6 on blaming people appealing to principles that one does not accept.

Third, one implication of my definition is that blame can be hypocritical without being deceptive.[10] Many accounts of hypocrisy imply that a necessary condition for hypocrisy is deception and, thus, imply that hypocritical blame, qua being a subspecies of hypocrisy, is a specific form of deception. Typically, the claim is that the hypocritical blamer attempts to deceive an audience into thinking that they are better than they in fact are by pretending to be serious about moral principles about which they are either indifferent or very cynical. However, there need not be anything deceptive about hypocrisy; nor need hypocritical blame suggest that the blamer poses as better than they are.[11] I might hypocritically blame someone knowing that they are completely aware of all my flaws (up until this moment) and, indeed, that my now blaming them for something that I am blameworthy for will lead them to infer correctly that I am even worse than they thought. This blame would be hypocritical blame all the same. We can make an even stronger point about how hypocrisy is not even remotely conceptually tied to trying to deceive people into thinking that one is better than one in fact is. For, say, strategic reasons I might exploit my hypocritical blame to deceive someone into thinking that I am worse than I am. For example, by deceivingly appearing to hesitate in my condemnation, I manipulatively convey the impression that I am even worse at violating the standards to which I appeal in my blame than in fact I am. On the background of these three preliminary points, let me elaborate on each of the four conditions in my definition.

1.2.1. The Blaming Condition

Here is the sense of paradigmatic blaming that shall occupy me in most of this book:

X blames$_p$ Y for ϕ-ing if, and only if
(5) X communicates to Y that Y's ϕ-ing was blameworthy (*the communication condition*) and[12]

---

[10] Cf. Kittay 1982, 277, 282; see also Crisp and Cowton 1994, 343–344; Taylor 1981, 144–145; Wallace 2010, 315; Ryle 1949, 173.

[11] This is not to deny that often hypocritical acts involve an intention to deceive. Nor is it to deny that when they do, they are wrongful in part because of this objectionable intention.

[12] Because I am defining blame in a paradigmatic sense, the appearance of "blameworthy" in the definiens does not render the definition viciously circular. If you disagree, substitute "wrong (or that Y should have regarded it as such) and that Y has no excuse for ϕ-ing."

(6) X communicates to Y that X demands a suitable uptake from Y in response to their communicative act (*the demand condition*: see Mason 2019, esp. 100–107).[13]

Call this account of blame *the moral authority account of blame*. On that account, two conditions must be satisfied for something to amount to blame. First, the blamer must communicate to the addressee of the blame that the blamee has acted wrongfully by certain moral standards. Often that communication involves an utterance, but it need not. In certain contexts, raising an eyebrow can do just as well. The communication also need not be sincere. I can blame someone without believing that they have acted in a blameworthy way; e.g., I believe that blaming my child for a certain action even though they do not satisfy an epistemic condition for having acted in a blameworthy way has good effects on the child's behavior (and character). In senses of "blame" other than the one I am interested in here, this might mean that in some of these senses, I do not really blame the putative blamee.

Second, the blamer must demand uptake from the addressee.[14] The demand condition leaves open what exactly the demanded uptake must comprise. However, my main interest lies in cases where the demanded uptake is a communicative response of some sort, e.g., an apology. Of course, blaming someone also often involves some kind of expectation that the blamee acts in a certain way or harbors a certain emotion, e.g., guilt or remorse. However, because it is not clear that one can directly bring oneself to harbor emotions and because, arguably, it makes no sense to issue demands to people when the demanders know that they cannot, directly at least, comply with the demands, it is disputed whether blame involves a demand for a certain emotional response.[15]

---

[13] Whenever someone blames someone else, the former thereby complains about—and in paradigmatic cases, also to—the latter. However, the reverse is not the case; e.g., if I complain about your stealing my bike because I want compensation, while conceding that you acted under duress, I might not blame you. Similarly, if I complain about something that I think you will do in the future, I am not blaming you (yet). And if I complain about a certain unfair outcome that no one is responsible for, I might not blame anyone. However, complaining often amounts to blaming. Whether it does or not, there is an issue about having the standing to complain, which, in my view, is quite parallel to the issue of having the standing to blame.

[14] As will become apparent below, it is because blame involves the demand condition, and not the communication condition, that a hypocrite lacks the standing to blame. Perhaps there are conditions that must be satisfied for one to have the standing to communicate some fact, but, if so, these are different conditions from the ones that are involved when we deny that a hypocrite has standing to blame.

[15] Others argue that blame might involve other and weaker directives than demands, e.g., encouragements or even invitations. I might blame you by communicating to you that you have acted in a morally abominable way and inviting you to publicly reflect on this matter, even if I end my

The demand condition reflects that to blame someone, one needs to do more than communicate the message to the blamee that what they did was blameworthy.[16] This condition implies that there is a difference between believing or communicating that someone has acted in a blameworthy way, on the one hand, and blaming someone, on the other hand (Bell 2013, 265–267; Sher 2006, 112; Smith 2007, 467–471; Wallace 2010, 366–369; Watson 2004, 226–227). The former is a necessary condition for blaming but not a sufficient one.[17] Different theorists offer different accounts of what that further condition is—in some cases because they are interested in different conceptions of blame. But most accounts of what blaming is entail that blaming is doing something in addition to believing or expressing the belief that the blamee did something blameworthy, although they differ regarding what that extra component is. Let us briefly review three accounts with a view to locating the moral authority account in a wider theoretical landscape.[18]

intervention by stressing that it is up to you whether you want to address the matter (Macnamara 2013a). I agree that such instances can amount to cases of (noninsistent) blame, and that a hypocritical blamer of this kind might lack the standing to invite the blamee to reflect on their wrongdoing. In fact, it is an interesting question whether one can lack standing to blame by way of demanding an uptake but have standing to blame for the same act by way of encouraging an uptake. However, in what follows I shall focus on demand-involving blame (see also Section 5.2). A different kind of case of blame, which does not involve a demand for an uptake in the form of a communicative response to the blame directed at the blamer, but which is not simply a matter of encouraging or inviting the blamee to do better in the future, is blame in hierarchical contexts; e.g., the privates being blamed by the officer are expected not to respond but simply to do better next time. I owe this observation to Daniel Statman.

[16] Those who think that merely communicating to an agent that they did wrong suffices for blaming the agent are invited to see my topic as one that concerns a subclass of blamings. Note also that the view defended here is consistent with accepting that, in some contexts, saying to someone that they acted in a blameworthy way *is* a way of blaming them, since, conventionally, it is taken to imply a demand for an uptake (for helpful discussion, see Tognazzini, forthcoming, 15–16). Clearly, however, not all contexts are like this. Suppose you are engaged in a philosophical discussion about the nature of blame. One discussant, a friend of yours, wants to make a philosophical point about the nature of blame and for the purposes of illustration needs an example of a blameworthy act. In the obvious absence of any ulterior motives, your friend points to something blameworthy that the two of you did in the past in the context of making a philosophical point about the nature of blameworthiness. Clearly, you would misunderstand what your friend was doing if you were to respond (whether indignantly or not) by refusing to be blamed.

[17] Perhaps this is too strong on some accounts of blame. If, say, one regards blame as a matter of harboring certain reactive attitudes like resentment, perhaps one can blame without believing or communicating that the blamee did anything morally wrong (Pickard 2013). It suffices that the blamee, say, did something that was very bad for me and that I had relied on them not to do and which I accordingly resent them for doing.

[18] For overviews of different theories of the nature of blame, see Brunning and Milam (2018, 145) and Coates and Tognazzini (2013, 7–17). The one account in Coates and Tognazzini's four-partite taxonomy that I omit is cognitive theories of blame, according to which to blame essentially is

First, some philosophers argue that blame, in addition to a judgment of a certain kind, e.g., that the blamee did something blameworthy, essentially involves an additional action-related element, e.g., a desire, an intention, or a disposition to act in a certain way. In blame, we do not simply form beliefs of a certain kind about the object of blame—we respond to it as well. Call such accounts *conative accounts of blame*. One example of this account is George Sher's theory, according to which blame for an action, in addition to the belief that the blamee "has acted badly or is a bad person," involves a desire that the blamee "not have performed his past bad act or not have his current bad character," issuing from the blamer's commitment to morality (Sher 2006, 112). Another conative account is Thomas Scanlon's. On his view, what blaming requires in addition to the judgment that the blamee has acted in a way that impairs the interpersonal relations, e.g., between blamer and blamee—the cognitive component of blame on Scanlon's account—is that the blamer holds "attitudes toward him that differ, in ways that reflect this impairment, from the attitudes required by the relationship one would otherwise have with the person" (Scanlon 2008, 145). On this account, blaming someone involves a revision of the way in which the blamer interacts with and regards the blamee. In short, the conative elements in Scanlon's account are more personal than in Sher's.

Second, another strand of thought on the nature of blame is much inspired by Strawson's seminal work on free will and moral responsibility and contends that blaming someone involves certain negative reaction emotions, e.g., most prominently resentment and anger. Several theorists whose work is prominent in the literature on hypocritical blame subscribe to this approach. For instance, Fritz and Miller (2018, 119) submit that

> Whenever R blames S for some item, A, R has a certain kind of belief-attitude pair: (i) a belief that S acted wrongly in A-ing (or in failing to perform some action, where A is that omission) or a belief that A is morally bad; (ii) a negative morally reactive attitude towards S on the basis of that belief (e.g., resentment, indignation, disapprobation, and, in cases of

---

to make a judgment of a certain kind, e.g., that the blamee's character is deficient in a certain way. Call this the cognitive account. Unlike the three other accounts, the cognitive account is not congenial to my purposes since, on that account, blaming is essentially just forming (or expressing) a certain belief. For challenges to the cognitive account, see Coates and Tognazzini (2013, 7–17) and Watson (2004, 226–227).

self-blame, guilt). (Cf. Driver 2016, 220; Strawson 1962; Wallace 2010, 323; 1994, 18–83)[19]

Like the conative account, this notion of blaming does not fit so well with the public notion of blaming. Suppose, in an angry tone of voice, R calls upon S to account for why they did A, to apologize, and to publicly reflect on how to avoid doing similar things in the future. There is a sense in which R blames S even if R neither believes that S acted wrongly in A-ing, nor has any negative morally reactive attitude towards S, but, say, Tartuffe-style, feigns seriousness about the norm in question to impress an audience. Call views such as this *emotion-based accounts of blame*.

A third account, a version of which is the one I am adopting here, is *the functional account of blame*. On this view, blame is defined not by a particular pair of belief and desire, or by a particular pair of belief and emotions, but rather by the function blame plays in human life, especially interpersonal interactions. On one influential account, an act is an act of blaming if it is a moral protest directed at someone's wrongful action (Smith 2013). In effect, the moral authority account introduced above is also a functional account, although the function in question is not to protest but to issue a demand. This function can be analyzed along Darwallian lines. On this account, blame has the function of publicly asserting the blamer's "authority to make demands on [the blamee's] behaviour" (Radzik 2011, 583; cf. Darwall 2006, 82–83).[20] That authority involves a liberty right on the part of the blamer to direct the blamee to respond in certain ways to the blame; i.e., the blamer has moral authority over the blamee if, and only if, the fact that the blamer makes a certain demand on the blamee results in the blamee now having some reason to comply with that demand.[21] No doubt it is controversial and contextual

---

[19] Another broadly Strawsonian account of blame championed by a contributor to the standing to blame literature is Rossi's (2018, 554) hostile attitudes account: "[W]here R and S are agents and A is an action, R blames S for A-ing only if: 1) R believes S is an agent of A. 2) R believes that S's A-ing is wrong or bad. 3) R believes that S is blameworthy for A-ing. 4) R experiences negative emotions (indignation, resentment, contempt, guilt) on account of (1), (2), and (3)." On Rossi's account, insincere expressions of (1)–(4) do not count as blame—he calls such cases false blame. However, if so, surely there is something like not being in a position to engage in false, public blaming of someone.

[20] Moral authority is a kind of authority that differs from the kind of authority that people might have by virtue of having a special social role invested with specific legal, etc. powers, e.g., being a police officer. It is an authority that one possesses by virtue of being a moral agent and by virtue of one's interaction with the recipient of the blame. It is compatible with the idea of moral authority that its demands are sometimes modified or counterbalanced by the kinds of authority that people have qua possessors of certain role.

[21] This is not to deny that the addressee had a reason to do so before being blamed; it is simply to say that now the addressee has an additional reason (see the distinction between alethic and constative oughts in Macnamara 2011, 91–92). Note also that blame typically involves two demands: that

what exactly a blamer can have the authority to direct the blamee to do, and the details are not important for present purposes. Typical examples of the sort of obligations a blamee has if blamed by someone with the standing to blame them are the duty to carefully listen and respond to criticisms; the duty to express remorse for the wrongful action; the duty to provide some kind of explanation of what led them to do what they did; the duty to accept and take more seriously than otherwise advice about how they can avoid performing similar blameworthy actions in the future; and the duty to openly deliberate on how they can improve in the future.[22]

For most of the purposes of this book, I can set aside the differences between conative, emotion-focused, and functional (including the moral authority) accounts of blame. What I do need to assume is that there is a distinction between merely judging someone to be blameworthy and blaming that person, and that the moral authority account captures at least an important aspect of much blame. Also, while I shall employ the moral authority account and focus on what I have called paradigmatic blame, I do not deny that other views of blame capture important dimensions of it. As already indicated, much blaming is not paradigmatic blame. First, in some instances the recipient of the communicative message—call this person the recipient of blame—is not the blamee, i.e., the wrongdoer who is being blamed, but a third party, who is, say, invited to join in blaming the blamee (Section 2.4). Second,

---

the blamee respond to the blame, e.g., apologizes, and that the blamee refrain from similar blameworthy actions in the future. In my view, a blamee can have a duty to respond positively to the first demand from someone with the standing to blame, even if, ultimately, the blamee believes correctly that the action in question is not blameworthy and, thus, that they are justified in rejecting claims of the latter sort.

[22] Examples of views along similar lines include: "[T]o blame someone to her face for some moral fault is a form of moral address and thus implicitly demands an apology or at least that the other person explain her behaviour" (Roadevin 2018, 138); "Blame begins, logically, as an accusation. Andy accuses Bertha of wrongfully destroying his marriage or his vase: he calls her to answer for that wrong, demanding an explanation and, unless the explanation is exculpatory, an apology" (Duff 2010, 123); "The notion of 'moral standing to blame' for a particular sort of wrongdoing should be defined directly as that status in virtue of which someone is entitled to blame another person for a particular sort of moral wrongdoing and have the blame taken seriously by other moral agents. This status can also be referred to as the 'authority' to blame. . . . A promising way of thinking about moral standing to blame for a particular sort of wrongdoing is that it is the entitlement to have one's blame heard and responded to by other members of the moral community. Someone who has moral standing is wronged on the face of it if their blaming of other persons is ignored" (Friedman 2013, 278, 281; cf. Friedman 2013, 275); "To issue a second-personal reason to someone (whether it be a sanction, a command or a request) is also to call for a response from her. To hold someone accountable for her behavior through a sanction is to demand an account from her. She is called upon to respond to her own behavior, perhaps in the form of an apology, a feeling of regret, or better future behavior" (Radzik 2011, 579).

sometimes blame is communicative, but does not involve any demand of an uptake. A spouse who leaves their partner on account of an affair, leaving an angry letter blaming their partner, would be an instance of that kind. Third, some instances of blame are not communicative at all. A resentful spouse who simply breaks off their relation to their partner might blame them in so doing (cf. Driver 2016, 219). Fourth, self-blame does not in any natural sense involve any attempt to communicate anything to the recipient of the blame (Section 2.3). Finally, some blame is private in the sense that the blamer never expresses their blame to anyone (Driver 2016, Chapter 2.2), so that neither the communication nor the demand condition is satisfied.[23] A full account of hypocritical blame would address these nonparadigmatic forms of blame too (see Sections 2.2–2.4). As will become apparent, I think that, in the case of some nonparadigmatic forms of blame, the notion of standing to blame is either nonapplicable or applicable in a derivative sense only.

1.2.2. The Incoherence Condition

In conjunction with the no-self-blame and the no-justification conditions, the incoherence condition, which states,

> (2) X believes or should believe that they themself have done something that is both relevantly similar to φ-ing and contextually relevant,

captures the widespread idea that hypocritical moral blame involves some sort of incoherence (cf. Wallace 2010, 307)—namely, the incoherence of responding differently to two cases that from the moral perspective of the blamer are relevantly similar in a way that is favorable to the hypocritical blamer. Sometimes this charge is put by saying that the hypocritical blamer applies double standards—a more lenient one for themself (or people whom they favor) and another more demanding one for others—despite the absence of any reason for using different standards in the two cases.

The incoherence condition consists of two separate conditions, each of which must be satisfied for blame to be hypocritical. The first condition is that the blamer believes or ought to believe that they have faults that are

---

[23] Mason's (2019, 112–123) discussion of "detached blame," which she thinks is not communicative (unlike ordinary blame), is another case of blame that might not be paradigmatic in my sense, though this is not reflected in the definition I offer.

relevantly like those of their blamee.[24] This requirement is subjective in the following sense. What is crucial for hypocritical blame is not that, as a matter of fact, the blamer has equally bad or even worse faults than their blamee. Rather, what matters is that the hypocritical blamer either believes this or that they ought to believe it given the evidence available to them.[25] Hence, whether I blame hypocritically when I blame someone for shoplifting does not depend on whether I actually have shoplifted myself, but on whether I believe or ought to believe, given my evidence, that I have shoplifted myself or engaged in some other relevantly similar wrongdoing. Suppose I have honestly and excusably forgotten about my own past shoplifting, but that my blamee is aware of my past wrongdoing. In that case, they can indirectly respond to my blame by denying that I have any standing to blame them—not because my doing so involves hypocrisy, but because I have done the very same thing for which I hold them accountable (cf. Lippert-Rasmussen 2013, 298; Todd 2019, 351–356). I shall refer to this indirect dismissal of blame as the *tu quoque* reply.

Speakers sometimes do not distinguish between the hypocrisy response and the tu quoque response (more on this in Section 4.2).[26] One reason why is that people tend to be aware of or to be in a situation where they ought to be aware of their own faults such that often when blame can be dismissed as hypocritical, it can also be dismissed on tu quoque grounds, and vice versa. Another reason is that once the blamee dismisses the blamer's criticism by informing the blamer that they have a similar fault, which, it so happens, they have honestly forgotten about, the blamer's blame might *then* become hypocritical if they persist in blaming the blamee.

When are faults relevantly similar? Obviously, φ-ing itself is relevantly similar to φ-ing. Thus, if the blamer believes that they have engaged in

---

[24] Some might press the distinction between a person being hypocritical and an act of blaming being so. They might contend that even in a case where someone blames someone else for a fault that they have themself but are culpably unaware of, this blame is not hypocritical. However, these facts about the blamer manifest that they have a hypocritical disposition. On this view, the act might be hypocritical in the derivative sense that it reflects a hypocritical disposition. It is irrelevant for present purposes whether we go with the proposed definition or the view suggested here.

[25] Suppose Al has no evidence suggesting that he is just as much at fault as Jack, but unreasonably thinks that he is. Normally, this would be seen as an indicator of being self-critical in a way that indicates a nonhypocritical character. However, if Al blames Jack, then he is blaming hypocritically even if, as a matter of fact, he would have the standing to blame were he aware of the facts regarding comparative faults.

[26] Nor do philosophers always do that: "[W]e are not merely blaming others for wrongs of a type that we have ourselves committed (which is, roughly, hypocrisy)" (Watson 2015, 178; see also Roadevin 2018, 144 and Crisp and Cowton 1994, 344.

φ-ing as well (or should believe that they have done so—henceforth I ignore this qualification in the interest of simplicity), then that fault is relevant to whether they are blaming hypocritically. This suggests

The qualitative identity condition: X's faults are relevantly similar to Y's if, and only if, they are qualitatively identical to the Y's faults.

However, faults can be relevantly similar even if they are not qualitatively identical. Suppose the blamer believes that they have engaged in behavior that is qualitatively different from what they blame the blamee for, but that it is at least as morally bad as what they blame the blamee for in light of the very same underlying moral principles that the blamer appeals to as the ground of their blame (Lippert-Rasmussen 2013, 303–304). Suppose that I condemn John for stealing on the ground that it harms the interests of innocent people and that I have often violently assaulted innocent people. In that case, the charge of hypocrisy is no less warranted than if I were a thief rather than a violent assaulter myself. This suggests

The greater fault condition: X's faults are relevantly similar if, and only if, they are qualitatively identical to or greater than Y's faults, as determined by the principles to which X appeals.

In fact, I want to defend a stronger claim. Suppose the blamer believes that they have engaged in behavior that is qualitatively different from what they blame their blamee for, but also believes that this behavior is only slightly less morally bad than what they blame their blamee for in light of the very same moral principles to which they appeal when blaming their blamee—e.g., suppose I blame you for robbing a bank ten times and that I am well aware that I have robbed a bank nine times. Even though many theorists write as if, provided the blamer's faults are lesser than the blamee's, then the blame is not hypocritical, it seems odd in such a case to deny that I blame hypocritically on the ground that according to the principles on which my blame rests, it is worse to rob a bank ten times than to do so nine times.[27] This suggests

[27] "Not significantly smaller" is difficult to render precisely. A mass murderer cannot dismiss being blamed for their wrongdoing on the ground that the blamer was once rude at the dinner table, even though they can dismiss blame from someone who has committed one fewer murder than they have. Where exactly between these two extremes the standing to blame kicks in is hard to say—if, indeed, any such point exists at all (Section 2.5).

The wider fault condition: X's faults are relevantly similar if, and only if, they are qualitatively identical to or at least not significantly smaller than Y's faults, as determined by the principles to which the blamer appeals.

Whichever of the three above-mentioned views we settle for, as indicated above there is a deeper and tricky issue—namely which of the following two accounts of degrees of faults we should accept:

The blamer-perspective-relative account of greater faults: the relative size of two faults is determined by the normative/evaluative principles to which the blamer subscribes or should reasonably subscribe given their other commitments.
   The objective account of greater faults: the relative size of two faults is determined by the true normative/evaluative principles.

Suppose that Adolf happens to think that bad table manners are a greater fault than being a genocidal mass murderer, and suppose, even more surprisingly, that given his other commitments he is not being unreasonable in holding this belief. In this highly unusual situation, Adolf's faults would not be relevantly greater than his son's on the blamer-relative account, but plausibly would be so on the objective account. While this might seem implausible initially, on reflection, we should accept the blamer-relative account of what counts as greater faults, because the fault of hypocrisy is, as it were, a fault that is internal to the hypocrite's own perspective. Thus, in this case, Adolf has a distorted view of morality, but it would be a mistake to dismiss his blame of his son's table manners as hypocritical. (Suppose that in the past he had bad table manners himself and that he repented for that for a long period of time, while fanatically striving to improve his table manners.)

Suppose we accept, as I think we should, the greater fault condition in its blamer-perspective-relative version. That leaves open what to say about the question of whether only actual or also hypothetical faults count. By "hypothetical faults" I mean faults that the blamer would manifest under certain counterfactual conditions. In relation to this question, I embrace

The circumstantial luck view: for the purpose of determining X's faults, it is not only faults manifested that count, but also faults that X would have manifested had it not been due to circumstantial luck.

Suppose a privileged person blames a homeless person for acting rudely in trying to squeeze money out of a passerby. Suppose also that it is obvious to everyone, including the homeless person, that had the privileged person been in their shoes—and the fact that they are not is simply a matter of their good circumstantial luck—they would have been at least as rude.[28] In such a case, the homeless person might indirectly dismiss the privileged person's blame as hypocritical, pointing out that, as the privileged person is very well aware, they would have been no better had they had slightly less luck.

Some might be skeptical of our ability to know about hypothetical faults and, generally, we might be less certain about such faults than actual faults. However, this is not a principled reason to deny that blame can be hypocritical in virtue of hypothetical faults. The most basic reason why this is so is in accordance with the blamer-relative-perspective view just exhibited—that what matters to hypocritical blame is not whether the blamer would have acted no better than the blamee were they in the blamee's shoes, but whether they believe, or should believe, that they would have acted no better were they in the blamee's shoes.[29]

One possible implication of the circumstantial luck view is that the range of cases in which one has standing to blame would be much more restricted if our views about how we would act were we in the blameworthy person's situation—when the reason why we are not is a matter of circumstantial luck—were true, or were the beliefs we should have in view of the evidence most educated persons are aware of, e.g., the evidence about how pessimistic we should be about our capacity for doing evil provided by Milgram's experiments (Piovarchy 2023; Todd 2019, 361). Some might see this as an objection to the circumstantial luck view on the ground that they infer from its truth that, typically, we should simply stay silent in the face of wrongdoing. This objection rests on a misunderstanding, to which I return later (Section 2.6).

---

[28] Are there other forms of luck that undermine standing to blame? Consider what Thomas Nagel (1979, 28) calls constitutive luck, e.g., luck in relation to one's character. Can a villain dismiss blame from an angel on the ground that it is just a matter of luck that the angel is such a better person than the villain? I think not. Perhaps this has to do with the fact, on the assumption that villainess is constitutive of the villain, that the villain could not have been (significantly) better and, thus, it is not a matter of bad luck that they were not. I thank Daniel Statman for reflections on this case.

[29] This is not to deny that a blamee can also indirectly deflect blame by asserting that the blamer would have acted no better had they been in the blamee's shoes even while conceding that the blamer thinks otherwise for good reason. However, it is not, I contend, to deflect blame on grounds of its being hypocritical. Rather the dismissal would be a case of a subjunctive tu quoque response, as it were (Section 4.2).

So much for the relevantly similar component of the incoherence condition. I now move on to the second component, i.e., the requirement of contextual relevance. The way I understand this requirement, a fault can be relevantly similar to the blamee's and yet not contextually relevant, e.g., because somehow the context is such that the blamer's fault is irrelevant to the dialogue. Often the location in time of the blamer's own fault is thought to be important to contextual relevance and, thus, to whether blame is hypocritical. More specifically, we tend to think that, typically at least, I might be aware that many years ago I engaged in exactly the same morally wrongful behavior I am now blaming someone else for without that making my blame hypocritical, despite the fact that had this wrongful act of mine taken place yesterday, my knowledge of that act would have made my blame hypocritical.[30] However, the fact that my fault lies so far back in the past might render it contextually irrelevant. Against this view, I am inclined to accept

The time-neutral view: for the purpose of determining X's faults, all of X's faults count, whenever in time they are located—be that the distant past or future.[31]

In defense of the time-neutral view, I offer two considerations. First, any attempt at determining when faults are old enough to become contextually irrelevant is bound to look arbitrary, and it is difficult to see why a fault's location in time should matter in itself.

The second, and more important, consideration is an error theory that explains why we might think time matters, appealing to the fact that distance in time often correlates with other factors that bear on whether blame is hypocritical, such that distant past faults often fail to satisfy the requirement of contextual relevance. If the blamer's wrong lies far back in time, chances are that they have already been blamed for that wrong and have engaged in

---

[30] To put this point in a way addressing future faults: If I know that I will commit the same wrong tomorrow, I cannot today blame someone else for that wrong today; perhaps, however, I can blame someone for a wrong that I know I will commit twenty years from now. This future-oriented view seems even more ingrained than the past-oriented view. A plausible explanation of why we rarely dismiss blame as hypocritical on the basis of the blamer's future faults is that blamers rarely believe, or have good reasons to believe, that potential blamees will have specific faults in the future. Admittedly, in some cases perhaps we can be confident about such future faults, and more so than about our present or past faults. In those cases, I suspect blame can be dismissed as hypocritical.

[31] There are some possible complications here in relation to a reductionist, Parfitian view on personal identity over time, which I ignore. In any case, these complications do not mean that location in time matters as such.

appropriate self-blame for that act. Perhaps the blamee forgave the blamer for the relevantly similar faults long ago (see Chapter 6). Additionally, if we think that hypocritical blame consists in a differential disposition to blame others more than oneself, one might think that if a wrong lies far back in the past, chances are that the blamer has since reformed and repented and would presently never do something similar, in which case the blamer's similar and temporally distant wrong is not a relevant fault for the purpose of applying the incoherence condition (cf. Fritz and Miller 2018, 121–122, 129–130). On both of the two views suggested here, distant past faults might, even though they tend not to, be as relevant as close past faults, e.g., because the blamer has never received blame for those faults or because the blamer is unreformed and unrepentant. If we were certain that the blamer's present self is completely continuous with their past bad self, and that they have not been forgiven by the victim nor repented their distant past faults, of which they hold a vivid memory, the blamer cannot dismiss the accusation that their blame is hypocritical simply by saying that their greater fault is far back in time, while at the same time conceding that they have not in any way improved, repented, been blamed, etc.

Distance in time, however, is not the only factor that might be thought to determine whether a fault that is relevantly similar is contextually relevant. Suppose a convicted robber meets with a fellow inmate every Tuesday afternoon to play cards. By mutual agreement, their entire social interactions are limited to card-playing activities. Suppose that the robber discovers that the fellow inmate cheats in the game and blames them to a degree that is fitting to cheating in card games. The prison mate responds by furiously complaining, "How come you're so worked up about my cheating in a game of cards, when you have nothing to say about your heinous robberies?" They would be right that the robber's past moral faults are much greater than the trivial fault of cheating in a card game. Still, possibly this fault is simply not contextually relevant given the permissibly consensually limited nature of the two parties' interaction and given the blamer's narrow target and, thus, is not a fault whose knowledge makes the robber's blame hypocritical.[32]

---

[32] If the robber's blame were inappropriate in the sense that they were implying that somehow their prison mate were a tainted person, then the robber's past crimes would be contextually relevant. However, to the extent that the robber is simply addressing the card-playing and not implying anything about the comparative virtuousness of themself and their blamee, their past greater fault might remain contextually irrelevant. However, perhaps there are some faults—say, ordering genocide—that are so grave that whenever one blames someone else, whatever the setting, that person can dismiss one's blame as hypocritical; e.g., Hitler would be in no position to blame someone who hits him on the nose for no other reason than that they wanted to hit someone on the nose. I take no stand

1.2.3. The No-Self-Blame Condition

I now move on to the no-self-blame condition of hypocritical blame:

(3) In a way that does not reflect a sheer coincidence, either X does not to a suitable degree or in a suitable way, make themself or accept themself being made the target of blame for their conduct that is relevantly similar to φ-ing.[33]

What this condition brings out is that, strictly speaking, one is not a hypocritical blamer simply by virtue of blaming someone for a fault when one believes that one has a relevantly similar fault. Rather, hypocritical blame requires additionally that the hypocritical blamer does not, and is not willing to, engage in a degree of self-blame that is proportionate to the severity of their blame of others and to the seriousness of their own relevantly similar fault.[34] To go back to the opening example in this chapter, in Jack's case Al would have to blame himself more than he blames Jack for Al not to be in a position to dismiss his blame on grounds of hypocrisy.[35] One can engage in self-blame vicariously, as it were, i.e., by accepting the blame that others subject one to.

The no-self-blame condition naturally suggests that, strictly speaking and unlike what is often assumed, one might be hypocritical when one blames someone whose faults are greater.[36] The reason for this is that one could

---

on this and, so I should state openly, I do not take the present paragraph to amount to anything that comes close to a theory of what contextual relevance of fault is in relation to blame and which factors determine it.

[33] Suppose I do not engage in self-blame, though I do not see what justifies my blaming my blamee for the same fault that I have but remain silent about. However, I would immediately accept blame from my blamee were they to blame me in response. Surely, in this case I am less hypocritical than I would be if I would refuse blame from my blamee. Still, perhaps I am slightly hypocritical, in which case the no-self-blame condition needs to be amended.

[34] I am focusing here on paradigmatic cases of blame, where hypocrisy involves taking a lenient view of one's own faults. However, there are also cases of third-person hypocrisy, where hypocrisy involves taking a lenient view of the faults of one's friends as opposed to the faults of one's enemies.

[35] Perhaps one also must blame oneself in a suitable way in addition to a suitable degree. If I blame myself privately to a suitable degree, but simply neglect to do so when I blame others publicly, then, possibly, my blamee can dismiss my blame as hypocritical even if, given the fact that I often blame myself, in one important sense of "hypocrisy" she cannot accuse me of being hypocritical—at least not in a typical way.

[36] Suppose Joe and Jill are in a supermarket together. Jill has stolen a lot from other people. Joe starts blaming Jill for stealing, while at the very same time putting a cheese in his large inner jacket pocket. Jill can dismiss Joe's blame as hypocritical even while conceding that her own faults are much greater. Hence, the fact that the blaming is concurrent with the blamer's doing something relevantly similar, even if much less bad, renders the complaint of hypocrisy appropriate (Section 1.2.2).

accompany such blame of others with a suitably milder form of self-blame rather than simply ignoring one's own lesser fault. More generally, once we notice that blame comes in degrees, what seems crucial is not so much the ordinal ranking of the faults of different individuals—roughly, whose faults are greater than the other's—but how their faults compare on a cardinal scale—roughly, how much greater one's faults are than the other's—and how this difference transforms into blame being hypocritical in varying degrees.

Finally, I should explain the qualification "in a way that does not reflect a sheer coincidence" in the no-self-blame condition. Suppose the blamer blames the blamee and intends to proceed to blame themself (recall again that I focus on communicative blame), but that the blamee interrupts the blamer before the blamer gets the chance to engage in the intended self-blame. Plausibly, the blamer can reject the charge of hypocrisy in this case, saying that it is a sheer coincidence that they did not engage in a suitable degree of self-blame. Next, consider a case where the blamer is simply confused. Sometimes they make a favorable exception for themself and blame others for faults that they have themself but does not blame themself for. At other times, they blame themself for faults they have and that they do not blame others for. In short, there is no discernible pattern behind whom the blamer lets off the hook blaming-wise. This blamer is incoherent, but not hypocritical. If it is just a fluke that one blames someone for a fault one has to a greater degree and the reverse were equally likely to happen, then the act is not hypocritical.[37] One plausible explanation for this requirement is that for blame to be hypocritical, it must be motivated in a certain way. Or, alternatively and more behavioralistically, the blame must be part of a particular pattern of blaming behavior for it to be hypocritical. Whatever is the correct explanation of this fact, this is what forms the background for the relevant qualification in the no-self-blame condition.

1.2.4. The No-Justification Condition

Consider the fourth and final condition in my definition of hypocritical blame:

---

[37] "The idea of disinterested hypocrisy boggles the mind" (Szabados 1979, 205).

(4)   It is neither (a) the case that X believes there are morally relevant differences between blaming their own conduct relevantly similar to φ-ing, on the one hand, and blaming Y's φ-ing, on the other hand, that justify their blaming Y for φ-ing and not blaming themself for their own conduct relevantly similar to φ-ing to the relevant degree or in the relevant way, nor (b) the case that X has a belief to this effect but that X has it for reasons that they can or should be able to see are not sufficient reasons.

The no-justification condition reflects the fact that blame is situated in a wider network of normative beliefs. Accordingly, even if the blamer has engaged in the same kind of behavior narrowly described and that fact is contextually relevant, it might be that, from the perspective of the blamer, the two instances of blame are relevantly different once one takes into account the wider context. To see the motivation of the (a) component in the no-justification condition, suppose that, unavoidably, I am much more sensitive to blame than my blamee is and that I believe that the justifiability of blame depends, inter alia, on the degree to which the blamee suffers because of being blamed. In that case, I might not be hypocritical when I blame my friend for shoplifting, but do not similarly burden myself with self-blame for the same conduct. To test this, consider a case where I can take blame and someone who is even more sensitive to blame than I am is just as blameworthy in some respect as I am. If, in such a case, I would not blame that person and would blame myself, perhaps I really am not engaging in hypocritical blame in the first case.[38]

Another possible difference pertaining to otherwise similar actions comes out in cases where the blamer and blamee stand in a certain hierarchical relation. Suppose a professor blames a student for being sloppy with the student's references in their writing. The student retorts correctly that so is the professor. Nevertheless, the professor might deny—sincerely, let us suppose—that they are blaming hypocritically on the ground that they believe that it is their job to educate the student and not the student's job to educate them and that this justifies their one-sided blame.[39] A third possible justification for

---

[38] Related to the present example, there is also a question about whether belief in something like an agent-relative prerogative can undermine accusations of hypocritical blame, i.e., that one believes that one can permissibly give greater weight to one's own interest in avoiding blame than others' and for that reason refrain from blaming oneself for a fault for which one blames others (see Section 7.4). In my view, it could, provided that the relevant blamer does not blame others for a relevantly similar exercise of their comparable agent-relative prerogative.

[39] Cf. footnote 20 on authority and special social roles. This is not to say that the professor's blame is appropriate. Blame can be inappropriate for many reasons other than that it is hypocritical.

differential blaming is that the blamee has consented to being blamed by the blamer even when the blamer has similar or even worse faults.[40] Plausibly in most such cases, the no-justification condition is not satisfied, i.e., the blamer believes that there is a morally relevant difference between their blaming the blamee (they have consented to being blamed) and blaming the blamer (they have not reciprocated the blamee's consent), but some cases might be different.

Specifically, regarding the (b) component in the no-justification condition, the motivation is the following. Often our beliefs about morally relevant differences are corrupted by our self-interest or our (typically overlapping) desire to see ourselves as being in the right. To the extent that this is so, we are being hypocritical, and blame motivated by beliefs about morally relevant differences, which are unwarranted for this reason, is hypocritical too.

1.2.5. Summary

This concludes my exposition of my definition of hypocritical blame. Just to recap: I focused on what I called a paradigmatic case of blaming, i.e., blame where the blamer confronts and blames their blamee for a blameworthy action of theirs. Not all forms of blame are paradigmatic. In Chapter 2, I address some complications in relation to my definition of hypocritical, paradigmatic blame; but before I get to that, I want to say something about what it is not to have standing to blame and, thus, what it is to dismiss blame as standingless.

1.3. Standing to Blame and Its Denial

Let us approach the question of what it is to have standing to blame by asking the question of what one does when one dismisses hypocritical blame as standingless. First, we need to distinguish between direct and indirect dismissals of blame. To dismiss blame directly is to deny that one is blameworthy. There are several ways of doing that (Duff 2010, 124). One way is to deny that one did the putatively blameworthy act (assuming that an act is the object of blame). Another is to concede that one performed the act in

---

[40] Perhaps, to some extent and more so in the very bad old days than now, such relations of consent color the relationship between professors and students.

question, but then deny that it was wrongful. A third direct response is to concede that what one did was wrongful but assert that one was excused for acting the way one did and for that reason did not act in a blameworthy way. Someone who dismisses hypocritical blame on grounds of the blamer's lack of standing might—and rightly so—concede that none of these direct replies to blame are justified in the case at hand. Jack can concede that, over the last year, he has flown more than 30,000 miles, that it is morally wrongful of him to do so, and that he has no excuse for doing so.[41] Yet he could intelligibly say to Al: "You're right. It is morally wrongful for me to fly as much as I do, and I have no excuse for doing so. Still, I refuse to accept blame from you on that account." He could not say that appropriately to Greta, I have contended, and that just shows why the essence of dismissing hypocritical blame is not a matter of directly dismissing blame. If it were, presumably Jack could and possibly should respond in the same way to Al and Greta. After all, both Al and Greta are claiming that what Jack does is blameworthy, i.e., they are putting forward the same claim about Jack. Hence, in dismissing blame as hypocritical and therefore standingless, one is not directly dismissing it on the ground that one is not blameworthy. Dismissing blame on the ground that the blamer has no standing to blame is to indirectly dismiss blame. In view of that, I suggest

> *The disjunctive account of indirect blame dismissal*: X indirectly dismisses Y's blaming$_p$ X for ϕ-ing if, and only if, X denies that Y has a liberty right against X to blame$_p$ for ϕ-ing *or* X denies that X has a duty to respond to Y's blaming$_p$ X for ϕ-ing.[42]

---

[41] There are many different indirect ways of responding to blame, and dismissing it on the ground that the blamer is hypocritical is one among other ways of doing so. For instance, often people dismiss blame from someone by trying to discredit them in ways other than by attributing hypocrisy to them, e.g., by calling them judgmental or by attributing discreditable motivations to their blame of them (Statman 2023), or for failing to understand the situation of the blamee. I examine some of these alternative indirect ways of dismissing blame in Chapter 4.

[42] There is an important variation of this view. Consider *the conditional liberty-right view of indirect blame dismissal*: X indirectly dismisses Y's blaming$_p$ X for ϕ-ing on grounds of lack of standing if X affirms that Y has a liberty right against X to blame$_p$ for ϕ-ing, but only if Y meets certain conditions that, in fact, Y has not met. One such condition might be that the blamer engages in suitable self-blame. Another such condition can be that the blamer also addresses some other issue; e.g., the blamee might contend that the blamer's indignation is grounded in certain objectionable mental states, e.g., jealousy, and not in the blamer's view that the action really is blameworthy (cf. Statman 2023). If the blamee deflects the blamer's blame indirectly in the latter way, they are not saying that they have nothing to account for (though, of course, one might think that standing to blame depends on having the right motivation, just like some think standing to blame requires not being complicit in that which one blames the blamee for [see Section 4.3]). Rather, they concede that they have, but they might be saying that the agenda in the two parties' dialogue should include more than the blamee's ϕ-ing. It should also include what motivates the blamer to blame. If so, perhaps one can dilute, but

This account is motivated by, though not entailed by

> *The conjunctive account of standing to blame*: Y has standing to blame$_p$ X for
> ϕ-ing if, and only if, Y has a liberty right against X to blame$_p$ for ϕ-ing *and* X
> has a duty to respond to Y's blaming$_p$ X for ϕ-ing.[43]

Both accounts have two components: one that is blamer-centric—(the denial
of) the liberty right of the blamer to blame; and one that is blamee-centric—
(the denial of) the duty of the blamee owed to the blamer to respond to the
blame (cf. Rivera-López 2017, 341–342). These two components are different. To deny that the blamer has any duty to the blamee not to blame them
does not entail that the blamee has a duty to the blamer to provide an uptake
to the blame. I may have no duty to respond to your offer to buy my house
even if you have the right to offer to buy it. Similarly, often when we dismiss
blame, we are not denying that the blamer has the liberty to blame us—we are
simply denying that we have any duty to them to respond. Conversely, it is
an open question whether the blamee has a duty to provide an uptake to the
blamer who has no liberty right to blame, even though such a duty must then
be grounded in something other than the blamer's demand for uptake.

One important feature of the conjunctive account of standing to blame
is that, by virtue of the second conjunct, to blame someone involves the assertion of a certain kind of moral authority over them, i.e., an authority that
can place them under a moral obligation directed to oneself by virtue of one's
blame to provide a certain uptake to one's blame.[44] Typically, the blamee

---

not deflect, blame without denying that the blamer has standing to blame. Another way to go than to
flesh out the underlying view in terms of rights and duties would be to say that to dismiss someone's
blame as standingless is to deny either that the blamer has any reason (overall or even pro tanto) to
blame their blamee, or to deny that the recipient of blame has any (robust) reason to respond to the
blame (see Herstein 2017). If one has a duty to one's blamer to respond to their blame, this entails that
one has a reason to respond to the blame.

[43] Suppose I have a liberty right to blame. However, in addition to that I might or might not enjoy
immunity against others eliminating this right, and I might or might not enjoy the power to renounce
my liberty rights to blame. Under what conditions one enjoys such immunities and powers is an
interesting complication. However, I do not think they bear on the question of dismissing standing
to blame; e.g., I do not dismiss your standing to blame if I deny that you enjoy immunity regarding
your liberty right to blame. A similar point about these two higher-order Hohfeldian moral statuses
applies to the disjunctive account of standing to blame.

[44] As Herstein, building on Searle and Vanderveken (1985), submits: blame involves directives. In
giving a directive, one purports "to trigger, generate or give reasons" (Herstein 2017, 3114–3115): "A
(valid) directive is the reason that it purports to be: a reason for the directive-subject to perform the
directive-action *because of the directive*. For example, in asking you to ϕ I intend for the request—my
asking you—to be a reason for you to ϕ" (Herstein 2017, 3115).

has no immunity, when confronted by someone with a standing to blame, against acquiring a duty to account for their action in the face of blame. Thus, one way to dismiss such blame on that account is simply to dismiss that one is under such a moral obligation to one's blamer or, to put the same point differently, that one is now under a moral obligation to one's blamer to respond to the blame in a certain way. Accordingly, I shall label a view of standing to blame that combines the disjunctive account of indirect blame dismissal and the conjunctive account of standing to blame *the moral authority view of standing to blame*.

This view has several virtues. First, it fits well with the moral authority account of public blame that I offered in Section 1.2.1. On this account, to blame someone involves, inter alia, the assertion that the blamee now has a duty by virtue of one's blame to provide a certain uptake to one's blame, e.g., to make amends. In dismissing hypocritical blame, one is denying that assertion.

Second, on the moral authority view of standing, to dismiss blame as hypocritical is not to deny that one is under a moral obligation *tout court* to provide an uptake to the blame one is being subjected to by the hypocritical blamer. However, it is to deny that one is under a moral obligation *to the hypocritical blamer* to provide an uptake to their blame due to their blaming one. It could be, say, that one's providing an uptake to the blame has valuable educational effects on third parties by virtue of which one is under an obligation—either to them or simply as an undirected, impersonal moral obligation—to provide an uptake to the blame. Or it could be that the blamee is under a duty to the blamer to respond to the blame on account of a previous promise to respond to future hypocritical blame.

This feature of the moral authority view of standing enables us to see that some common objections to the idea that hypocrisy undermines standing to blame rest on misconstruing the nature of dismissing blame. Some object to the idea that someone can lack the standing to blame by contending that if the blamee really has done something wrong, then it is morally worse if the blamer does not blame the blamee than if they do. Even assuming this claim is true, the moral authority account does not entail a denial of the claim about betterness that the objection rests on. It is consistent with saying that it is morally better—indeed that the blamee has a duty to respond to the blamer's standingless blame, *though not a duty to the blamer on account of that person's blame*—if the blamee responds to the blamer's standingless blame. Not being under a duty to the blamer to respond to their blame is not the same as not having the liberty to do so. Hence, a friend of the moral authority account of standing can agree with the point that is being pressed against them in the wrapping of an objection; to wit, that it is better that the blamer blames the blamee for their wrongful action than if no one does.

Third, the moral authority account of standing fits well with the plausible view that someone who simply states that another person has acted in a blameworthy way but without blaming the person cannot be dismissed on account of hypocrisy. After all, such a person is not making any demand that the blamee apologizes, etc. The same goes for the blamer who precedes the other-blame with a suitable dose of self-blame, or, strictly speaking, the same goes for the blamer whose self-blame serves to communicate that the blamer does not impute any asymmetrical obligations on the part of the blamee.

Finally, the phrases we use when we dismiss hypocritical blame are typically quasi-legal, thus invoking the notion of authority, e.g., "Who are you to judge me?" The moral authority account cashes out the legalistic metaphors that are often involved in discussions of standing to blame.

Before proceeding in Section 1.4 to examine three alternative accounts of (dismissing) standing to blame, let me respond to an important challenge to the present account. Suppose I have wronged someone and now they blame me. On the moral authority account of standing, I now have a reason by virtue of this person's blaming me to respond in a certain way to the blame, e.g., to apologize. But does it follow from this account, absurdly, that I had no reason to apologize before the person blamed me and, more generally, that we have no reason to apologize to people whom we wrong and who are, say, too kind to blame us (cf. Enoch 2011; Anonymous, forthcoming, 6–7)?[45]

I agree these implications would be absurd. However, they are not implications of the moral authority account of standing. Nothing in it rules out that blamees have independent—and perhaps even stronger—reasons to do that which their being targets of blame gives them additional reasons to do. Some who deny that blame can give blamees reasons they would not have had in the absence of the act of blaming might deny this, because, more generally, they doubt that agents can have reasons they would not have had in the absence of directive speech acts addressing them. However, this is out of tune with how we think. Surely, I have a reason to give you water because you are thirsty, independently of your requesting water from me. But now that you request it, I have an additional reason or, if you prefer, I have the same

[45] I thank Paul Bou-Habib and Kartik Upadhyaya for pressing this question.

reason as I had before, but its weight is boosted by the fact that you request it (cf. Herstein 2017, 3116–3117; Tognazzini, forthcoming, 11–14). And this additional reason—or this strengthening of the prior reason—results at least in part from your demanding or requesting it and not, say, the fact that you demand it and that ignoring your request would be disrespectful. Similarly, I might have good reason to give you water because you are thirsty, but once I have promised to do so, I have an additional reason. This concludes my defense of the moral authority account of (dismissing) standing.

1.4. Other Accounts of What It Is to Dismiss Blame on Grounds of the Hypocrite's Lack of Standing

There are other accounts of what standing to blame is and, thus, other accounts of what it is to dismiss blame as standingless aside from the moral authority account. In this section, I will review three alternative accounts—the infelicity, moral wrongness, and incoherence accounts—arguing that all of them are problematic, thereby indirectly supporting the moral authority account of standing.

The first account is modeled on Austin's (1962) account of infelicitous illocutionary acts; e.g., a person marrying a couple without being authorized to do so tries to marry them but fails to do so:

> *The infelicity account*: Y has the standing to blame$_p$ X for ϕ-ing if, and only if, were Y to try to blame$_p$ X for ϕ-ing, Y would succeed in performing an act of blaming. Thus, X indirectly dismisses Y's blaming$_p$ X for ϕ-ing if, and only if, X denies that Y's attempt to blame$_p$ X for ϕ-ing is, or would be, a successful attempt at blaming.

On this account, standingless blame amounts to trying to perform a speech act with a particular illocutionary force but failing in that attempt because certain presuppositions of performing such a speech act are unsatisfied. In the case of standingless hypocritical blame, the relevant condition is, setting aside complications addressed above, that the blamer's faults are not greater than the blamee's.[46]

---

[46] In Chapter 4 I review some other ways in which one can deny that the blamer has standing to blame. Arguably, the infelicity account must claim that these other forms of standingless blame too involve failing to meet certain presuppositions of the illocutionary act of blaming. More generally,

The basic idea here can be captured by a comparison of two cases: one in which a nonhypocrite and another in which a hypocrite utter the same words in similar contexts. According to the infelicity account, it might then be the case that the nonhypocrite succeeds in blaming the blamee, whereas the hypocrite does not. The hypocrite tries to blame, and says things that sound like blaming—just like the nonauthorized person says things that sound like marrying a couple—but that, really, are not. In our opening example: while Greta succeeds in blaming Jack, Al does not.

Isserow and Klein suggest an account along those lines. On their view, an "act of condemnation . . . is a kind of speech act that an agent must be in a position to perform. When we declare that we are 'not in a position' to criticize others, we refer to some kind of 'disabling fact' about ourselves that undermines the illocutionary force of our utterance. And one prime candidate for such a disabling fact would surely be that we ourselves are guilty of the relevant vice" (Isserow and Klein 2017, 198; see also Dworkin 2000, 184).[47]

One advantage of the infelicity account is that it can explain why we can preface negative moral judgments about others with utterances like "I am not in a position to point fingers, but what you did was wrong," and in so doing avoid engaging in hypocritical blame even if, in the situation, simply saying, "What you did was wrong" might amount to hypocritical blame. The infelicity account can explain this by saying that, through the relevant prefacing, the speaker makes it the case that the utterance does not have the illocutionary force of blame and that simply expressing the view in a nonblaming way that what someone did was wrong or blameworthy does not have among its illocutionary presuppositions that the speaker's own track record is better than that of the recipient of the message.

Unfortunately, either the infelicity account reduces to the moral authority account or, to the extent that it is distinct from it, it is flawed. In support of the first disjunct, note that if hypocritical blame is infelicitous, then it must fail to have the illocutionary force that successful acts of blaming have. The obvious candidate regarding this illocutionary force is the demand for the sort of uptake that the moral authority account identifies. But then the infelicity

---

presumably our account of standing applies to all forms of (what we normally think of as involving) a lack of standing to blame or, for that matter, to perform other related illocutionary acts.

[47] Cf. Fritz and Miller (2019a, 382) on moral pronouncements having "illocutionary force"; Darwall (2006, 4) on normative felicity conditions.

account seems substantially reducible to the moral authority account, even if we may differ on whether we want to call relevant acts that lack the relevant duty-producing illocutionary force "blame" or "failed attempts to blame." Some might point out that this reply ignores the liberty right to blame component in the moral authority account and argue on that ground that the two proposals are different. I am skeptical of this suggestion. This takes us to the second disjunct.

I have two main reasons for thinking that the infelicity account so construed is flawed. First, it is revisionary in that standard conditions of hypocritical blame are offered as an account of exactly that and not as conditions of hypocritical attempted blame. To the extent that philosophers largely fail to capture the conditions that lie behind their classificatory intuitions, standing is not a necessary condition of blame.[48]

Second, in terms of how people respond to hypocritical blame when they complain about being subjected to it, they do not think of their complaint as being about having been subjected to an unsuccessful attempt at blaming. Rather they think that they were wrongfully subjected to blame and that is what they, say, want a recognition of.[49] Perhaps when an alternative way of describing the situation is offered—to wit, that what we are outraged by in such cases is being subjected to something that appears to be or pretends to be blame, but that, really, is not—we might see little reason not to go with the novel understanding of the situation. However, unless there are positive reasons in favor of conceptual revision, we should continue with our standard ways of describing the situation.[50]

The second account grounds standing to blame in considerations about moral wrongness:

---

[48] If it were and if hypocrisy always undermines standing, then there is no such topic as what makes hypocritical blame wrong, since that idea is a contradiction in terms. However, there is a closely related topic of the wrongfulness of hypocritical attempts at blaming.

[49] Here I agree with the following passage: "[S]tanding in . . . contexts [like the standing to bring legal suit or the standing to command (i.e., authority)] is an *enabling* condition on the very activity involved. The status makes possible the pertinent activity; one *cannot* do it without the requisite standing . . . one can act as if one is commanding a subordinate, or try to do so, but without the relevant authority, one simply fails to command. . . . In contrast, hypocritical and meddlesome blamers, even if they lack standing, do not *fail* to blame. It's precisely their blame to which we're objecting" (King 2019, 270; see also King 2015, 1). Unlike King, I would add that, on my account, that to which we are objecting is either the blamer blaming without a liberty right to blame, or the moral authority to impose a duty on the blamee to provide an uptake to the blame.

[50] On my definition of communication blame, for something to count as such, it is not required that the blamer has standing to blame; e.g., I can succeed in demanding an uptake even if I have no liberty right to make such a demand.

The moral wrongness account: Y has the standing to blame$_p$ X for φ-ing if, and only if, were Y to blame$_p$ X for φ-ing, Y would not perform a morally wrongful act. Thus, X indirectly dismisses Y's blaming$_p$ X for φ-ing if, and only if, X asserts that Y's blaming$_p$ X for φ-ing is morally wrongful.

The moral wrongness account might seem promising for two reasons at least. First, many instances of hypocritical blame are morally wrongful and, indeed, are morally wrongful by virtue of the hypocrisy they involve.[51] Certainly, to describe someone as engaging in hypocritical blame sounds like a moral criticism, and since the moral wrongness account implies that it *is*, this supports the account.[52] Second, if hypocritical blame is morally wrongful, all things considered, it also makes sense that one is not morally required to provide it with an uptake, since the act of blaming should not have occurred in the first place. No wonder, then, that it can be appropriately dismissed. At any rate, the moral wrongness account is widely accepted in the literature. Benjamin Rossi (2018, 553), for instance, approvingly observes: "Hypocrisy is widely thought to be morally objectionable in a way that undermines the hypocrite's standing to blame others." Fritz and Miller (2018) seem to be making a similar claim when they submit that it is (the affirmation of) "equality of persons" that grounds the standing to blame others and, thus, the denial thereof—something that they think is involved in what they call a differential disposition to blame—that undermines the standing to blame. The same is true of Wallace (2010, 320): "Hypocrites lack the standing to blame . . . insofar as their own behaviour makes it morally objectionable for them to adopt the stance of blame."

Even so, the moral wrongness account is wrong. At best, the determinants of standing to blame overlap with some of the determinants of moral wrongfulness of blame. In dismissing hypocritical blame, one is simply either denying that the blamer has a claim right that the blamee respond to the blame, or denying that the blamer has a liberty right to blame. And if

---

[51] This is not to deny that one can be improperly outraged when subjected to hypocritical blame. After all, one can be blameworthy for what the hypocrite blames one for and, in many cases, the blameworthiness of one's action should be more firmly on one's mind than the perhaps relatively minor slight of being subjected to hypocritical blame.

[52] I do not think this reason is particularly persuasive. Sometimes people dismiss hypocritical blame in a completely calm and friendly matter—not very common, I suppose, but it happens—without displaying any moral indignation. Presumably, we want our account of standing to blame to explain that sort of case, and if the moral wrongness account explains that cases of dismissal of hypocritical blame involve moral indignation, by parity of reasoning the cases not involving moral indignation constitute counterexamples to that explanation.

hypocritical blaming involves doing something one has no right to do or demanding something to which one has no right, this does not entail that the hypocritical blamer acts in a morally wrongful way, all things considered. It could be that the blamer is morally required to engage in blaming that they have no standing to engage in, e.g., because of benefits for third parties. Similarly, it could be the case that the blamer is morally required to abstain from blaming even when they have the standing to do so, e.g., because the occasion—say, the funeral of the blamee's partner—is inappropriate (cf. Bell 2013, 275; for a reply, see Fritz and Miller 2018, 128).

The latter—denying that the blamer has a liberty right to blame—might not be so clearly different, since if the blamer has a duty to the blamee not to blame them, then to the extent that they nevertheless do that, this seems a source of wrongfulness (cf. Fritz and Miller 2018, 122). To say this is to say that blaming without having the standing to do so is a pro tanto wrong-making feature. Clearly, there could be other and non-standing-related wrong-making features. But if the wrongfulness is what grounds the lack of standing to blame, then, assuming that that which grounds something must be different from it, it follows that lacking the standing to blame is different from one's blaming being pro tanto wrongful. Hence, I reject the moral wrongfulness account (see also Section 7.3 on epistemic blame, which despite being standingless might not be wrongful).

A third account focuses on the incoherence involved in hypocritical blaming:

> *The incoherence account*: Y has the standing to blame$_p$ X for ϕ-ing if, and only if, there is no incoherence between Y's blaming X for ϕ-ing and, in the absence of proportionate self-blame or openness to proportionate other-blame, Y's own conduct, i.e., Y themself engages in ϕ-ing or something relevantly similar. Thus, X indirectly dismisses Y's blaming$_p$ X for ϕ-ing if, and only if, X asserts that Y's blaming$_p$ X for ϕ-ing involves such an incoherence.

One advantage of the incoherence account is that by definition—my definition, at any rate—hypocritical blame involves incoherence of the kind whose absence constitutes standing to blame. Indeed, in certain paradigmatic cases of hypocritical blame, this incoherence is a foregrounded feature of the cases.[53] Additionally, the incoherence account is compatible with the distinction I have been urging between the factors that undermine standing

---

[53] In some of the dialectically most forceful critiques of hypocritical blame, the incoherence only becomes apparent to the hypocritical blamer after the blamer's angry reaction, cf. the prophet

to blame and the factors that determine wrongfulness of hypocritical blame. One reason for this is that sheer incoherence does not seem like a moral fault. It is only when it is motivated—i.e., when the blamer systematically makes a favorable exception in their own favor—that the incoherence turns into a moral flaw.[54]

Even so, the incoherence account of standing to blame is flawed because it is tied too narrowly to hypocritical blame. As we shall see in Chapter 4, there are other ways of lacking the standing to blame, which do not involve any sort of incoherence between the blamer's principles and the blamer's own conduct. Take meddlesome blame (Section 4.4). A perfectly coherent meddlesome blamer lacks the standing to blame, even if there is no incoherence between their meddlesome blame and their own response to other people's meddlesome blame of their conduct in matters that are none of the blamers' business. But if a perfectly coherent meddlesome blamer can lack the standing to blame, then it cannot be the case that the standing to blame consists in the absence of incoherence between the blamer's standards and their own conduct.[55] This concludes my critical review of three alternative, general accounts of standing to blame.

1.5. Conclusion

This chapter opened with the appropriate dismissal claim; to wit, the claim that one has a reason to dismiss hypocritical blame even when one is (or believes one is) blameworthy. My opening example of the philosopher with the large (as far as individuals go) carbon footprint was meant to show that this claim has strong intuitive support. I then offered an account of the necessary and sufficient conditions for paradigmatic blame, i.e., cases where the blamer confronts the wrongdoer with the wrongfulness of their action and demands a response to their blame, to be hypocritical. On that basis, Sections 1.3 and 1.4 assessed various accounts of what it is to have standing to blame

---

Nathan's story of the rich and the poor man and King David's anger with the former, who takes the poor man's lamb, unaware that, by virtue of his having Uriah killed so that he can marry his wife Bathsheba, he is the main character of Nathan's story (McNaughton 1988, 59).

[54] The not "sheer coincidence" requirement of the no-self-blame condition might entail that hypocritical blame is motivated, if the only way of being noncoincidental is by being motivated.

[55] A similar argument could be made appealing to standingless blame that is vulnerable to the tu quoque reply (Section 4.2), complicitous blame (Section 4.3), or uninformed blame (Section 4.4).

and to dismiss blame as standingless. I defended the moral authority account of having the standing to blame and dismissing blame as standingless. In a nutshell, to have standing to blame on this account is to hold a liberty right against the blamee to blame that person for their wrongdoing and to hold a claim right against the blamee to a response to one's blame. To dismiss blame as standingless is to deny that the blamer has any of these rights.

While this chapter has provided a sketch of the essentials of my account of what it is to have (and to lack) standing to blame and what it is to dismiss blame as standingless, many complications remain. The most important of these are addressed in the next chapter. While doing so, I will put some more flesh on the bare bones of the moral authority account of (dismissing) standing to blame.

2

Complications and Defeaters of Standing

2.1. Introduction

In the previous chapter I offered a definition of hypocritical blame (Section 1.2) and of what it is to dismiss hypocritical blame as standingless (Section 1.3). In many ways Chapter 1 provides the conceptual groundwork for much of what goes on in this book. This chapter builds on it by considering finer details pertaining to these two matters that were not addressed in Chapter 1, e.g., in relation to how we should understand nonparadigmatic hypocritical blame and, thus, dismissals of nonparadigmatic blame. Chapter 2 also takes up two new, general issues, i.e., the skeptical view that there is no such thing as standing to blame and the question of why hypocrisy undermines standing to blame. Answers to these questions presuppose definitions of what hypocritical blame is and what it is to dismiss hypocritical blame, but these definitions do not by themselves determine the answers to these questions.

Sections 2.2–2.5 discuss my definitions of hypocritical blame and my definition of what it is to dismiss blame as standingless and, in light of four complications, that blame might be unexpressed and thus not involve any expressed demand for an uptake from the blamee (Section 2.2); that it is possible to blame oneself and that, similarly, doing so does not involve any demand for an uptake (Section 2.3); that it is possible to blame bystanders or, to use a different term for the same referent, third parties to the communicative interaction (Section 2.4); that blame comes in degrees such that the dichotomous distinction between having and not having the standing to blame is too simplistic (Section 2.5). Section 2.6 critically discusses and rebuts several reasons to be skeptical of the notion of standing to blame in general. Section 2.7 examines the moral equality and the commitment accounts of what undermines the standing to blame, defending the latter. Section 2.8 concludes.

The Beam and the Mote. Kasper Lippert-Rasmussen, Oxford University Press. © Oxford University Press 2024.
DOI: 10.1093/oso/9780197544594.003.0003

2.2. Private Blame

The disjunctive view of what it is to dismiss blame defended in Chapter 1 applies to paradigmatic blaming. However, as I noted there, not all forms of blame are paradigmatic. For one thing, sometimes people blame others without ever expressing that blame to those whom they are blaming, or for that matter without ever expressing it to anyone.[1] Hence, the analysis offered in Chapter 1 is problematic—not in the sense that private blame shows that it is false, but in the sense that its scope is restricted. However, there is an additional worry, which is that a private blamer can blame hypocritically, and do so in a way that we might characterize as involving standingless blame. If the object of such hypocritical blame were to learn about the fact that the blamer hypocritically blames them, we can easily imagine that, despite the absence of any blame in my communicative sense, the blamee might dismiss the private blame, exclaiming: "Who are they to blame me? That hypocrite has no standing to blame me." But if the complaint in this context means the same as the similar complaint in the context of paradigmatic blame and if, in privately blaming someone, one does not make any demands on one's blamee for a certain uptake to one's blame, then it seems to follow that the disjunctive view cannot be right. Dismissing blame cannot be a matter—or at least not simply a matter—of denying that one's blamer has a liberty right to blame (since, possibly, the blamee has no moral claims on what goes on in the mind of someone else, the blamer included), or a matter of denying that one has a duty to provide any uptake to the blame demanded by the blamer (since, surely, the private blamer has made no such demand).

While I agree with much in this challenge—to wit, that there is such a thing as private blame, e.g., harboring unexpressed resentment against someone, and that we might characterize what a private blamer does as engaging in standingless blaming—I do not think it points to any flaw in the disjunctive view. First, one can respond to the present challenge simply by saying the disjunctive account only provides an account of what it is to dismiss public blaming and that, obviously, the reasons, or at least some of the reasons, that exist for dismissing such blame are different from the reasons that exist for dismissing hypocritical private blame. Thus, it is no flaw in the account

---

[1] This is not to say that their blame has no behavioral manifestations at all, so for that reason my notion of private blame is neutral on the relationship between mental states and behavior.

that it fails to account for how *other* forms of blaming can be dismissed as standingless.

In response, some might say that, ideally, one would like an account of hypocritical blame and of what it is to dismiss hypocritical blame that is unified in the sense that it applies to both public and private blame and identifies the common feature of them that makes both morally wrong. This, however, presupposes that the moral wrongs in question really are relevantly similar across private and public blame, and this one might dispute. One might say that while people who engage in private hypocritical blaming have an objectionable character, such people do not wrong their blamees, who after all hold no rights against the blamers regarding the contents of their mental states; and while we might say that the hypocritical private blamer blames without having the standing to do so, what we mean is really something quite different from what we mean when we say that a hypocritical public blamer engages in standingless blame.[2]

Some people might think that we can wrong others simply by virtue of the content of our mental states; e.g., I have a right against others that they do not (or at least a justified moral complaint against others if they) think of me in racist or sexist ways, even if they never express these attitudes (see Basu 2019a, Chapter 7.5). However, if we take that route, then it becomes unclear why something like the disjunctive view might not apply to private blame, and this is my second response to the challenge from private blame—to wit, that the disjunctive view applies or can easily be tweaked to apply to standingless private blame. One reason why the disjunctive view is easily tweaked to apply to hypocritical standingless private blame if we can have claim rights on other people's mental content is that I then might have a claim right against others that they do not privately blame me and, thus, that they have no liberty right to do so.

Another reason that one can offer is something like an extension of the blamee-focused component of the disjunctive view, saying that private blame is standingless if, and only if, were it communicated to the blamee, the blamee

---

[2] Here are two views to the effect that others have no rights regarding what goes on in other people's minds. According to Warren Quinn (1993, 170–172): "A person is constituted by his body and mind. . . . For that very reason, it is fitting that he have primary say over what may be done to them. . . . We feel, I believe, most strongly about assaults on our minds. . . . Here it seems the sense of our own rightful say leads almost to absolutism." Sher (2021, 1) takes a marginally stronger view, which, unlike Quinn's, leaves no room for self-regarding duties pertaining to the content of one's mind: "[U]nlike actions in the world, which morality is properly said to constrain, each person's subjectivity is a limitless, lawless wild west in which absolutely everything is permitted."

would acquire no obligation to provide an uptake to the blame (cf. Mason 2019, 100–107; McKenna 2012, 69–70). Tweaking the account in this way is not ad hoc, since, arguably, it is not possible to blame someone privately and not to think that were one to express one's blame to the blamee, then the blamee would be obligated to provide an uptake to the blame. If one thinks not, then presumably that is either because one does not really blame the blamee, or one does, but only ambivalently so; e.g., one is ambivalent about whether what the blamee did was blameworthy. I conclude that the challenge from private blame can be met, either because the disjunctive view should not account for standingless private hypocritical blame or because it should but also could—perhaps with a few, non-ad hoc amendments.

2.3. Self-Blame

The challenge from self-blame to the disjunctive view is in some ways like the challenge from private blame. The challenge starts from the observation that we often blame ourselves, and sometimes that blame is moral blame and not, say, prudential blame. Yet it seems strained to say that in morally blaming myself I communicate to myself that what I did was morally blameworthy and that I demand a certain communicative uptake from myself in response to my blame. This would suggest that my account of hypocritical blame is inapplicable to the case of self-blame.[3] Yet hypocritical self-blame is possible—indeed, widespread. Suppose I am at fault in a very minor way—say, as a dart player—and in a very fundamental way—say, as a parent. I never blame myself for my much more serious and fundamental flaw as a parent, but often blame myself, publicly and privately, for my dart player deficiency, perhaps even too severely. However, this blame pattern is motivated in that it reflects my desire to see myself and to make others see me as a better parent and person than I am, even if deep down I have some not-completely-articulated self-awareness that I am much worse than I pretend to myself to be. In this case, it would, so I contend, be correct to think of myself as engaging in hypocritical blame, even though I am only blaming myself. Moreover, there seems to be something at play that is like not having the standing to blame. That is,

---

[3] To be clear, it makes perfect sense to blame oneself, and for that matter to forgive oneself. Arguably, being in a position to forgive oneself presupposes being in a position to blame oneself (see Chapter 6).

having the standing to blame myself for my dart player faults requires that I face and blame myself for my much more serious flaws as a parent. Others can say to me: "How can you be so obsessed with your faults qua dart player, when you completely ignore your faults as a parent?" They might properly refuse to listen to the former because I ignore the latter.[4]

I think there are two reasons why the complication of self-blame does not defeat my analysis. First, clearly self-blame does not fit my analysis of blame even if we disregard Condition (3)—to wit, the condition that blamer and blamee are different (see Section 2.1). It is odd to say that in blaming one-self, one communicates one's blameworthiness to oneself and demands a certain uptake from oneself.[5] Still, as in the case of private blame, I can still say that the topic of other-blame is an important topic in its own right and that the mere fact that it is possible to blame without blaming others does not show that I have not correctly delimited and analyzed *my* topic. Moreover, my analysis of paradigmatic blame can perhaps cast light on what it is to blame oneself. Perhaps something like the second condition in my analysis of paradigmatic blame must be satisfied for something to constitute self-blame (Section 1.2.1); e.g., the self-blamer must believe that were the victim of their wrongdoing someone else and were this person to blame them for their wrongdoing, they would be entitled to an uptake to their blame.

The previous paragraph does not address the worry that the possibility of self-blame shows that one can engage in standingless hypocritical blame. This is a worry because the difference between standingless and standingful self-blame seems to consist neither in the self-blamer having a liberty right to blame themself in the latter but not the former case—intuitively and absent special conditions, e.g., a promise to someone else to abstain from self-blame, we are at liberty to blame ourselves—nor does the difference consist in the self-blamer having a duty to provide an uptake to their self-blame in the latter, but not the former, case. In neither case does the self-blamer have any of these duties.[6]

---

[4] In refusing to listen to me, they need not blame me. Hence, it is irrelevant for the present point whether the "none of your business" reply is appropriate (Section 4.4).

[5] If you think that one can communicate a certain view to oneself, e.g., by repeatedly saying something to oneself, and make demands on oneself, then my analysis of blaming does fit self-blaming, and that aspect of the complication disappears.

[6] If you think one can have duties to oneself, then perhaps my account of having the standing to blame oneself might apply. Still, I am not sure that duties to self makes sense, and for that reason I do not want my argument to rest on the assumption that they do. Also, I do not find it obvious that if I blame myself for violating a lesser duty to myself and ignore my violating a greater duty to myself, my blame is standingless (cf. Shoemaker 2022).

In response to this worry I make two replies. First, while it might be the case that we sometimes speak about not having the standing to blame oneself, I suspect that this—at least when we are talking about private self-blame—is really a loose way of talking and that, in any case, the moral flaw that we have in mind in such cases is different from the one involved in paradigmatic hypocritical blame. Specifically, I think the moral fault at stake in such cases is an aretaic fault, i.e., a fault in our character or at least in the way that we on this occasion think about the relevant faults and not a fault that consists in wronging anyone.

Second, at least in some contexts, something like my analysis might apply when suitably amended. Suppose I—a lousy parent—blame myself in front of my children for my faults as a dart player. In doing so, I am inviting them to provide an uptake to self-blame. Given the addressees of my self-blame— self-blame can be public—there is, however, another set of faults that I should much more urgently address in their presence; i.e., I have no liberty right to blame myself for my dart-player faults in their presence (I might have a liberty right to do so in other contexts), nor do they have any duty not to simply ignore my self-blame qua dart player. I conclude that while self-blame points to a possible limitation of my analysis, it does not show that it is flawed, where one way for an analysis to be flawed is for it to fail to be suitably generally applicable.[7]

2.4. Third-Person Blame

Often when we blame, the addressee is some third party rather than the wrongdoer themself, whom the blamer does not and sometimes never will be able to blame face-to-face, e.g., because the blamee is dead. Such blame is quite common and can be hypocritical in a way that we will often say undermines the standing of the blamer to blame. Fortunately, however, it is possible to see how my analysis can be extended to such cases.

Take first my account of (hypocritical) blaming. It seems easy to extend it to third-person blame. We can say that X blames Z addressing Y—the relevant third party—if, and only if

---

[7] Self-blame where the self-blamer is the addressee of the blame is the form of self-blame that, arguably, fits my analysis of paradigmatic blame in Chapter 1 the least. Self-blame where the addressee is someone else, as in my lousy parent example, is different.

(1*) X communicates to Y that X believes that Z's φ-ing was blameworthy and that, under the right circumstances, Z would be under a duty to provide X with a suitable uptake were X to communicate this view and a demand for an uptake to Z.

(2*) X communicates to Y that X demands a suitable uptake from Y in response to X's communicative act.

(3*) X, Y, and Z are three different persons.

Clearly, the uptake that the blamer demands from the third party is different from the uptake they would demand from the wrongdoer, were the blamer to communicate their views to this person; e.g., it cannot involve a demand for an apology, since the addressee of the blame has not done anything blameworthy (or, if they are not utterly exceptional, they have, but this is not what is at stake in the conversation). Typically, the sort of uptake demanded would be participation in a joint act of blaming (cf. Cohen 2013). When I blame some third party for being unfaithful and my interlocutor rejects my standing to blame—either because I am unfaithful to a greater degree or because there is someone whom I like and do not blame, but whose unfaithfulness is greater—this is the sort of uptake we refuse to provide.

The last remark also indicates how my analysis of standing to blame$_p$ and dismissing blame$_p$ on grounds of lack of standing can be extended to cases of third-party blame. On this amendment, the blamer has the standing to blame the wrongdoer while addressing the third party if it is either the case that the blamer has a liberty right in relation to the wrongdoer to do so or if the third party has a duty to provide an uptake to the blamer's blaming the wrongdoer. Similarly, when we dismiss third-party blame, we either submit that the blamer has no liberty right to blame the wrongdoer in the presence of the relevant addressee or that the addressee has no duty to respond. In a case influentially discussed by G. A. Cohen: the Israeli ambassador has no liberty right to blame Palestinian terrorists, and his addressees, e.g., UK citizens, have no duty to join him in condemning Palestinian terrorists (or whatever they, or some of them, are other than terrorists), given the ambassador's silence both on Israeli killings of a greater number of Palestinians than the number of Israelis killed by Palestinian terrorists (whether this is justifiable or not) and given Israeli complicity in whatever grievances Palestinians have that make the Palestinian terrorists engage in the attacks condemned by the ambassador (whether these attacks are morally much worse than Israel acting in the relevant grievance-producing ways or not) (cf. Cohen 2013,

116). I conclude that the analysis I propose of blame$_p$ and standing to blame$_p$ can be amended to cover third-party blame as well.

One interesting implication of extending my analysis to third-party blame is that blame can be dismissed as hypocritical in two ways. As in the case of paradigmatic blame, it can be dismissed because the blamer's faults are at least as great as the blamee's. But it can also be dismissed if the blamer's faults, e.g., in relation to the addressee, are much greater than the addressee's faults. If, when addressing Peter, Mary blames John for always being late to their meetings and Mary has without exception been late for all of Mary and Peter's meetings, Peter can dismiss her third-party blame as hypocritical by responding: "Who are you to blame John when addressing me?" This is so even if John is indeed notoriously untimely and even more so than Mary; i.e., Mary cannot respond: "I can because Peter is much worse than I am."

2.5. Degrees of Blame and Degrees of Standing

I now turn to a complication that arises not due to my focus on paradigmatic blame, but that arises for all analyses of hypocritical blame and standing to blame that exist and which is usually ignored. Thus far, I have written about having the standing to blame as if it is a nonscalar, "either you have it or you don't" matter (cf. my blamer- and blamee-centered definitions of standing to blame); i.e., I have been writing as if the following view were true:

> *The simple threshold view*: it is either the case that, for any degree of blame, X has a standing to blame Y, or it is the case that, for any degree of blame, X has no standing to blame Y.

Yet, once we zoom in on it, the threshold view seems false. Both blame and standing come in different kinds and in different degrees (cf. Upadhyaya 2020; Mason 2019, 94).[8] To illustrate how blame comes in different kinds, note that there is a difference between implying that while one is a morally virtuous person, with regard to the action in question one acted in a blameworthy way, on the one hand, and implying that on this particular occasion one acted in a blameworthy way and that this reflects a more general and

---

[8] To foreshadow an issue that becomes relevant in Chapters 5 and 6, I also think praise and forgiveness are scalar phenomena.

serious moral flaw in one's character, on the other hand. To illustrate the latter, there is a difference between someone disapprovingly raising their eyebrow—in most contexts a mild form of blame—and someone expressing severe censure by shouting; there is a difference between blaming one in a sentence and lecturing one for hours on one's faults; there is a difference between conveying blame in a one-to-one setting and blaming one in front of an audience. Plausibly in some cases one has standing to engage in some form of mild blame, but not in severe forms of blame, rather than that one either has standing to do both or the standing to do neither.

Not only blame, but also standing, comes in degrees. This should be obvious in light of some of the factors that are said to bear on and undermine standing to blame. Take, for instance, hypocritical blame. There is a scalar difference between people who hypocritically blame others for lying, depending on whether they lied on a particular occasion on a matter that was rather insignificant to the blamee or whether they have massively lied to and deceived their blamee on a wide range of very important matters. Perhaps it is much too simplistic to say that this group of blamers falls into two, mutually exclusive groups, namely those with standing and those without standing to blame. Presumably, this ignores important distinctions between those blamers. Suppose it is morally required, all things considered, that somebody blames a wrongdoer. Unfortunately, only two hypocrites are available to do so. One is massively guilty of the same fault as the wrongdoer, while the other is guilty of the same fault to such a degree that if his fault were slightly lesser, then he would have the standing to blame on the threshold view. In such a case, arguably it would be better, morally, if the latter hypocrite were to do the blaming, which one might explain by saying that this person has more of a standing to blame than the former.

While I think this complication is important and will return to it on several occasions below, for many of the arguments in this book it is not crucial. Therefore, generally I shall simply write as if the simple threshold view were true. However, strictly speaking we should think of standing to blame as a scalar matter, where standing and blaming both come in degrees (however difficult it might be to distinguish precisely between different degrees of severity of blame) and where the standing requirement says that for a certain degree of blaming—say, mild censure—a certain degree of standing—say, not strongly objectionable similar faults—is required. This leaves open the possibility that a person with the standing to engage in mild blaming does not have the standing to engage in stronger forms of blaming and, conversely, that a person who does not have the standing to engage in a certain degree of blaming might have the standing to engage in milder forms of blaming. In short, instead of the threshold view we should accept:

> *The proportionality view*: X has the standing to blame Y to degree d_1 for ϕ-ing if, and only if, X's aggregate score on standing-undermining factors is not higher than d_2. X has greater standing (e.g., the claim right to an uptake is more stringent) the lower that score is.

In short, one's blaming should be proportionate to one's score on standing-undermining factors. This is compatible with the view that, in some cases, one has no standing to blame at all, and the view that, in the case of some triplets of blamers, blamees, and blameworthy actions, the blamer has a standing to engage in any degree of blaming of the blamee for the blameworthy act in question. Thus, in a sense, the proportionality view is a threshold view too, but it is a more nuanced threshold view than the simple threshold view.

2.6. Skepticism about Standing to Blame

Up to this point, I have contended that we have reason to dismiss hypocritical blame; that this is due to the fact that the hypocritical blamer lacks standing to blame; and that this notion of standing to blame can be cashed out in terms of the blamer's liberty right to blame or the blamee's duty to the blamer to provide an uptake to the blame to which they are subjected. While I think few would deny that these assumptions have considerable intuitive force or that, at the level of our psychological dispositions, we are very averse to being subjected to hypocritical blame, some philosophers think that, nevertheless, one or more of these assumptions should be rejected and that, basically, the whole idea of standing to blame and the idea of dismissing standingless blame is suspect. In this section, I review five such challenges. I argue that none of them succeed and that the assumptions described in the opening sentence of this paragraph can be defended.

First, some skeptics of standing to blame think that dismissing standingless blame is analogous to committing an ad hominem fallacy; i.e., you reject an argument not because you offer reasons to doubt its premises or whether its conclusion follows from them, but because the arguer has certain undesirable features.[9] Call this the *ad hominem objection*. Since one should avoid committing ad hominem fallacies and since dismissing standingless blame is analogous to committing that fallacy, one should avoid dismissing standingless blame on account of its being standingless. Or so the objection goes.

I believe the ad hominem objection is flawed. The basic reason for this is that dismissing standingless blame is not a matter of dismissing an argument. Recall that in indirectly dismissing blame, one is neither denying the conclusion posited by the blamer (if the blame takes the form of an argument), i.e., that one is blameworthy, nor denying that the conclusion follows from whatever true premises the blamer appeals to in support of the conclusion. Thus, dismissing blame does not involve the fallacy of an unmediated inference from the poor qualities of the arguer to the poor qualities of the argument (assuming the arguer has one). Whether the premises of the argument are true and the conclusion follows from the premises are matters that are unaffected by features of the arguer (setting aside special cases where the premises concern features of the arguer). However, whether one incurs any obligations through being subjected to blame—as my account of blame implies—plausibly might depend on features of the blamer.

Second, some skeptics of standing to blame submit that if blame requires standing and blamees can dismiss standingless blame, that would have or justify morally bad consequences. This is due to the fact that, in many cases, it is morally better that someone engages in hypocritical blame than that they do not (cf. Turner 1990, 264).[10] For instance, if the blamee has indeed acted in a wrongful way, being subjected to blame might make this person less likely to act in a similar wrongful way in the future and, generally, that would be a good thing, morally speaking.[11] Even if blame does not have such a motivating effect, some might think that hypocritical blame is warranted

---

[9] Cf. Mackie 1967, 177. Admittedly, in some cases hypocrisy might constitute metaevidence about the quality of the arguer's arguments (Aikin 2008, 165; Govier 1983), so assessment of the arguments per se and the arguer are not entirely separate.

[10] "Would it be better if I convinced myself that vegetarianism is not morally superior, just to avoid hypocrisy?" (Turner 1990, 264). This is a malformed challenge, since the standing account does not say that nonhypocrisy is better than hypocritical blame, just that the hypocritical blamer has no standing to blame.

[11] Often we improve more from being subjected to nonhypocritical blame than from being subjected to hypocritical blame. In the latter case, our indignation at being subjected to hypocritical blame comes between us and the moral improvement. However, all of this is a contingent matter, and perhaps in some unusual cases hypocritical blame might be more effective in making us improve in the future.

nevertheless, e.g., for retributivist reasons (cf. Bell 2013, 275). Call this the *bad consequences objection.*

Basically, the bad consequences argument fails for three reasons. First, the only alternative to blaming people is not to simply shut up. As noted in Section 1.2, one can express one's view that some act is blameworthy without blaming the agent. Since people typically become very defensive when being blamed, it surely requires some argument for why blaming people standinglessly has better consequences than simply expressing the view that they have acted wrongly but without blaming them.

Second, even if the moral fact of there being such a thing as standing to blame has or would justify morally bad consequences, I do not think this is a reason to believe that there is no such thing as (not having) standing to blame. For instance, the putative fact that there is an agent-relative prerogative that justifies that people bring about suboptimal outcomes, morally speaking, is not in itself a reason to reject the idea of an agent-relative prerogative.

The third reason why the bad consequences argument is flawed is the following: holding that there is such a thing as standing to blame and that standingless blame is in one way wrongful is consistent with thinking that many instances of standingless blame are morally permissible, even morally required, all things considered. On a pluralist view, many other morally relevant factors might bear on whether, in a particular instance, one should blame, even if doing so would be hypocritical. This is also why the account offered here does not condemn most institutional instances of blame, e.g., a judge condemning the offender for his wicked crime, assuming, as some do, that most instances of institutional blame are issued by institutions that are at fault in ways no less bad—often much worse—than the faults of those citizens it punishes, etc. So much for the bad consequences objection (see also Lippert-Rasmussen forthcoming).

A third source of skepticism about standing to blame is the worry that if one can dismiss hypocritical blame on the ground of its being hypocritical even when, considered on its own, the blame is completely warranted, then that is likely to lead blamees to ignore the content of the blame being expressed and, thus, to avoid facing their own wrongdoing (Bell 2013, 281). Call this the *distraction objection.*[12]

There are at least two reasons why this objection is flawed. First, like the bad consequences objection, it involves a sort of category mistake, i.e., the

---

[12] Perhaps the distraction objection is a specific version of the bad consequences objection.

mistake of inferring from the putative fact that people's accepting or acting on a certain norm will have certain bad effects that this norm is not a valid norm. This is a category mistake, if for no other reason than because it is not the norm being valid, but people applying it in a particular way, that results in the relevant bad effects. Second, a norm that permits blamees to dismiss blame coming from hypocritical blamers is different from a norm permitting blamees to be indifferent to the content of the blame. I could consistently believe that a blamee can dismiss their blamer's hypocritical blame, e.g., refuse to accept that they owe *their blamer* an explanation, but also think that the fact that the blamer brings the blamee's blameworthy action to the blamee's attention means that now it is even more objectionable if the blamee does not engage in self-blame for their blameworthy actions (see Section 2.2). In short, nothing in the standing view of blame implies that it absolves one of duties to take blame seriously.

A fourth objection attacks specifically the idea that blame that is hypocritical is for that reason standingless. It appeals to the fact that hypocrisy is defined relative not to the right moral standards, but relative to the moral standards to which the hypocrite appeals (see the blamer-relative account of the size of faults expounded in Section 1.2.2). Suppose I blame someone for acting against their own interests by following the prescriptions of Peter Singer in relation to global poverty, appealing to ethical egoism, i.e., the view that we have a moral duty to do what is best for ourselves. Suppose also that I am a hypocrite, since I have given even more to the global poor and, thus, have acted even more wrongly than the blamee according to the principles to which I appeal. According to the assumptions sketched initially, I have no standing to blame my interlocutor for their moderate benevolence. I could regain that—at least as far as considerations about hypocrisy are concerned—in two ways: I could retract my charitable donation (if possible) or I could revise my moral principles such that they permit charitable giving. The conception of standing to blame is indifferent between these two options. However, clearly morality instructs us to do the latter. Hence, the notion of standing to blame is indifferent between the two options. Thus, the idea of standing to blame is morally inert and, if so, irrelevant even if intelligible. Call this the *indifference objection*.[13]

---

[13] There is an analogous challenge to hypocritical blaming being pro tanto wrong. Since one way in which I could have retained my standing to blame would have been by my not giving anything to the fight against global poverty in line with the requirements of ethical egoism (let us suppose), which I embrace, it seems that people who think hypocritical blame is pro tanto wrongful are committed to saying that it would have been in one respect morally better if I had not given anything to the fight

In response, one might note that there is nothing in the notion of standing that is inconsistent with a moral preference for avoiding hypocritical blaming by revising the blamer's moral principle. The idea about standing is supposed to capture one moral principle. It is not supposed to exhaust morality and, accordingly, it is no objection to it that it does not imply all moral judgments that we want to make. Similarly, it is no objection to the principle that deception is wrongful that it does not imply that deception with harmful consequences for the deceived is worse than deception without harmful consequences for the deceived. It just shows that the principle needs to be supplemented with other moral principles.

Fifth, an argument along the following lines has been proposed by Matt King (2015) and Macalaster Bell (2013) as a reductio of the claim that the hypocrite loses their standing to blame:

(1) Almost always all of us are guilty of faults of the kind for which we blame others.

(2) If almost always all of us are guilty of faults of the kind for which we blame others, then almost always we have no standing to blame others.

(3) But: it is not the case that almost always we have no standing to blame others.

(4) Thus, it is not the case that if one is guilty of faults for which one blames others, then one has no standing to blame (i.e., (2) is false).

Call this objection the *obliteration-of-blame objection*. Given a certain account of guilt and faults, (1) is an empirical premise. I suspect "almost always" is a bit too pessimistic. Even if almost all of us are bad, even setting aside concerns about constitutive luck, we are not equally bad and, presumably, given this variation among us, for a lot of pairs of people, one of them is not guilty of the same fault for which they blame their counterpart, e.g., violence, being abusive in one's marriage, or engaging in serious tax fraud. Still, if we accept, as I have argued above that we should, that one can blame hypocritically even if one's faults are lesser than those of one's blamee and that there is such a thing as counterfactual hypocrisy, perhaps this premise is true after all, or true in an only slighter weaker form.

against global poverty and, thus, had avoided being a hypocritical blamer. But this, so the objection goes, is absurd. Surely, there is no way in which a world where I do not give anything to charity and blame others for doing so is better than a world in which I do give something to charity and (hypocritically) blame others for doing so.

(2), however, is too strong. Even if, say, I was once late to a meeting, it is not clear that because of this I have no standing to blame someone who is almost always late for our meetings.[14] My main quarrel with (2), however, is with the assumption that a person who is guilty of the same fault for which they blame someone else is a hypocrite. This assumption is false, since, if this person engages to a reasonable degree in blaming themself for their similar faults, they do have the standing to blame their addressee (see Condition (3)) in the definition of hypocritical blame offered in Section 1.2. Once this is specified, it is also clear that the consequent in (2) is false (Roadevin 2018, 150–151). Even if, almost always, we have no standing to blame others without engaging in a suitable dose of self-blame, it does not follow that, almost always, we have no standing to blame others full stop. After all, we could and should engage in appropriate self-blame.

For a reason like the one mentioned in the previous sentence, (3) needs to be specified with regard to the issue of whether self-blame accompanies other-blame or not. If (3) is a claim about being in a position to blame while properly addressing one's own faults, it does indeed appear true. However, that is not a threat to the position developed here. If instead (3) is a claim about being in a position to blame without addressing one's own faults, it bears on the issue at hand, but it is also clearly false—in very many cases, because of our own similar faults we have standing to blame only if we address our own faults—and thus cannot support skepticism about how hypocrisy undermines standing to blame. I conclude that the obliteration-of-blame objection is flawed.

There might be reasons to be skeptical about the idea of (not) having the standing to blame other than those examined here. However, to my mind these are among the most powerful ones, and if I am right they do not suffice to justify skepticism about standing to blame or, more specifically, skepticism about hypocrisy undermining standing to blame. Accordingly, I shall proceed as if the notion of standing to blame is a real normative phenomenon to be described and accounted for rather than rejected as illusory and explained away.

---

[14] Premise (2) reminds one of the following biblical passage: "He that is without sin among you, let him first cast a stone at her" (quoted in Duff 2010, 127; see however Section 1.2.2 on why the lesser faults of a blamer might negatively affect the blamer's standing to blame the blamee).

COMPLICATIONS AND DEFEATERS OF STANDING   59

2.7. Why Does Hypocrisy Undermine Standing to Blame?

Above I have defended a certain view of what it is to indirectly dismiss blame on grounds of hypocrisy—the disjunctive view—but I have not yet said anything about why a hypocrite has forfeited their standing to blame by virtue of those faults that render their blame hypocritical. In this section I address two such views: the moral equality account and the commitment account.[15]

The moral equality account of lack of standing to blame: what deprives the hypocrite of their standing to blame others is the fact that by virtue of their own fault, the hypocrite's blaming the blamee involves relating as people with unequal moral status, e.g., by implicitly denying the blamee's equal moral status.[16]

This account is attractive. Apparently, hypocritical blame involves the blamer making an exception in their own favor. The hypocritical blamer treats themself better—generally, but not necessarily always, blaming someone is treating them disadvantageously—than others for no good reason. This amounts to treating people unequally for no good reason and, arguably, treating people unequally for no good reason is relating to them as people without equal status. Thus, implicitly (at least), the hypocrite denies the moral equality of persons. Specifically, the hypocritical blamer implies that the blamee has a lower moral standing than the blamer.

Not only is the moral equality account appealing, but it is also an account that plays a central role in much contemporary theorizing on hypocrisy and the standing to blame. R. J. Wallace, for instance, argues that "hypocritical moral address"—hypocritical blame inter alia—"offends against the commitment to the equality of persons that is constitutive of moral relations in the first place" (Wallace 2010, 308). Similarly, Kyle G. Fritz and Daniel Miller (2018, 118) submit that hypocritical blame involves rejecting "the equality of persons, which . . . grounds the standing to blame others." My concern here is not with the details of these, or other specific, versions of the moral equality account (cf. Lippert-Rasmussen 2018, 105–110).[17] I mention them simply

---

[15] Much of the material in this section draws on Lippert-Rasmussen (2020).

[16] I treat "relating as people with unequal moral status" as a bit of a placeholder here.

[17] Neither Wallace nor Fritz and Miller use the phrase "relating as people with unequal moral standing." I intend the phrase to cover their views as well as additional equal-moral-standing-focused ones.

to show that the moral equality account has traction. My concern is with the equality account as such. I want to show, first, that the moral equality account, and a closely related account, cannot be correct.

Hypocrisy is common. What I shall call hypercrisy is rare, but it exists (and, in any case, for my purposes all I need is that it could exist) (cf. Nelkin 2022).[18] Hypercrisy is when a blamer blames themself in a disproportionately severe way for their relatively minor faults in the presence of relevant others whose much graver faults they either completely ignore or blame the others for, but to a degree that is disproportionately mild in view of the severe self-blame they subject themself to and the relative mildness of their own faults. In short, the hypercrite is the complement to a hypocrite—someone who makes an unfavorable exception of themself.

If the hypocrite implicitly denies moral equality of persons by implicitly affirming their own elevated moral standing, then so does the hypercrite, by implicitly affirming their own lowly standing relative to other persons.[19] If all persons are moral equals, then neither is one oneself a superior or an inferior, so there can be no relevant difference in relation to the implicit denial of moral equality of persons between the hypocrite and the hypercrite.[20] However, setting aside perhaps extreme cases where the hypercrite's pattern of blaming manifests a basic lack of understanding of the concept of blame, the hypercrite's standing to blame others is not undermined (see, however, Fritz and Miller 2021, 851–854). Suppose Adrian severely blames himself for, say, stealing ten dollars from a rich person, while at the same time expressing mild disapproval of Beth's theft of all the possessions of a poor person. Surely Beth cannot dismiss Adrian's mild disapproval on the ground that, due to his hypercrisy, he has no standing to blame her.[21] But if the hypercritical blamer does not lose her standing to blame and if either hypocrisy and hypercrisy both involve implicitly denying moral equality of persons or neither does, or both involve relating as equals or neither does, then it is not the case that denying moral equality of persons is why hypocrisy undermines the standing to blame.

---

[18] "Hyper" is the antonym to "hypo."

[19] Some hypercrites might only be superficial hypercrites; i.e., they hold themselves to much higher standards than others because deep down they think of themselves as superior (see Cohen 2013, n. 14). Here I (largely) set aside superficial hypercrites.

[20] The same point applies to whether the hypocrite relates to others as equals and whether the hypocrite relates to themself as an equal (as opposed to an inferior).

[21] Perhaps this point applies even if Adrian is a superficial hypercrite.

In response, some might doubt that the hypocrite—even implicitly—denies moral equality of persons. However, you might subscribe to this denial and still accept the conditional claim I am putting forward. Additionally, it is not a response that friends of the moral equality account are in a position to offer, since their account rests on the putative fact that hypocrisy involves an implicit denial of moral equality. Hence, the argument in the previous paragraph amounts to a compelling objection to the moral equality account. Still, its primary significance lies in the fact that it makes us see that what we might really be committed to is not the moral equality of standing to blame account, but something closely related to it:

> *The anti-moral superiority account*: what deprives the hypocrite of their standing to blame others is the fact that by virtue of their own fault, the hypocrite's blaming the blamee involves relating to the blamee as someone with a lower moral standing.[22]

The antisuperiority account fits the intuitions invoked above, since the hypercritical blamer, unlike the hypocritical blamer, does not affirm their own superiority. It is a good question why these two ways of denying moral equality of persons are relevantly different when it comes to standing to blame.[23] However, we can set this question aside, because as we shall now see, independently thereof, there is a compelling reason to reject the antisuperiority account. Consider:

> *The inegalitarian norm*: aristocrats ought to prevent severe harm to other aristocrats when they can do so, even at a moderate cost to themselves, and to prevent severe harm to commoners only when they can do so at a small cost to themselves. Commoners ought to prevent moderate harm to other commoners when they can do so at a small cost to themselves, and to prevent even small harm to aristocrats even when they can do so only at a severe cost to themselves.

---

[22] In my view, this account applies also to cases where a hypocrite implicitly asserts the superiority of the moral status of third parties relative to their blamee.

[23] Perhaps it is significant here that the hypercritical blamer implicitly consents to being disproportionately blamed, whereas the target of the hypocritical blamer (typically at least) does not. However, if it is the denial of a certain moral truth about the moral equality of persons that undermines standing to blame, it is unclear how consent comes into the picture even if, no doubt, it is relevant to the overall moral permissibility of blame.

Surely, to affirm the inegalitarian norm is to affirm hierarchy of moral status among persons and, thus, to deny—implicitly, if not explicitly—the moral equality of persons.[24]

Suppose two aristocrats, both of whom subscribe to the inegalitarian norm, blame you for having acted contrary to the inegalitarian norm. Both think of you as an aristocrat like themselves and believe that you have often helped commoners when doing so involved accepting moderate costs for yourself. Suppose also that the first blamer is nonhypocritical—this aristocrat knows that they themself have never violated the inegalitarian norm— while the second blamer is hypocritical—this aristocrat knows that they have often violated the inegalitarian norm, helping commoners even when doing so required them to bear moderate costs.[25]

In this case you can dismiss the blame you are being subjected to in either of two ways (which, of course, means that you can dismiss the blame in both ways). First, you can do so directly by denying that what you did was morally wrong or morally blameworthy. The inegalitarian moral norm is false and, accordingly, acting in a way that violates it is neither ipso facto morally wrong nor ipso facto blameworthy. This direct dismissal—warranted as it is—however, does not amount to denying that your critics are not in a position to blame you. As noted, denying that someone is in a position to blame you is an indirect response to blame in the sense that it brackets whether what you did was morally wrong or blameworthy. Indirect responses to blame attack the critic's standing to blame the blamee for the relevant act, not the blameworthiness of the act (Section 1.3). Hence, the grounds for this dismissal are irrelevant to the truth of the antisuperiority account, which concerns the standing to blame, not blameworthiness.

---

[24] If some moral norms are incompatible with the moral equality of persons, surely the present norm is. However, readers who think it is not, but think that some moral norms are incompatible with the moral equality of persons, could simply substitute their favored candidate of hierarchical norms for the one I present here for purposes of illustration only.

[25] Possibly, friends of the moral equality account are committed to holding that, through their helping deeds, this hypocritical blamer implicitly affirms the moral equality of persons. At this point some might respond by pointing to the fact that by appealing to the inegalitarian norm, the hypocritical blamer explicitly affirms the inequality of persons. But, by parity of reasoning, then, the hypocrite who hypocritically blames someone for violating a norm whose content derives from moral equality of persons similarly explicitly affirms the equality of persons. Hence, if this hypocrite has no standing to blame despite their explicit affirmation of moral equality—as, *ex hypothesis* and plausibly so, they have not—then why should the former hypocrite lack standing to blame by virtue of their explicit embrace of inequality of persons? This is a serious challenge to the anti-moral superiority account, but it is independent of the one I explore here.

Second, you can dismiss your hypocritical aristocratic blamer by pointing out that, since they themself have often violated the inegalitarian norm, they are not in a position to point fingers at you for doing so. You cannot say the same to your nonhypocritical aristocratic blamer. But then it follows that the antisuperiority account is false. Both of your blamers affirm their (and that of other aristocrats') superior moral standing. Yet one of them has the standing to express their (for other reasons directly dismissible) blame, while the other has not. The fact that accounts for this difference in standing must result from some other difference between them.

At this point, friends of the antisuperiority account might say that there are two aspects of antisuperiority. First, there is, as it were, an issue about first-order moral norms, i.e., moral norms that regulate, say, the distribution of benefits and harms, the respect for others' will etc. In relation to those norms, one can distinguish between egalitarian and inegalitarian norms—my example of an antiegalitarian norm pertaining to helping others being of the latter kind. Second, there are second-order moral norms about how we assess our conduct considering these first-order norms. For instance, do these norms imply, in a hierarchical fashion, that some people can hold others to account for their failure to comply with the relevant first-order principles, but not the other way around? Some might suggest that to have a standing to blame, one must not affirm superiority in relation to these second-order norms and that the relevant difference between my two aristocratic blamers is that the hypocritical aristocratic blamer denies moral equality in this way, while the nonhypocritical aristocratic blamer does not. True, the latter thinks that the interests of commoners count for less, morally speaking, but accepts that aristocrats and commoners are symmetrically located when it comes to holding each other to account for their failures to comply with the relevant hierarchical, first-order norms.

Unfortunately, this reply will not do. Consider the following norm, which consists of a conjunction of the original inegalitarian norm and:

The inegalitarian, second-order norm: when reasoning about moral norms and our compliance with them, aristocrats ought to treat the contributions etc. of other aristocrats as equally significant, i.e., as something that demands an uptake, e.g., an apology or a display of an intention to improve, but to treat the contributions etc. of commoners as insignificant, i.e., as something that does not demand any uptake. When reasoning about moral norms and our compliance with them, commoners ought to treat the contributions etc. of other commoners as equally significant, but to treat the contributions etc. of aristocrats as more significant, i.e., as something that demands a more extensive uptake compared to similar contributions from commoners.

Call the norm conjoining the original inegalitarian norm and the inegalitarian, second-order norm *the complex inegalitarian norm*. The complex inegalitarian norm enables us to see that shifting attention to moral equality at a second-order level simply moves the underlying problem one level up. Consider a case where two aristocrats who both subscribe to the complex inegalitarian norm blame you for violating the complex inegalitarian norm, e.g., for your often taking the blame of commoners as meriting a response. One aristocrat always acts in compliance with the complex inegalitarian norm, while the other, hypocritically, often violates it. This situation invites a parallel response to the one I gave in relation to asserting first-order-level moral superiority. You can directly dismiss the blame coming from the first aristocrat because you rightly dismiss the complex inegalitarian norm. But you can also dismiss the blame coming from the hypocritical aristocrat for an additional reason: to wit, that their failure to comply with the norm to which they appeal undermines their standing to blame. Yet both deny the second-order-level moral equality of persons. Hence, this denial cannot be what explains the second critic's lack of standing to blame. If it did, then the first critic would also lack the standing to blame.

Why do the egalitarian and the antisuperiority accounts seem plausible when, in fact, they are flawed? Here is a conjecture. Second-order moral norms are norms that are, and that we believe to be, consistent with or indeed somehow flowing from the moral equality of persons. Accordingly, it is not natural for us to think of an egalitarian hypocrite who violates hierarchical norms pertaining to assessing noncompliance with moral norms, and we therefore mistake what is a contingent feature of blame that is hypocritical in a way that undermines standing to blame—that it involves implicitly denying moral equality—for a necessary feature of standing-undermining hypocritical blame.

Can we say something in light of the criticisms of the egalitarian and the anti-moral superiority accounts about why hypocrisy undermines the standing to blame? I think we can, and this takes us to the second and alternative account of what undermines standing to blame:[26]

---

[26] I discuss the two accounts as if they are alternatives. However, some might think that they can be combined because both relating as unequals and being uncommitted undermine standing to blame.

The commitment account of lack of standing to blame: what deprives the hypocrite of their standing to blame others is the fact that by virtue of their relevantly similar flaws, which render their blame hypocritical, they show themself to lack commitment to the norm that they appeal to in their blame.

All the hypocrites that we have encountered so far have one common feature: they are not serious about the norm that they blame others for not complying with. Their lack of seriousness manifests itself in their being relatively unconcerned about their own violations of the norm to which they appeal.[27] Thus, one hypothesis that the present critique suggests is that lack of seriousness about a norm undermines one's standing as a critic of others' noncompliance with that norm.

It speaks in favor of the commitment account that it explains why one can regain one's standing to blame through one's moral improvement and self-blame even when one has violated the relevant blame-inducing norm severely in the past—now one is serious about the norm and so one's role as enforcer of the norm is not in question (cf. Fritz and Miller 2018, 121–122; Shoemaker and Vargas 2021).[28] It also explains why a critic can be in a position to blame violators of a certain norm that, out of weakness of the will, they themself have often violated despite being serious about it (Fritz and Miller 2019a, 382). Finally, it explains why it would appear that one's standing to blame can be undermined by facts other than the fact that one is not serious about a moral norm by virtue of violating it oneself. Suppose that I blame you for failing to live up to a principle that I reject myself, even if I have never violated it, nor am disposed in a way that would lead me to do so

---

[27] One worry here is that my selection of examples is one-sided. Consider someone who largely—and to a higher degree than others—complies with all lightly demanding norms they subscribe to and appropriately blames themself and others for failures to comply with those norms, setting aside the facts that this person also consistently—and more so than others—fails to comply with all more-than-lightly demanding norms and that they never blame anyone for failures to live up to those norms. None of this person's acts of blaming might be hypocritical when considered in isolation. However, the person's overall pattern of blaming is hypocritical. Might the hypocrisy involved in the overall pattern transfer to individual instances of blame coming from this person, such that others might refuse to be subjected to blame from this person for their failings to comply with lightly demanding norms only? Or should we instead say that while this person is a hypocrite by virtue of their overall pattern of blame, in no individual instance do they engage in hypocritical blame?

[28] Admittedly, this view does not explain why, in relation to blame and with some qualifications, we care about commitment at the time of blaming and not commitment at other times as well. The need for "with some qualifications" is brought out by a case where I am blamed by someone who appeals to a moral principle that for a long time they rejected, but now very recently became committed to. Even if there is no doubt about the blamer's commitments, a blamee is likely to deflect from the blamer by pointing to the fact that not so long ago the blamer would have responded very differently.

in the future. Plausibly, I have no standing to blame others for failing to live up to this standard about which, obviously, I am not serious myself. As Rawls (2000, 190) puts it: a "person's right to complain is limited to violations of principles he acknowledges himself" (see Section 4.6).

Despite these attractions, the commitment account also faces at least five challenges. First, what about hypercrites? If they too lack commitment to the norm to which they appeal when blaming themselves, e.g., all they care about is the opportunity to engage in "self-punishing behavior," as manifested in their refraining from blaming others for violating that same norm, and if they nevertheless have standing to blame others, then the case of hypercrites seems like a counterexample to the commitment account for a reason similar to why the case serves as a counterexample to the moral equality account of standing (Tierney 2021, 4). Perhaps the challenge represented by the case of hypercrites is symmetrical in the sense that while hypocrites lack standing to blame others, hypercrites lack standing to blame themselves (Tierney 2021, 6; see also Fritz and Miller 2021, 850–854).

In response, note first that on the assumption that one can hold no liberty or claim rights against oneself, then on my account of what it is to lack standing to blame, it makes no sense to say that the hypercrite lacks standing to self-blame—standing is a matter of a right one holds against others. However, it does seem that a hypercrite who blames themself in my presence might lack a conversational claim right against me to an uptake to their self-blame. Second, while I contended above that the hypercrite does not lack standing to blame others, in view of Tierney's critique I now think this claim must be revised. In those cases where hypercrisy is indeed an indication that the hypercrite is not committed to the norm to which they appeal when engaging in self-blame, e.g., all they care about is punishing themself and they simply opportunistically exploit the norm in question despite not really caring about it, others can dismiss both self- and other-blame from the hypercrite's side, were they to engage in it, as standingless. For what it is worth, however, I conjecture that in the vast majority of cases of hypercrisy, the hypercrite does care about the norm in question, but for other reasons (e.g., shyness or dislike of conflicts) refrains from blaming others, whereas in the vast majority of cases of hypocrisy the hypocrite does not care very much about the norm in question, and that whatever commitment they do have to the norm is overwhelmed by other of the hypocrite's concerns.[29]

---

[29] Hence, I disagree with Tierney (2021, 2) when she writes: "[J]ust as hypercrites are relevantly

The second challenge to the commitment account concerns what sort of commitment bears on standing to blame and how degrees of commitment affect standing to blame. Regarding the nature of the relevant commitment, it seems that the mere fact that one strongly believes that a certain moral principle is correct does not secure one's standing to blame. A hypocrite who really believes in the principle that one ought not to lie, but nevertheless often lies and never addresses their own lying, has no standing to blame, even if they sincerely and strongly believe lying is wrong.[30] Mere cognitive commitment is not enough (Todd 2019, 355; see also Fritz and Miller 2021, 836–837, 851). Noncognitive commitment, e.g., strong motivation to act in accordance with the principle, is needed too (even though in light of the akratic person we might not insist that the motivation manifests itself in the agent doing what they are motivated to do).[31] Presumably, we could allow that an akratic person who is strongly committed to the relevant norms both cognitively and motivationally but nevertheless fails to mobilize the willpower required to comply with them has the standing to blame others.[32] We should also note, however, that if the akratic person fails to address their own wrongful, akratic conduct, that is at least one way—perhaps a particularly important way—in which they score low on a determinant of lack of commitment. In any case their standing to blame might be undermined by the mere fact that, at least given a somewhat coarse-grained level of description,

similar to hypocrites in denying equality of persons, they are also relevantly similar in failing to take norms seriously." I accept, however, that there might be cases of hypocritical blame where the hypocrisy does not manifest lack of commitment to the norm; e.g., it might reflect fear of social sanctions if one accepts responsibility for one's own violations. However, most likely standing to blame in those cases is undermined on tu quoque grounds, not on hypocrisy grounds. The blamee can say: "I realize you are strongly committed to the norm that you blame me for violating. Even so, in view of your own more serious violations, you have no standing to blame me." A similar response is not available to the hypercrite, whose hypercrisy does not manifest lack of commitment. In that sense we should treat the two cases asymmetrically, unlike what Tierney suggests. Moreover, we can reject Tierney's asymmetry: while hypocrites have no standing to blame others, hypercrites have no standing to blame themselves.

[30] As this passage shows, I am skeptical of strong forms of internalism about moral judgment and motivation.

[31] Other complex mental states and mental dispositions might also bear on commitment, e.g., the degree to which one's long-term plans are constrained by the relevant norm. Perhaps things other than mental states narrowly construed, e.g., one's unreflective habits, might bear on one's level of commitment too.

[32] This is not to imply that, generally, akratic behavior is an indicator of lack of commitment to the relevant norms. People are more likely to engage in akratic behavior when it comes to not eating sweets than when it comes to avoiding (imminently) life-threatening situations.

they have the same fault as that for which they blame others (see the discussion of the tu quoque response in Section 4.2).[33]

This brings us to the third challenge. Commitment comes in degrees, because just like belief—at least when understood as subscription to a certain credence—motivation comes in degrees.[34] On a threshold view of standing and commitment, once one's level of commitment reaches a certain intensity on an absolute scale, one's standing to blame is secure. However, on a scalar view, along the same lines as suggested in Section 2.5, standing to engage in severe blame requires greater commitment than standing to engage in mild blame. I am inclined to favor the scalar view. However, I also think that the present challenge only defeats dichotomous commitment accounts of standing to blame, and scalar ones that involve some kind of proportionality between the severity of the blame being imposed on the blamee and the severity of the blamer's own acknowledged wrongdoings.

Fourth, for the commitment account to be fully satisfying we need a rationale for why lack of commitment undermines one's standing to blame.[35] This question is particularly pressing because other moral relations are not undermined by lack of commitment. Suppose that I promise you I will do a certain thing. Suppose, moreover, that you are not committed to the principle that people should keep their promises. This lack of commitment would not seem to undermine your standing to demand that I fulfill my duty; e.g., it is not as if I can dismiss your demand on me to do as I promised on the ground that given your lack of commitment to the moral principle that one is obligated to keep one's promise, I am absolved of my duty. Why, one might reasonably ask, is blaming any different? I do not have a satisfying answer to this question. Intuitively, lack of commitment undermines standing to blame, but pointing to that fact does not provide an answer to the challenge. It would make sense that lack of commitment undermines standing to blame if we see morality as a collective project or club that one can join. Being a contributor to the project or a member of the club requires that one is committed to, and

---

[33] The akratic person is likely to respond to a dismissal of their blame by noting that they really wanted to do better, unlike the person whom they blame, and for that reason they have the standing to blame the other without addressing their own wrongdoing. In my view, this reply has some force, but not enough to completely undermine an indirect dismissal of their blame.

[34] Could the hypocritical blamer say: "I am strongly committed to this principle. However, I have little commitment to applying the principle to this specific case"?

[35] Some might say that the quest for a rationale rests on a misunderstanding. There is no explanation for why lack of commitment undermines standing to blame—it just does (Todd 2019). Or as Riedener (2019) puts it: the fact that lack of commitment undermines standing is simply a fact about the philosophical grammar of blame.

therefore committed to obeying, the relevant conditions and rules.[36] Doing so confers certain rights on one, notably, to demand that other contributors or members do their fair share and to hold them accountable when they do not. I am doubtful that this is the right way to look at morality, but at least it would cast some light on why lack of commitment undermines standing to blame.

Finally, it is unclear that commitment has the right shape to explain lack of standing. On my view, hypocrisy is a comparative matter; i.e., whether one's blame is hypocritical depends on how one's faults in one's view compare to those of others. But, presumably, if someone's degree of commitment depends on noncomparative factors, e.g., how often I think of the relevant norm, it should be possible for someone to be at greater fault in relation to some norm than another person, whom the former blames for violations of that norm, even though the blamer is more committed to the relevant norm. But then, on the commitment account, one would expect this person to have standing to blame, unlike what, generally, we take to be the case. Consider my opening example of Jack, Al, and Greta. Suppose we say that Al has no standing to blame Greta for flying too much and the reason why is that he is not sufficiently committed to whatever is the relevant norm here. If so, and if standing to blame depends on one's absolute level of commitment as measured by noncomparative features, then it follows that Jack has no standing to blame Al either. However, intuitively Jack has standing to do so. Admittedly, we could focus on how the commitment of the hypocritical blamer compares to that of the blamee, but there seems to be no conceptual guarantee that the commitment of the hypocritical blamer to the norm in question is lower than that of the blamee, one reason being that a blamee can dismiss hypocritical blame as ipso facto standingless even if the blamee is not committed to (or even is committed against) this norm. Despite these challenges, especially the last one, which I concede to be serious and to require more work than I supply here, based on the strengths of the account I nevertheless believe that the commitment account is the most promising account of standing to blame of the two accounts that I have discussed.

---

[36] Perhaps we can give a contractualist account of the relevant rule, i.e., to order one's social relations with others based on principles that no one can reasonably reject.

2.8. Conclusion

In this chapter, I have done three things. First, I have addressed certain complications that arise in connection with my account of hypocritical blame and of what it is to dismiss standingless blame (Sections 2.2–2.5), e.g., that not all forms of blaming involve paradigmatic blame. For instance, private blame is not paradigmatic blame in my sense. I argued, inter alia, that both (lack of) standing and blame come in different degrees, and I suggested that, strictly speaking, it is better to adopt a scalar view of standing to blame rather than to think of standing to blame (whatever the degree of blame) as a binary thing. Second, I examined and rejected five arguments in favor of skepticism about the whole idea of standing to blame. Third and finally, I asked what deprives hypocrites of standing to blame. I suggested that the view that it is because their hypocritical blame somehow clashes with moral equality is wrong and instead argued, with a number of reservations, that what undermines standing to blame is the hypocrite's lack of commitment to the moral or evaluative principles to which they appeal when blaming others.

All of this leaves quite open what makes hypocritical blame wrongful. This is the question I turn to in Chapter 3, where we will see both the moral equality and the commitment accounts return, though this time not as accounts of what undermines the hypocrite's standing to blame, but instead as accounts of what makes it morally wrong, when it is. In this form, I am more sympathetic to the moral equality account.

3

What, If Anything, Makes Hypocritical Blame Morally Wrong?

3.1. Introduction

Chapter 1 defined hypocritical blame. It also offered an account of standing and of what it is to dismiss hypocritical blame on the grounds that the blamer has no standing to blame. Chapter 2 elucidated these accounts in view of various complications—especially in relation to blame that deviates from paradigmatic blame—and proposed the commitment account as an account of what undermines the hypocrite's standing to blame. Chapter 3 builds on these two chapters and asks what makes hypocritical blame morally wrong, when it is.[1]

One important claim I should highlight from the outset is that, in my view, what makes hypocritical blame wrong is different from what undermines standing to blame. I suspect that, offhand, many readers assume that the features that undermine it are the same features that make hypocritical blame wrong. Some readers might even think that what undermines the standing to engage in hypocritical blame is its moral wrongfulness (Section 2.7; Rossi 2018, 553). Ultimately, my view that the two come apart must be assessed based on the strengths of the arguments that I provide in favor of my account of what undermines standing to blame in Chapter 2 and in favor of my account of what makes it wrong in this chapter. However, the view I take here

---

[1] I am assuming here that something can be said in response to this question. However, we should be open to the possibility that nothing really can be said in response to it—that it is simply a fundamental fact, not derived from any other fact, moral or otherwise, that hypocritical blaming *just is* wrongful (cf. Todd 2019, 372). Still, this would be surprising if I am right that hypocritical praise, acts of forgiveness, etc. can be wrongful too, for similar reasons as hypocrisy. Interestingly, Friedman's (2013, 273) account implicitly suggests such an explanation. On her view, "Blaming is a social relationship that assumes shared membership in the moral community." If membership in the moral community in turn is conditional on commitment to act in accordance with moral norms (as one sees them), we have an explanation of why lack of commitment undermines standing to blame; i.e., in virtue of one's lack of commitment one is not a member of the moral community. This explanation is in some way analogous to Fritz and Miller's account of why the hypocrite lacks standing to blame (cf. Fritz and Miller 2019a, 384).

The Beam and the Mote. Kasper Lippert-Rasmussen, Oxford University Press. © Oxford University Press 2024.
DOI: 10.1093/oso/9780197544594.003.0004

is not radically unorthodox. What makes something a lie, i.e., an utterance made by the liar in the knowledge that it is false and with the intention to make the recipient believe the falsehood, might be different from what makes a lie wrong, e.g., on some accounts the harm to the interests of the recipient from being lied to, even though the typical kind of harm that lies produce reflect what lies are. Perhaps such a harm-based account of the wrongness of lying has only limited validity or is even false altogether. That is not the point. The point is that it is not an objection to this account that it implies that what makes something a lie is different from what makes it wrong—not even if lies are wrong as such. I suggest a similar point applies to the standing to blame and the wrongness of standingless blame.

Another important preliminary issue is the need to see the question of what makes hypocritical blame wrong in a slightly broader context, i.e., its relation to the more generic question: What makes blame morally wrongful, when it is?[2] Most would agree that sometimes it is not morally wrongful to blame, i.e.:

The simple view: for some pairs of people X and Y, if Y has done something that is blameworthy and X can blame Y, it is not morally wrongful for X not to blame Y.

To see the force of the simple view, suppose the blamee's action is not particularly blameworthy, that the blamee is going through a difficult period in their life, during which harsh words are likely to deeply affect them, and blaming the blamee is unlikely to prevent further wrongdoing on the blamee's part; e.g., suppose the blamee repents their wrongdoing and has embarked on a plan of moral improvement anyway. In that case, blaming the blamee for their blameworthy action seems morally impermissible. Indeed, it seems in no way wrong not to blame the blamee. Thus, there is no direct inference from blameworthiness to the moral permissibility of blaming.

---

[2] I say "when it is" because I do not think that, under all circumstances, the fact that blaming is hypocritical is a feature by virtue of which blaming is pro tanto wrong. Consider a case of consensual hypocritical blaming, i.e., one in which two persons have made an agreement with one another that they can hypocritically blame each other. Suppose they think that it is very important that they are blamed for their faults and fear that if they do not permit the other to blame even when the blame will be hypocritical, they will not be blamed enough. In such a case, the fact that the blamer blames the blamee for a fault that the blamer has to a greater degree might not even be a pro tanto wrong-making feature of the act. Mutual, consensual hypocritical blaming wrongs no one.

In further support of this claim, consider the fact that publicly blaming someone is often a way of harming people. Most people find it unpleasant to be blamed, e.g., because of the shame involved in being publicly singled out and confronted with one's wrongdoing; so, offhand, one would suspect that norms that pertain to harming in general at least also have a bearing on norms of blaming (cf. Isserow and Klein 2017, 217). Specifically, the mere fact that a person is "harmworthy"—assuming that it is possible for a person to be that, as retributivists think it is—does not imply that, always and for any potential distributor of harm, it is morally permissible for that distributor to harm the harmworthy person. Even if we assume that an evil aggressor deserves to be harmed, many will say—appealing to considerations about necessity—that if a defender could thwart the aggression in a way that imposes less defensive harm on the harmworthy aggressor, then it is impermissible to impose the harm on the aggressor that this person deserves.[3] However, it is also clear that norms about blaming cannot simply be a special case of norms about harming, one reason being that sometimes blame will benefit the blamee in the long run, e.g., because the person's relations to others will improve and the person will learn valuable lessons from being blamed (cf. Dover 2019). And, of course, there are special cases of blamees who do not find it unpleasant to be blamed. After all, being blamed is one way of getting attention—sometimes intense attention.

There seem to be at least four respects in which we should be looking for an answer to our core question of what makes hypocritical blaming wrongful, which is not too ambitious, as it were. First, given that the reasons why, sometimes, one ought not to blame others even if they are blameworthy would seem to apply to cases of nonhypocritical and hypocritical blame alike, arguably in looking for an answer to the question of what makes hypocritical blame wrong, we should not be looking for an answer to the effect that hypocritical blame is *always* wrong. Just as it is sometimes morally wrong to blame blameworthy persons nonhypocritically, sometimes it is morally permissible to blame—even nonblameworthy persons—hypocritically. Arguably, the former involves the impermissibility of treating a person in a way that would

---

[3] Interestingly, most who write on the ethics of self-defense think that liability to defensive harm, not desert, is crucial to the permissibility of self-defense. Few theorists who write on blame think that liability to blame, and not whether one deserves to be blamed, is crucial to the permissibility of blaming. No doubt, part of the reason for this is that, unlike self-defense, blame's primary function is not thought to be the prevention of morally undesirable future events (though I suspect that few will deny that this is, in some sense, an important function of blame). It is an interesting question, though, to what degree this asymmetry between blame and self-defense is defensible.

not wrong him, whereas the latter merely involves infringing a right not to be blamed.

Second, there is a difference between monistic and nonmonistic accounts of the wrongfulness of hypocritical blame. The former holds that there is one and only one feature by virtue of which hypocritical blame is wrongful. The latter denies this claim and allows that there is more than one such feature. Nonmonists could consistently claim that whereas some instances of wrongful hypocritical blame are wrong because they have all the features by virtue of which hypocritical blaming can be wrong, other instances are wrong because they have one, and only one, of the features by virtue of which hypocritical blaming can be wrong. Perhaps it is good to be open to the possibility that hypocritical blame can be wrong for several reasons, when it is wrong, and perhaps there is no specific wrong that is common to all cases of wrongful hypocritical blame.[4]

Third, there is a question about whether hypocritical blaming is a distinctive wrong. This question is orthogonal to the monism-pluralism question (cf. Isserow and Klein 2017, 192). Suppose that, unlike what I think is the case, hypocrisy necessarily involves deception, and that deception is pro tanto morally wrong. Since hypocritical blame is a form of hypocrisy, it follows from this assumption that, necessarily, hypocritical blame involves deception and, thus, is morally wrong for this reason. If so, hypocritical blame is morally wrong, but possibly not for any distinctive reason, i.e., not for any reason that applies specifically to hypocritical blaming and not to other forms of wrongful acting—it is possibly wrong simply because it falls under a broader category, i.e., acts of deception, and is morally wrong for the same reason as any other act that falls under this category is wrong. Offhand, it seems wise to be open to the possibility that the wrong of hypocritical blame is not distinctive in this way.[5]

Finally, we do well to remember that, as noted in the introduction, hypocritical blaming is in a different league of wrongful actions than some of the other wrongful actions often discussed in ethical theories, e.g., unjust wars or bringing people into existence whose lives are worse than not living. While important for the reasons I offered, the wrong of hypocritical blaming

[4] If moral pluralism is true, it would be very surprising if instances of hypocritical blame could not be wrong for several reasons.

[5] On the moral equality account that I defend below, the wrong of standingless blame is not distinctive—there are ways of relating to others as inferiors other than by subjecting them to standingless blame (Section 3.9).

belongs to microethics, as it were (cf. Sher 2017, 88–108).[6] Accordingly, in answering our core question, perhaps we should not expect our answer to what constitutes the wrong of hypocritical blame to belong to the moral Super League.

Sections 3.2 to 3.9 critically assess eight different accounts of the wrongfulness of hypocritical blaming. Sections 3.2 to 3.8 review seven accounts that I am critical of to varying degrees, to wit, the desert, lack of commitment, wrong attention, moral authority, reciprocity, moral community, and falsehood accounts. Section 3.9 defends my favored moral-equality-based account of the wrongfulness of hypocritical blaming. We have already encountered something analogous to that account in the previous chapter, although in that chapter the moral equality account was an account of what undermines standing to blame. Here, however, I am going to defend the claim that hypocritical blaming is wrongful whenever it involves treating the blamee as an inferior. The eight accounts that I discuss sort into three different kinds: distribution- (Section 3.2), blamer- (Sections 3.3–3.4), and blamer-blamee-relation-focused accounts (Sections 3.5–3.9).

In accordance with the cautionary remarks about the ambitiousness of the answer to the chapter's main questions, I shall not be claiming that no cases of wrongful hypocritical blaming are wrong for reasons other than those identified by the moral equality account; that all cases of hypocritical blaming involve the blamer treating the blamee as an inferior (e.g., consensual hypocritical blaming might not); that hypocritical blaming is wrong in a distinctive way in that there are no other ways of treating people as inferiors than by hypocritical blaming; or that treating people as inferiors is always a serious moral wrong compared to other wrongs. Section 3.10 concludes.

3.2. Lack of Desert

One vice of hypocrisy that theorists often draw attention to is trying to deceive others into thinking that one is better than one in fact is. It is thus natural to think that the wrongfulness of hypocritical blaming derives from its having this feature. Without explicitly asserting such a view, Isserow and

---

[6] That is one reason why some might find it odd to say that one has a right not to be blamed hypocritically. They might think that moral rights protect only important interests, e.g., an individual's interest in their life or liberty. I disagree and think of rights as a normative structure that can attach to morally less important interests as well.

Klein (2017, 209) suggest that a view along these lines or, at least, a view like this often motivates our condemnation of hypocritical blame:

> We are also likely to be moved to anger by the *unmerited esteem* that they [hypocrites] garner. . . . But esteem, being inherently comparative, is a good in limited supply . . . esteem is ultimately a zero-sum game. . . . It is therefore unsurprising that hypocrites are traditionally met with disdain; for they have ultimately shown themselves to be undeserving of [the elevated esteem that comes with being a moral authority].[7]

There are two distinct objections here, which Isserow and Klein do not distinguish clearly between, nor whether they subscribe to neither, both, or one and only one of those.[8] One objection derives from the ideal of absolute desert:

> *The absolute desert account*: hypocritical blaming is wrongful because it involves trying to acquire (or actually acquiring) more esteem in the eyes of others than one deserves, absolutely speaking.[9]

The other objection appeals to comparative desert:

> *The comparative desert account*: hypocritical blaming is wrongful because it involves trying to acquire (or actually acquiring) more esteem in the eyes of others than one deserves relative to what one deserves in comparison with others.

It is particularly obvious why the issue of how esteem is a zero-sum game is relevant and important on the comparative desert account. On this account, if esteem is a zero-sum game, then if some acquire more esteem than they

---

[7] McKinnon suggests a similar objection to hypocrisy. She thinks that the reason one should not be a hypocrite is that the hypocrite "is collecting unwarranted moral kudos or avoiding merited blame and we resent her for that" (McKinnon 1991, 326; cf. Tosi and Warmke 2016). Coates (2016, 462) writes: "It still seems inappropriate to blame (absent good reasons for believing the would-be blamee to be morally responsible). This is because, I think, most of us attach some significance to be value of innocence and also to the value of *just* deserts."

[8] As indicated, they are not putting their weight behind the desert account, but simply pointing to something along those lines as something that captures an important reason why hypocrisy is often met with (moral) anger. Hence, I do not see my present observation as a criticism of the main thrust of their insightful article.

[9] I use "merited" and "deserved" interchangeably here.

deserve in comparison with others, it follows logically that others will have less esteem in comparison with the hypocritical blamers than they deserve, comparatively speaking. No such thing follows logically on the absolute desert account. Even if I have more esteem than I deserve as a result of my hypocritical blame, that does not entail that others must enjoy less esteem than they deserve, absolutely speaking. Perhaps the constant sum of esteem available to be distributed across all is greater than it would be if everyone enjoyed exactly the amount of esteem they deserve, absolutely speaking.

I am skeptical of the desert objection in both of its versions. While it might account for part of what we find objectionable about extreme characters like Moliere's Tartuffe to the extent that they blame, there are many cases of hypocritical blame that we would find morally objectionable even if they clashed neither with absolute nor with relative desert. Consider absolute desert. Suppose I am unjustly being denied the esteem that I deserve. I engage in hypocritical blaming, thereby conveying the impression that I am better than I actually am and, thus, boost my esteem to the level that I do in fact deserve. From the point of view of a distribution of deserved esteem, there is nothing morally objectionable about my hypocritical blame. However, there might well be, in which case what makes this the case cannot derive from considerations about how distribution of esteem fits degrees of absolute desert. There can also be cases where I am aware that by acknowledging my own faults, others will see me as a saint and, thus, I will enjoy more esteem than I deserve. Yet this fact would not seem to make my blame a case of wrongful standingless blame. Even if it is wrongful—it results in my getting more than my deserved esteem—it is wrongful for the same reason as an otherwise identical instance of standingful blame.

Consider next comparative desert. Accounts of the moral wrongness of hypocritical blame by appeal to relative desert are vulnerable to a similar objection. Suppose a blamer is undeservedly esteemed less than their blamee. By hypocritically blaming the blamee, the blamer brings about that their comparative levels of esteem satisfy comparative desert. Yet it might well be morally objectionable for the blamer to hypocritically blame their blamee.

The remedy to both counterexamples seems obvious. In the case of absolute desert—I think it is clear how the comparative desert account can be similarly revised (and refuted), so I will not discuss it—one might propose:

The revised absolute desert account: hypocritical blaming is wrongful because it involves trying to acquire (or actually acquiring) more esteem in
the eyes of others in a way that is underserved.[10]

The idea here is to give up on the idea that hypocritical blame is wrongful by
virtue of how it clashes with the proper distribution of esteem. Rather, the
idea is that there are certain ways of acquiring esteem that make the extra
esteem one acquires deserved if one's attempt to do so is successful; e.g., one
performs a praiseworthy deed that others notice and as a result esteem one
more than one merits on account of one's deed; and ways of acquiring esteem that imply that the additional esteem is undeserved, e.g., by the moral
grandstanding involved in hypocritical blaming.

One implication of the revised absolute desert account is that hypocritical
blaming can be wrongful even when it results in one getting the overall level
of esteem that one deserves.[11] Some might find this problematic. Second,
there is a much more serious problem with the revised desert account, which
is that we can imagine cases of hypocritical blaming where the act of blaming
neither affects the esteem of the blamer, nor is expected—let alone intended—
by the blamer to do so. Presumably, such cases of hypocritical blaming can be
wrongful, in which case the revised desert account must be rejected. Third,
like the unrevised desert account, the revised desert account fails to fit the
relational nature of the wrong of hypocritical blame. Suppose I hypocritically
blame someone who has consented to being hypocritically blamed by me in
the presence of others, aiming thereby to increase my esteem in their eyes in
a way that is undeserved.[12] On the desert account, whether revised or not,
this case of hypocritically blaming is not different, morally, from a similar
case where the blamee does not consent to being blamed. This shows that the
desert account—revised or not—fails to capture how hypocritical blaming is
a wrong specifically of the blamee.

One possible lesson to take away from the failure of the desert account
is that accounts of the wrongfulness of hypocritical blame that either focus

---

[10] Perhaps the parenthesis suggests an indefensible form of disjunctivism. The wrong-making
features of hypocritical blame are all present in the case of (unsuccessfully) trying to boost one's esteem such that one enjoys more esteem than one deserves, and adding that the attempt succeeds is
not adding an additional wrong-making feature.

[11] Hence, the revised absolute desert account is not an exclusively distribution-focused account.

[12] The fact that the blamee consents to being hypocritically blamed does not—or least might not—
change the fact that any additional esteem the hypocritical blamer acquires through their blame is
undeserved.

on how it affects the general distribution of some good or on the (intended) effects (on the blamer or others) of hypocritical blaming fail as general explanations of the wrongfulness of hypocritical blame. This, of course, is not to deny that some cases of hypocritical blaming might be wrong in part by virtue of how the hypocritical blamer seeks or gets undeserved esteem. However, it suggests that instead of looking for the source of the wrongness of hypocritical blame in how it affects distributive patterns, we should look after its source in the hypocritical blamer. This is what the next two accounts do.

3.3. Lack of Commitment

If lack of commitment is what undermines standing to blame, it is natural to suppose that it is also lack of commitment that makes hypocritical blame wrong. Probably the clearest example of this view is provided by Roger Crisp and Christopher Cowton, though their account applies to hypocrisy in general and not just to hypocritical blame, and their proposition below concerns moral blameworthiness and not moral wrongness. On their view (1994, 347), "[H]ypocrisy is a failure to take morality seriously. This also explains much of what is bad about hypocrisy. If anything is morally blameworthy, the lack of concern for morality itself surely is."[13] So in this section I will address:

The lack-of-commitment account: hypocritical blaming is wrongful because the hypocritical blamer is insufficiently committed to the norms to which they appeal in their blame.[14]

---

[13] Strictly speaking, hypocrisy does not imply that the hypocrite does not take morality seriously. At best, it implies not taking what one takes to be morality, or even more precisely what one takes to be the specific moral norm to which one's blame appeals, seriously. After all, one could be wrong about morality (and even serious about norms that one subscribes to and, mistakenly, does not think of as norms of morality). In any case, where the blamer has a wrong view about morality—perhaps even an obnoxious view—it is hard to see why they are blameworthy for not being serious about morality as they take it to be. The agent with false beliefs about morality might be unconcerned with morality de re, but much concerned with morality de dicto. Such an agent might even be committed to the norm in question though from a different perspective, e.g., prudence or aesthetics. It is not clear that a person committed to what is in fact a moral norm, though the person thinks of it as, say, a prudential norm, lacks the standing to blame a norm violator (though the blame in question that the blamer has standing to impose is prudential, not moral, blame).

[14] Like some of the others that I have discussed, this view implies that mental states make a difference to wrongfulness. Note also that the lack-of-commitment account makes the ethics of blaming distinct in that, arguably, in relation to many other wrongs it is not lack of commitment to a certain norm that generates the relevant wrong; e.g., the wrongfulness of killing does not derive from—perhaps is not even affected by—the killer's lack of commitment to, say, a norm to the effect that one should not kill the innocent.

Obviously, this description needs to be fleshed out in different ways. First, commitment can have different aspects, e.g., cognitive as well as motivational aspects (see Section 2.8). Second, whichever aspect one has in mind, commitment is a matter of degree. Hence, to fully specify the lack-of-commitment account, one would either have to go for some kind of threshold view—i.e., there is a threshold degree of commitment such that once one surpasses that level of commitment one can blame without standinglessness-related wrongfulness—or some kind of more complex proportionality view—i.e., a certain level of commitment implies that one can engage in a certain degree of blaming without wrongfulness, and the greater the commitment the more severe the blaming one can engage in (see Sections 2.5, 2.8). Third, it must be explained whether hypocritical blamers per se manifest lack of commitment to the norms to which they appeal. Standard hypocritical blamers do indeed satisfy this requirement; i.e., they are not really concerned about their own norm violations but are strongly upset (or at least act as if they are) about the norm violations of others. However, it seems possible to imagine a hypocritical blamer who appears more committed to the norms in question than most ordinary norm subscribers, e.g., someone who is very agitated about their own norm violations—more so than people generally are agitated about similar norm violations by others that affect them negatively—but even more agitated about the norm violations of others.[15] This hypocritical blamer might act wrongly even if there is a sense in which they are clearly sufficiently committed to the norm to which they appeal.

One attractive feature of the commitment account of the wrongfulness of hypocritical blame is the fact that we often dismiss hypocritical blame directed at fictional characters—e.g., characters in *Game of Thrones*—precisely because often the blamer has the same faults for which they blame a fictional character.[16] This is hard to explain on some of the other accounts that are examined below; e.g., insofar as the reciprocity norm only applies to reciprocity between actual persons, the reciprocity account cannot explain the wrongfulness of blaming a fictional character for a flaw that one possesses oneself (cf. Section 3.6). Similarly, providing that, plausibly, the interests of fictional characters do not matter morally, Wallace's moral equality account

---

[15] On my account of hypocritical blame, it seems to follow that this strongly committed, but hypocritical, blamer lacks standing to blame. If so, this defeats any commitment account of standing to blame that defines degree of commitment in simple, absolute terms.

[16] See Driver (2016, 219) on blame directed at fictional characters.

is hard pressed to explain the wrongfulness of blaming a fictional character for a flaw that one possesses oneself (cf. Section 3.9).[17]

Despite these attractive features of the lack-of-commitment account, it is false. First, consider someone who is not very serious about a certain moral norm, because they are not very serious about when others violate that norm, but that, generally, they are very serious about not violating that norm themself and for that reason they have never violated it (cf. the discussion of the hypercrite in Section 2.8), though on several occasions they have called the norm into question. Suppose that, for once, this person blames another for violating the norm in question. Compare this person to another who, in the same way, is not very serious about violations of the norm in question, but who differs from the first blamer in two ways. While they have never called the relevant norm into question, on a couple of occasions they have, and they understand that they have, violated it themself. On the assumption that these two blamers are equally uncommitted overall to the norm in question, it seems that the commitment account implies that their blame is equally wrong. In response, I submit that the second and hypocritical blamer's blaming is wrongful in a way that the former and nonhypocritical blamer's is not. This suggests that the wrongfulness of hypocritical blaming is not due to lack of commitment—at least not lack of commitment per se.[18]

I suspect the commitment account can be partially amended to accommodate the present counterexample. For instance, the account could be revised as follows:

> *The revised lack-of-commitment account*: hypocritical blaming is wrongful because, in relation to their own conduct, the blamer is insufficiently committed to the norms to which they appeal in their blame.

Since both of my two blamers might be sufficiently serious about the norm in question in relation to their own conduct (though not perfectly so in the case of my second blamer), the revised lack-of-commitment account

---

[17] My subordination-focused version of the moral equality account is immune to the fictional-characters-blame objection, provided the concern for absence of subordination takes an impersonal form in addition to a personal one. Admittedly, if the commitment account has a similar dual-focus shape, it too is compatible with the wrongfulness of hypocritical blame of fictional characters.

[18] Assuming that the two blamers are equally committed to the norm and yet differ in terms of hypocrisy and, thus, in terms of standing, it also seems like a potential problem for the commitment account of standing to blame (Section 2.7). At least, mere degree of commitment cannot be all that matters—the shape of commitment must matter too.

accommodates my first intuition. However, it fails to accommodate the intuition that despite equal levels of commitment to the norm in question in relation to their own conduct, there is something wrongful about the second and hypocritical blamer's blame that is absent in the first and nonhypocritical blamer's case. (Recall that the first and nonhypocritical blamer is less committed than the second and hypocritical blamer by virtue of their doubts about the norm in question.) Moreover, the revised account faces the task of explaining why it matters whether the relevant lack of commitment derives from a lack of commitment when it comes to the blamer's own norm conformance or the norm conformance of others. After all, both involve lack of commitment, and the most obvious explanation seems to point in a different direction than the (revised) lack-of-commitment account, e.g., in the direction of something like not treating others as inferiors or the like (see Section 3.9).

There is a second reason to be skeptical of the lack-of-commitment account. Consider a case where someone blames me for something and is not serious about the norm to which they appeal. They are not hypocritical in that they have never violated the norm themself. They would not even violate the norm if they were in a circumstance where doing so would be opportune for them—say doing what the norm proscribes just seems unattractive to them for nonmoral reasons—so they are not even being subjunctively hypocritical. However, they are just not very serious about the norm—the norm does not motivate them at all, and while they think it is more likely than not that it is a valid norm, they consider the arguments in its favor just slightly stronger than the arguments against. Arguably, there is nothing wrongful about their blame, in which case the (revised) lack-of-commitment account is false.

There are two considerations that support my second objection. First, rejecting the lack-of-commitment account for the reasons indicated is consistent with saying that I have no particular reason to respond to someone's blame if that person does not really care about the norm on which the blame rests—I am under no duty to provide that person with an uptake, just as if I ask you a question but manifestly do not really care about whether I get an answer; perhaps I have less of or even no entitlement to one; e.g., the husband who asks his wife how her day was while surfing the net on his iPhone, clearly manifesting indifference to the answer he receives, is not really entitled to an answer to his question. So even if commitment is irrelevant to the wrongness of hypocritical blame, it can still bear on having the standing to blame, as I argued in Section 2.8.[19]

The second supporting consideration is the fact that often when people blame someone appealing to norms that they do not really care about themselves, they have various objectionable ulterior motives, e.g., to shame and thereby manipulate that person into doing something they suspect that they would otherwise not have done. This might give the impression that the lack of commitment renders the hypocritical blame wrongful, when what makes hypocritical blame wrongful in these cases is not the lack of seriousness about the relevant norm per se, but the ulterior motive, e.g., the attempt to shame and thereby manipulate the person. While, for reasons indicated here and in Section 2.8, lack of commitment bears on standing to blame, I conclude that we should reject the lack-of-commitment account of the wrongfulness of hypocritical blame. Some might find this dual stance strange. Note, however, that while there cannot plausibly be a duty to have greater manifested seriousness about a norm to which one appeals in one's blame than one's blamee, it is not clear why difference in manifested commitment cannot affect standing to blame (see the fifth challenge in Section 2.9).

3.4. Wrong Attention

Matt King has suggested a different view, which, like the commitment account, focuses squarely on the blamer. On his view, blaming is an attentive activity, and, like meddlesome blamers, hypocritical blamers are misdirecting their attention in a way that they have moral reasons to avoid:

> [T]he basic problem with hypocritical blame is that one's blame of others has taken precedence over a reevaluation of one's own attitudes and conduct. This principal moral defect is a failure to prioritize the proper moral features of one's situation. . . . Hypocritical blaming is thus an instance of a more general case of failing to have one's moral priorities straight. (King 2020, 1434, 1436)[20]

---

[19] Admittedly, it seems less plausible that the uncommitted, but nonhypocritical, blamer has no liberty right to blame than denying that the blamee has any duty to provide an uptake. However, in light of the gradualist view of standing to blame that I have appealed to, I find it sufficiently plausible that lack of commitment somewhat erodes standing to blame.

[20] King thinks that the idea of standing to blame is misconceived—see Section 2.7—and that we should simply focus on morally inappropriate blame instead. On his view, we should simply explain

In the interest of facilitating comparison with the previous accounts, I shall discuss the following view, which I take to capture the essence in King's account:

> *The wrong attention account*: hypocritical blaming is wrongful because it involves a wrongful misdirection of the blamer's attention.

I agree with King that, typically, hypocritical (and meddlesome) blamers are misdirecting their attention and fail to get their moral priorities straight in terms of where they direct their attention.[21] Hence, I agree that, in an assessment of the blamer's character or deliberations, facts about misdirected attention are relevant. Nevertheless, misplaced attention on the part of the blamer is not what explains—or at least not what primarily explains—the wrongfulness of hypocritical blame. Below I offer four reasons why not.

First, consider a case where a blamer blames a blamee for a flaw that the blamer has themselves—so, on my view the blamer has no standing to blame their blamee—but where the consequences for third parties are such that, all things considered, the blamer is morally required to blame the blamee. Suppose also that in blaming the blamee, the blamer attends to those consequences and, thus, in that important respect, gets their moral priorities straight—they focus on the morally most relevant feature of the situation, i.e., the one that determines what they should do all things considered.[22] Nevertheless, this blamer has no standing to blame. What this case brings out is that when we ask whether a hypocritical blamer gets their moral priorities straight, there are two different questions that we might be asking. First, we might be asking—call this *the coarse-grained question*—whether the blamer attends to what they ought to do all things considered. Some passages in King (2019, 268) suggest that this is the question he has in mind:

that inappropriateness "in terms of norms of attention—norms that have nothing to do with rights, authority, or jurisdiction" (King 2019, 266). However, he also proposes his wrong attention account as one that does not rest on a rejection of the idea of standing to blame. It is in this spirit that I discuss it in this section.

[21] Note, however, that blaming understood as a speech act is something that can be performed absentmindedly.
[22] Admittedly, on my view there is a morally relevant fact that they do not attend to; to wit, that they have a similar flaw themself and that by virtue thereof they have no standing to blame the blamee, even if their blaming themself for the relevant fault or inviting the blamee to join them in blaming themself for that fault has no comparable good effects on third parties. More on this later.

[A] better explanation of what goes wrong with hypocritical and med-dlesome blame is that the blamers are misconducting themselves. That is, they are unjustified under the circumstances: they have more reason not to blame than to blame . . . the inappropriateness of the blame is explained, not by some loss of status, but by the overall balance of moral considerations. Such blamers aren't disqualified; they just shouldn't blame.

Second, we might be asking—call this *the fine-grained question*—whether the blamer attends in a suitable way to each of the morally relevant factors that together determine what they ought to do all things considered.

With the distinction between the coarse- and the fine-grained questions foregrounded, we can see that the wrong attention account faces a di-lemma.[23] If proper attention only requires proper attention to what is mor-ally right, all things considered, then a hypocritical blamer could have their moral priorities straight and, thus, improper attention cannot explain what is morally objectionable about hypocritical blame. If instead proper attention additionally requires proper attention to the different moral factors that to-gether determine what is morally right all things considered, then the wrong attention account cannot serve as an account of what makes standingless blame morally objectionable. For assuming that this is a fact to be explained, then one fact that the hypocritical blamer fails to attend to is the fact that they have no standing to blame and that this means that their blame is morally objectionable in one respect. But if so, then misplaced attention is a result of this fact about lack of standing and not an explanation of it (though, perhaps, one might think that certain ways of failing to attend to this fact compound moral wrongness).

Second, there are cases where talk about standing to blame aligns very badly with norms of attention. Consider a case where the blamer's faults in some dimensions are much worse than the blamee's. However, the blamee consents to—perhaps even invites—the blamer's blame. In this case, we might think that even though the blamer now has the standing to blame the blamee—the blamee is no longer entitled to deflect blame by saying, "Who are you to blame me?"—the blamer still ought to focus on their own faults

---

[23] King (2019, 269) says that both on the "orthodox view" and on his own view, "it should be no surprise that the relevant explanation for that inappropriateness will be independent of an explana-tion of the blamee's blameworthiness. After all, in both cases the problem is generated by something to do with the blamer herself." However, it is important not to forget that it also has something to do with the blamee, e.g., whether the blamee's faults are lesser than the blamer's (in cases of hypocritical blame) or whether the blamee has consented to being blamed (e.g., in cases of meddlesome blame).

rather than the blamee's. If they fail to do so and engage in a full-scale attack on the blamee, we might criticize them for misdirecting their attention even if we agree that the blamee holds no standing-related complaint against them, since the blamee acted in a way that restored the blamer's standing to blame. If so, there is work to do for the concept of standing to blame, which cannot be captured in terms of norms of attention (unless, perhaps, we contend that norms of attention incorporate facts about the blamee having consented to being blamed).

Third, while this does not show that the wrong attention account is correct—only that it is unfounded—several of the arguments King offers in its defense are inconclusive. For instance, King (2019, 274) submits that "standingless blame seems no less objectionable if held privately. Huey's blame of Louie is inappropriate regardless of whether he confronts Louie about the lie." I agree with the last sentence. However, it does not support the first sentence in the quotation, which, unlike the latter, makes a comparative claim. Moreover, it is more objectionable, as well as objectionable in a different way, to publicly express one's standingless blame than to simply blame privately without standing. And, precisely for that reason, it cannot be that the inappropriateness of hypocritical blame is simply a matter of an attention disorder. That inappropriateness might be equally present in the private and the public case, and yet the latter is more objectionable.[24] It is more objectionable to the extent that demanding something from someone that one is not entitled to is wrongful, and that element is lacking in the case of private blame. In short, our account of the wrongfulness of hypocritical blame must appeal—or at least *also* appeal—to what hypocritical blame is doing to the blamee.

Finally, according to King (2019, 276–277, 280):

> In the case of hypocritical blame, the blamer is critiquing others when their attention and efforts ought to be directed at improving their own conduct. Indeed, I argue that hypocritical blame is best understood as running afoul [of] norms counseling improvement of one's own moral house, which I call *norms of priority* . . . it is more important (ceteris paribus) to do better than to be accurate with one's blame.[25]

[24] Some might make the reverse point. However, this point seems less plausible in view of the element of deception involved in public blame not corresponding to any reactive attitudes etc. on the part of the blamer.

[25] A converse point applies to the case of the hypercritical blamer, whose attention to their own faults comes in the way of their contributing to the improvement of others. Note also that King seems

In part at least, norms of attention here seem grounded in considerations about the good consequences in terms of one's moral improvement resulting from doing what the norm enjoins; to wit, to attend to one's own flaws rather than blame others. If that is the case, then King's contention regarding the superior explanatory power of norms of attention is false. Suppose I am irredeemably flawed and know myself to be so. Hence, there is no (narrow) consequence-based point in blaming myself or accepting blame from others, since it will not make me improve.[26] I now blame someone else whose faults are much lesser, and they point to my lack of standing to blame. At this point, I suspect the reply—"It is appropriate for me to blame you without blaming myself, since blame is wasted on me, whereas chances are that you might actually improve as a result of my blaming you"—lacks force.[27] There are two reasons why. First, norms of attention are less consequence-oriented than King seems to imply—one should give some attention to one's faults even when one is unlikely to improve. Second, the relevant dismissal of blame is about standing to blame and not so much about proper attention—one can improperly attend to something one has a right/standing to attend to, just as one can properly attend to something one has no right/standing to attend to.

I conclude that the wrong attention account fails to explain the wrongfulness of hypocritical blame. This, I repeat, is not to say there is nothing to the wrong attention account. After all, it does seem that a hypocritical blamer is typically manifesting bad character, or at least flawed deliberations, through misplaced excessive attention to faults of others etc. However, this is not what explains the wrongfulness of the hypocritical blame. In light of the argument in this and the previous section, it seems natural to extend the scope of the

---

to adopt a rather rationalistic view of self-improvement, whereby to improve one must attend to one's faults. Thus, on King's view blaming others easily comes in the way of self-improvement, because "it is more difficult to blame another while at the same time keeping one's own wrongdoing clearly in focus" (2019, 281). However, one might self-improve in ways that do not involve one's attending to one's faults; e.g., hypocritical blame of others might have civilizing effects on oneself behind one's back, as it were (Elster 1998, 110).

[26] Admittedly, there could be good, broader consequences of an irredeemably bad person criticizing themselves (publicly); e.g., it could be that it would result in listeners improving. However, we can assume that there are no such good broader consequences either.

[27] This raises a question about whether this reply does not point to a justification for differential blame, in which case the blame is not hypocritical on my definition. One thought here might be that, in almost all cases, we reject the relevant reply because we think the blamer could improve, so the factual presupposition of the reply is false. But if we really thought the blamer were irredeemably flawed, then we would accept the differential blame as not being hypocritical.

focus of an account of wrongful blame from just the blamer to the relation between the blamer and the blamee.[28]

3.5. Transgression of Moral Authority

In Chapter 1 I defended an account of public blaming according to which blaming involves communicating to the blamee that one demands a certain uptake from the blamee. If, however, the blame is hypocritical, typically the blamee has no duty to provide what the blamer demands, i.e., an uptake of some sort, e.g., an apology or public deliberations about how to improve. At least in some cases, it is wrongful to demand something from someone who has no duty to give it; e.g., if, standing in a position of formal authority over you, I demand an apology from you for something, implying that you owe a duty to me to apologize even though I know very well that you were entirely within your rights to do what you did. Making such a demand for something to which you have no right seems wrong—if for no other reason than that demanding such an apology when the blamer has no moral demand on the blamee for an apology amounts to humiliation. Something like this forms a natural line of thought motivating the following account:

> *The moral authority account of hypocritical blame*: hypocritical blaming is wrongful because it involves demanding something from the blamee that the blamee has no duty to the blamer to provide.[29]

It is natural to amend the moral authority account in such a way that it makes the relevant wrongfulness vary with the nature of the uptake demanded; e.g., there is a difference between demanding that the blamee cursorily explain to the blamer why the blamee did what they did, on the one hand, and demanding that, in addition to this, the blamee supply a much broader account, express regret over an extended period, regularly apologize not just

---

[28] There is also the possibility of a purely blamee-focused account of the wrongness of discrimination, e.g., one that appeals to the negative effects of hypocritical blame on the blamee to account for its wrongfulness. However, because the effects of hypocritical blame vary and are contingent, such an account is unlikely to account for what makes hypocritical blame wrong as such. Also, to my knowledge no such account has been proposed in the literature.

[29] Roadevin (2018) suggests that hypocrisy involves making a demand one has no authority to make. However, she does not claim that this is wrong as such, only that it is wrong when it involves a violation of reciprocity.

for their specific fault but also for their obnoxious character in general, and publicly announce written and ambitious plans of self-reform. If the blamer has no standing to demand any of this and if making demands on others that one has no right to or that others have no duty to comply with is wrongful, then making greater demands plausibly is more wrongful than making lesser demands.[30]

Basically, there are two potential problems that motivate my skepticism about the moral authority account of the wrongness of hypocritical blame. First, there are cases where hypocritical blaming is not wrongful, but that involve demanding something from the blamee that they have no duty to the blamer to provide. Second, there are cases where hypocritical blaming is wrongful, but where it is either the case that it does not involve demanding something from the blamee that the blamee has no duty to the blamer to provide, or, alternatively, where it does involve that but where it is not because of this feature that it is wrongful. Both kinds of cases exist.

First, there are cases where hypocritical blaming involves demanding something from the blamee that they have no duty to the blamer to provide, but where hypocritical blaming is not wrongful. Consider again the disjunctive account of having the standing to blame (see Section 1.3). One disjunct says that some blame is standingless because the blamee has no duty to the blamer to provide an uptake, and that, as I noted in Chapter 1, is consistent with the hypocritical blamer having a liberty right to blame. Perhaps in some such cases it is not wrongful to blame just as sometimes there is nothing wrongful about demanding something from others that they have no duty to provide us with; e.g., if I am drowning and I sternly, but tactfully, demand that you do something to rescue me, realizing that it will be so costly for you to rescue me that you have no duty to do so, plausibly I am not wronging you in making this moral demand on you. After all, you can simply refuse to meet my demand. To suggest that it is wrongful to make any demand on others for something they have no duty to provide, when they can—setting aside slight social embarrassment—costlessly and easily reject one's demand, seems like an extreme position. Saying this is consistent with saying that in other cases, demanding an uptake in response to one's blame that the blamee has no duty to provide is wrongful analogously with cases of

---

[30] I set aside here the complication noted in Section 2.5 that standing and blaming are scalar phenomena such that the blamer might be in a position to make small demands on the blamee, but not in a position to make large demands.

people exercising their liberty rights in a wrongful way, e.g., spending one's own money in a wrongful way. However, I suspect that in such cases what makes such demands wrongful is something other than the mere fact that the blamee has no duty to provide an uptake, such as the fact that in blaming that person in this way, one is treating them as an inferior (see Section 3.9 below). This takes me to the (second variant of the) second objection to the moral authority account.

According to this objection, there are cases of wrongful hypocritical blaming that are not wrongful because the blamer is demanding a certain uptake from the blamee that they have no duty to provide, but wrongful for some other reason. Consider the case of the inconsistent blamer, who, on this occasion, blames their blamee for a fault they know themself to have.[31] This, however, does not reflect any bias on their part in their own favor, but simply that their blaming patterns are erratic—they are just as likely to blame themself for a fault in the presence of others with similar or even worse faults whom they would not blame. Compare this blamer to the consistent (at least in the way that is at stake here) hypocritical blamer, who blames the same blamee for the same fault that the hypocritical blamer knows that they also have. Both blamers are making a demand on the blamee that the blamee has no duty to fulfill. However, the hypocrite's blame is wrongful in a way that the unpredictable blamer's blame is not. Since both of them are demanding an uptake from the blamee that the blamee has no duty to provide, this cannot be what renders the hypocritical blamer's blame additionally wrongful. Thus, it cannot explain the wrongfulness of hypocritical blame. Hence, the moral authority account of the wrongfulness of hypocritical blame must be rejected.

3.6. Failure of Reciprocity

In a recent paper, Cristina Roadevin (2018) develops an account of the wrongfulness of hypocritical blame, which like the moral authority account addresses the relation between blamer and blamee, but which, unlike that account, focuses on reciprocity:

---

[31] Inconsistency here is what involves, what Rossi (2021, 59) labels "normative inconsistency": "[I]t consists of a doxastic attitude or assertion that represents a *normative* proposition as true, and an action or attitude that does not 'satisfy' the proposition."

[T]he moral interaction between us also requires that we pay attention to our own faults and change our behaviour, especially if we want our demands to be taken seriously when we ask others to answer to us. . . . If Harvey expects that Laura owes something to him (that she should examine and acknowledge her faults), he should also realize that he also answers to her in the same way—he owes it to her to critically examine his own behavior. . . . As a matter of justice, he needs to clear himself of his "moral debt" before he can be in a position to demand an explanation from Laura regarding her moral faults.[32] Otherwise, he opens himself to moral criticism and justified blame. (Roadevin 2018, 147–148)[33]

We can reconstruct this view, or at least one important aspect of it, as follows:

The reciprocity account of hypocritical blame: hypocritical blaming is wrongful because it involves a failure to reciprocate to the blamee on part of the blamer, i.e., the blamer demands something from the blamee, but rejects a relevantly similar demand from the blamee.[34]

There are other formulations in Roadevin's insightful article that suggest slight deviations from this view or, indeed, nonreciprocity-based objections to hypocritical blame. However, I shall focus on the merits of the in-dented view.

There are several problems with the reciprocity-based account. First, it is not so clear that the account is distinct from the moral equality account (see

---

[32] This sentence suggests that Roadevin does not distinguish in the way I want to between an account of the wrongfulness of standingless blame and an account of what renders blame standingless (see Section 3.1).

[33] Cf. "The hypocrite refuses or culpably fails to admit her own mistakes, while at the same time demands that others admit theirs. The paper argues that this lack of reciprocity—expecting others to take morality seriously by apologizing for their faults, without one doing the same in return—is what makes hypocritical blame unfair" (Roadevin 2018, 137). Here the relevant duty is presented as being a conditional one, i.e., as a duty one is under if one has certain expectations of others. However, the duty to take morality seriously whatever one demands of others in this regard seems a no less plausible candidate for a moral duty than Roadevin's corresponding conditional duty, in which case hypocrisy would seem wrong on account of involving a violation of that duty too.

[34] Presumably, the reciprocity account of the wrongness of blame rests on a more general reciprocity norm to the effect that it is wrong to demand something from someone else, whether that pertains to blame or not, while rejecting a similar demand from that person. This is relevant to points made in Chapter 7. Roadevin refers to Duff's account of what makes hypocritical blame "inappropriate" as "the reciprocity account"—see next section—and distinguishes it from her own account. As far as I can tell, her account differs from Duff's mostly in terms of the sort of reciprocity required, i.e., more than simply a willingness to address one's own faults when one blames others for similar faults.

Section 3.9 below), to the extent that it is attractive. Let me explain. Here is the case for believing that the two accounts are distinct.[35] First, you can affirm moral equality without acknowledging any requirements of reciprocity in relation to that norm, e.g., if you think that persons are to be respected in accordance with their equal moral status and that what counts as doing so does not depend on how they treat others (e.g., Scanlon 2008). Some might find this an attractive ideal, but, whether it is or not, it is one that friends of the reciprocity norm cannot appeal to. Their point is precisely that what it is to treat someone as a moral equal depends on whether that person is willing to reciprocate. Second, you could have a norm of reciprocity that is incompatible with moral equality, e.g., because what, according to the relevant norm of reciprocation, counts as reciprocating differs across persons depending on their differential moral status (cf. the hierarchical norm introduced Section 2.8). An inegalitarian reciprocity norm, however, is one that we would (and should) reject and, accordingly, it cannot explain the moral wrongness of hypocritical blame. Moreover, if we appeal to an egalitarian reciprocity norm, the suspicion is that it is the egalitarian aspect of the norm that does the normative work. Consider a case where failing to reciprocate does not clash with moral equality. It is hard to think of such a case, but imagine one in which the blamee has consented to being hypocritically blamed and the blamer hypocritically blames the blamee, not reciprocating by not being willing to accept being blamed by the blamee for their own similar fault.[36] In such a case, arguably, there is a failure of reciprocity, which, however, does not clash with moral equality. Additionally, the blamer does not seem to wrong the blamee. Thus, failure of reciprocity is morally inert with respect to the wrongfulness of hypocritical blaming, and it is the equality aspect of the egalitarian norm of reciprocity that does the normative work.

---

[35] Roadevin (2018, 145) argues that not all cases of hypocritical blame offend "against a presumption in favour of the equal standing of persons," because it is not true of all cases of hypocritical blame that the blamer puts their interests above the interests of the blamee, e.g., because a hypocritical blamer might have forgotten about their own faults that are comparable to those of their blamee. I have reservations against this challenge to the moral equality account (including that I do not think the case really is a case of hypocritical blame [cf. Fritz and Miller 2019b, 554; Section 4.2]). Note also that if the challenge is valid, a similar challenge can be mounted against the reciprocity account. That is, it is true of the forgetful blamer that they do indeed realize that for them to hold others to account for their faults, they should also hold themself to account for their own forgotten faults. Thus, in this sense they do not violate any norm of reciprocity.

[36] The reason why it is not clear that it is a failure of reciprocity that does not clash with moral equality is that, arguably, it involves no failure of reciprocity at a deeper level, i.e., the level of consent. The hypocritical blamer accepts that the blamee can relieve them of their duty not to blame hypocritically and expects the blamee to similarly accept that the blamer could relieve the blamee of such a duty (though they have not chosen to do so).

There are also two additional, lesser weaknesses with the reciprocity account, at least in the form given to it by Roadevin. The second weakness is that the reciprocity account fails to explain what I shall call *the specificity condition* in relation to the undermining of the standing to blame:

The specificity condition: if a blamer is guilty of a fault that is relevantly similar to the blamee's fault, then the blamer has no standing to blame the blamee for that fault. However, the blamer might have the standing to blame the blamee for other faults that are not relevantly similar to any fault of which blamer is guilty (cf. Section 1.2.2).

According to Roadevin (2018, 146):

His [the hypocritical blamer's] attitudes towards his own wrongdoing show that he does not understand what is morally significant for our moral interactions—that is, that we have to live by the same moral standards we hold others to; he needs to critically examine his own faults, if he expects others to examine their own in return.[37]

The problem with this account of why the hypocrite has no standing to blame is that it does not fit well with the specificity condition. Suppose that my engaging in hypocritical blame reveals a very general illusion I am under with respect to my duty to critically examine my own faults, given that I hold others accountable to the moral standard according to which the relevant faults of mine are indeed faults. If so, why is it not the case that I lose my standing to blame *tout court* by virtue of my hypocrisy and not just, as the specificity condition implies, my standing to blame others for the faults of which I am guilty myself? The reciprocity account has no good answer to this question, and while it might be true that other accounts also fail to explain the specificity condition, this is at least one reason to reject the reciprocity account.[38]

Third, while the reciprocity account casts some light on our practice of rejecting hypocritical blame, there is a further aspect of it that it fails to

---

[37] The use of "understand" suggests that Roadevin thinks of the relevant error as a cognitive error. But perhaps the hypocrite fully understands the relevant facts about moral significance and just does not care about them.

[38] The moral equality account (Section 3.9) can explain the specificity condition to the extent that it is not the case that any blame exchanges between people with different, but in some sense equally serious, faults must involve one relating to the other as an inferior.

elucidate. Compare that practice to a different hypocritical practice, where, if someone engages in hypocritical blame, then he "opens himself to moral criticism and justified blame"; i.e., others can justifiably blame him for his hypocritical blaming, but he does not lose his standing to blame on that account. This means, on the disjunctive account defended in Chapter 1, he still has the liberty right to blame others and others owe him an obligation to respond to his blame. In a sense, such a practice would embody a higher-order norm of reciprocity—I can sanctionlessly blame you for your fault only if I blame myself for my comparable fault—only the sanction for violating the norm of reciprocity would be different; i.e., the sanction is not losing one's standing to blame, but becoming morally liable to blame for one's hypocritical blame.[39] Even if what makes hypocritical blame morally blameworthy is a violation of a norm of reciprocal self-examination, that leaves it completely open what the relevant sanction for violating that norm is. Hence, the reciprocity account is unable to explain at least one important feature of our practice of dismissing hypocritical blame. In light of this and the two additional problems exhibited, I conclude that the reciprocity account is unpromising.

3.7. Moral Community

In defending her account, Roadevin appeals to Anthony Duff's account of standing to blame and the wrongfulness of hypocritical blame. Duff has developed this account in tandem with his communicative theory of punishment. According to this theory, punishment involves a communicative message to the punishee amounting to a form of blame. When someone dismisses blame indirectly, what the blamee does is to deny that they are answerable to the blamer for that for which they are being blamed (Duff 2010, 125). To be answerable to another, one has to belong to the same moral community:

> Blame requires a suitable relationship between blamer and blamed, as
> fellow members of a normative community whose business the wrong is: it

---

[39] The fact that I have a liberty right to blame hypocritically does not entail that I cannot be rightfully blamed for exercising that right.

is an attempt at moral communication, appealing to values by which blamer
and blamed are, supposedly, mutually bound. (Duff 2010, 125)

There are two ways to understand Duff's position as expressed in this passage.
On one understanding, he has no independent account of what it is to stand in
relations of normative community with one another other than that two persons are members of the same normative community if, and only if, they are
accountable to one another. If that is what normative community comes down
to, then the notion really does no explanatory work and, specifically, it cannot
answer the question of when we are accountable to one another. If this reading
is the correct one, his position might overlap extensionally (if not more) with
a version of Roadevin's reciprocity account, given that Duff thinks members
of a moral community are accountable to one another in an egalitarian way.[40]
On another understanding, Duff has (and wants his account to involve) an
independent account of what it is to stand in relations of normative community with one another and that account can explain why members, and only
members, of the same normative community are accountable to one another.
In that case, his account appears distinct from Roadevin's reciprocity account
even though, like her account, its focus lies on the nature of relations between
blamer and blamee.

Consider a case where "Ian has committed a wrong that is, in principle,
Hilda's business: he lied to her; or he stole money from their flatmate,"
and where Hilda has either committed a similar wrong or is involved in
Ian's wrongdoing so that Hilda has no standing to blame Ian (Duff 2010,
126, 128).

What makes it improper for Hilda to criticise Ian, whilst refusing to answer
to him, is that this denies the fellowship on which her criticism depends
for its legitimacy. In criticising Ian, she must purport to address him as a
fellow member of a normative community to which the wrong belongs: as
a friend, as a colleague, as a flat-mate. . . . But members are answerable to
each other: if she is to treat Ian as a fellow member who must answer to her,

---

[40] The following passage naturally supports this interpretation: "Rather, her [Hilda's] standing
is undermined if she demands that Ian answers to her (which is what she does in blaming him),
whilst refusing to answer to him for what she has done. Calling others to answer must be a reciprocal
activity—if they must answer to me, I must be ready to answer to them; it is the lack of such reciprocity that would undermine Hilda's standing to blame Ian" (Duff 2010, 129).

she must also be ready to answer to him. (Duff 2010, 128–129; cf. Friedman 2013, 273; see Cohen 2008, 41–46)[41]

While the following might not be Duff's exact view, this is the one that I shall address:

The community account of hypocritical blame: hypocritical blaming is wrongful because it involves a denial of a fact without which the blamer would have no standing to blame; to wit, the fact that the blamer and the blamee are members of the same moral community.

My use of the term "standing to blame" here is meant to capture what Duff has in mind when he talks about "legitimacy."[42] Sometimes when people use this term, they mean something like morally permissible. However, if that is what is meant here, then Duff would be saying that it is not morally permissible for a blamer to blame their blamee if they deny that they are members of the same moral community. That, I take it, is an extreme position. If the blamer blames the blamee for something that is none of the blamer's business, surely, this could nevertheless be morally permissible in light of the good consequences such blame might have.

Is the community account of the wrongfulness of hypocritical blame plausible? I think not. First, suppose that I believe that I am indeed accountable to you, but that I also deny that you are accountable to me, so that, on Duff's account, I deny that we are members of the same moral community. Suppose also that there is no good reason for this belief—I simply happen to be a very self-effacing person—and suppose that, despite my denial of the stated reason for our membership of the same community, I blame you for some blameworthy action. In this case, I am not acting wrongfully or in any way wronging you. On the contrary, it might well be that I am responding in the way I morally ought to respond to your wrongful action. More generally, there are many cases where performing a certain action in such a way that one is denying a fact that one's standing to perform that action presupposes does not make one's action wrongful on account thereof. Suppose I pay you

---

[41] This might introduce a slight change in Duff's view. It is one thing to deny that one is answerable to another, and it is another thing to be disposed to answer the other if called upon to do so (and in that sense be "ready to" answer for oneself).

[42] Given my analysis in Chapter 1, this can mean two things. It might mean that we have liberty right to blame each other. Or it might mean that we have duties to respond to each other's blame.

back some money that I owe you in such a way that I am denying that I am in a position to do so, e.g., because I am somehow affirming that the money is not mine, in which case the transaction is normatively inert—the money you receive is not now yours for you to dispose of as you see fit. Surely, in doing what I do, I am not acting wrongly.

In reply, one might say that this is only because we assume that I do not really believe, though I might somehow claim otherwise, that the money I am using to repay my debts is not mine and that if I did, in the relevant sense, deny that, then my action would be wrongful. However, this reply is a tricky one to mount in the relevant context, given that it is unclear that very many hypocritical blamers in the relevant sense really believe that they are not equally accountable to others. Most likely, they present to themselves various strained accounts of why, despite being equally accountable, they have nothing to account for—they think, despite the fact that they ought to know better, that what they did is morally different from what their blamee did; or they do have something to account for, but for some reason, they need not. They think, implausibly, that various bad consequences would follow if they were to be open to criticism. This takes us to the second reason for being skeptical of the community account.

Second, there could be cases of hypocritical blame not involving any denial of co-membership of the same community that nevertheless are morally wrong. Take the case of someone who is strongly committed to an antihypocrisy norm, but nevertheless from time to time ends up hypocritically blaming others against their own will, as it were. In hypocritically blaming their blamee, such an akratic blamer would in no way be denying either that they and their blamee are members of the same moral community, nor that they are not bound by the same norms as their blamee. After all, they are acting against their own better judgment. Even so, we might think that they are acting wrongly. If so, this is something the community account cannot explain. In conjunction with the previous objection, this strikes me as a good reason to have little faith in the community account.

3.8. Implying Falsehoods

I now turn my attention to a different account of the wrongfulness of hypocritical blaming, which is however related to the community account in that this account locates the wrongfulness of hypocritical blaming in denying, or implying a denial of, a certain fact; to wit, a fact about whose actions impaired the social relations between the blamer and the blamee. This account, or at least something close to it, has been proposed by Thomas Scanlon (2008).

According to Scanlon, blaming someone for an action "is to take that action to indicate something about the person that impairs one's relationship with him or her, and to understand that relationship in a way that reflects this impairment. . . . To *blame* a person is to judge him or her to be blameworthy and to take your relationship with him or her to be modified in a way this judgement of impaired relations holds to be appropriate."[43] So, unlike what is the case on my account of paradigmatic blaming, blaming in Scanlon's sense is not tied to demanding an uptake of sorts from one's blame. Nor does Scanlon's account, unlike typical reactive-attitudes-based accounts (see Section 1.2.2), imply that to blame someone one must have certain negative reactive attitudes directed against them. Finally, on Scanlon's account blaming neither involves assessing the character of the blamee, nor imposing—or wanting to or finding it justified to impose—some sanction on that person.

There are several attractions of Scanlon's account of blame. First, it implies that blame is personal in the sense that what blaming amounts to depends on the relationship you have with the person you are blaming. Blaming your spouse for betrayal differs from blaming a business partner for betrayal, because of how trust plays a much greater role in the former kind of relationship and, thus, that betrayal undermines it to a much greater degree.

Second, his account seems readily generalizable to illocutionary acts other than blaming. In Scanlon's view, "[I]f praise is the [mere?] expression of a positive appraisal, it is not the opposite of blame" (2008, 151; see also Section 5.2). An attitude like blame, though with the opposite valence, must involve "awareness that one's relationship" with the person toward whom one has this attitude "has been altered by some action or attitude on that person's part" (Scanlon 2008, 151). Scanlon suggests that gratitude is the "clearest example" of a "positive correlate of blame." It involves not just a positive appraisal, but a change in the sort of relationship that one now considers appropriate. When one is grateful, one typically has "a greater readiness to help a person who has

---

[43] Scanlon 2008, 122–123, 128–129; cf. Section 1.2.2. This appears not to fit the case where Adam acts in a way that is blameworthy, but less so than what Beatrice had, for good reason, expected. Presumably, Beatrice might blame Adam for what he did even if she now thinks that their mutual relationship has improved relative to what it was prior to Adam's blameworthy action. It is also unclear whether Scanlon's account fits cases of incoherent blame, where the blamer blames the blamee for something the blamee has done to a third party.

gone out of her way to help [one], should the occasion arise" and to think that such help is required by the nature of their relationship (Scanlon 2008, 151).

Third, Scanlon's account motivates a principled account of how much the blamer's fault must resemble the blamee's to undermine the blamer's position to blame (see Section 2.6). If, in blaming you, I suggest that your fault disqualifies you from participating in a specific, normal kind of moral relationship, I can be in a position to blame you for this fault despite my own greater, but different and for our relationship irrelevant, faults. If, however, I blame you and imply that your fault disqualifies you from participating in a wide range of normal moral relationships ("If you can do *this*, you can do anything"), my greater but different faults deprive me of the entitlement to blame since, in doing so, I would falsely imply that it is only your conduct that impairs a wide range of moral relationships between us.

Assuming this is the correct account of blaming, what makes hypocritical blaming wrongful? Here is what Scanlon writes about how hypocritical blame involves lack of standing to blame, which might indicate something about why, in Scanlon's view, it is wrongful:

> I cannot claim that the attitudes revealed in your willingness to stand me up constitute an impairment in our relations, because the mutual expectations and intentions that constitute those relations were already impaired by my own similar attitudes, revealed repeatedly in my past conduct . . . In blaming you I would be holding that your willingness to behave in this way makes you someone toward whom I cannot have the intentions and expectations that constitute normal moral relations, such as the intention to trust you and rely on you. But insofar as these normal expectations and intentions are *mutual*, my own conduct already reveals me to be a person who cannot be a participant in these relations . . . So there is something false in my suggesting that it is *your* willingness to act in ways that indicate untrustworthiness that impairs our moral relationship. (2008, 176–177)[44]

There are several ways to read Scanlon at this point. Perhaps Scanlon simply takes this to bear on having the standing to blame and does not intend it as (suggesting) an account of or even relevant to the blameworthiness or even

---

[44] Probably, the intended meaning in the last sentence is captured better if "it is your willingness" is read as "it is *only* your willingness," since otherwise the blamer is not implying anything false.

impermissibility—an important distinction, Scanlon insists[45]—of hypo-critical blame, even though the quoted passage appears in a section on the ethics of blame and he applies it to the Bill Cosby controversy (referring to an event predating his conviction as a sexual offender) to "make sense" of the—so I assume—moral "criticisms" that Cosby was exposed to when criticizing many poor blacks in the United States for not being good parents etc. (Scanlon 2008, 210; see also Wallace 2010, 320, on how to understand Scanlon's account).[46] Perhaps he does intend it to highlight what renders hypocritical blame wrongful. Whatever his intentions are, the account—whether that account is Scanlon's or not—of the wrongfulness of hypocritical blame that the quoted passage suggests is the following:

> *The falsehood account*: hypocritical blaming is wrongful because it involves the suggestion of a false claim; to wit, that the blamer's and the blamee's moral relationship is impaired as a result of the blamee's faults, not the blamer's faults.

One implication of the falsehood account is that there is nothing distinc-tively wrongful about hypocritical blame. On this view, hypocritical blame is wrongful in the same way as other ways of suggesting false claims, e.g., by giving a misleading appearance or skillfully exploiting an implicature.[47] This,

---

[45] Scanlon might simply say that while hypocritical blaming is blameworthy and, in that respect, morally inappropriate, it is not morally impermissible provided that the blamee has acted in a blame-worthy way.

[46] I have my doubts as to whether it succeeds in that respect also. Even if incoherent blame always implied a false claim about what impairs the blamer's and the blamee's relationship (see the first ob-jection to the falsehood account below), this in itself would not explain what undermines standing to blame. Suppose I blame you for having told me a white lie and that in so doing I suggest that it is such that our relationship is now impaired, and I imply falsely that I can no longer trust you, whatever the matter. Here, my implying a false claim about what impairs our relations in no way undermines my position to blame. No doubt, my blaming you is unjustified, but there is nothing specific about me to render it less proper for me than others to put forward such unwarranted condemnation. It follows that the mere fact that a condemner implies such a false claim cannot in itself explain how that undermines his position to blame.

[47] This answers Wallace's (2010, 320–321) worry: "This distinctively moral objection disappears on Scanlon's interpretation, however. His position seems to be that you have undermined the factual basis of your complaint about other persons if you have already impaired your relationship with them through behavior of the kind that you would object to in their case. But why should it be thought to be morally problematic to adopt a stance that in this way lacks a factual basis? Doing something that meets Scanlon's description would seem to leave you in a position that is conversationally awk-ward, but it would not open you to a distinctively moral complaint." The moral wrongness lies not in *adopting* a stance that lacks a factual basis, but in adopting a stance *implying* that its factual basis is satisfied. Note also that if hypocritical blame requires that the blamer believes or should believe that their own faults are at least as great, so Wallace's (2010, 321 n. 24) comparison of the hypocritical blamer to a blamer who is "honestly mistaken about whether another person's negligence has caused them harm" is misplaced.

of course, connects nicely with the view held by many that hypocrisy involves deception, and it implies that hypocritical blame is wrongful for the same reason as other forms of hypocrisy that do not involve blaming.

Despite the attractions of the falsehood account, there are at least three reasons why it is unable to account for the wrongfulness of hypocritical blame. First, hypocritical blame need not imply any false claims about what impairs the blamer-blamee relationship and yet still is wrongful. This much emerges in a case of hypocrisy where the blamer falsely believes that their faults in a certain dimension are greater than the blamee's and where, accordingly, the hypocritical blame implies a true claim about what impairs their moral relationship: namely, that it is the faults of the blamee that do so.[48] Such hypocritical blame might be wrongful, or at least blameworthy, despite the absence of the feature the falsehood account invokes to explain these properties of hypocritical blame.[49]

Second, the degree of wrongfulness of the hypocritical blamer's and the blamee's actions could vary independently of how their relative actions impair their relations, even though this variation seems to make a difference to their standing to blame. Consider a case where the person who blames has different and greater faults than the blamee, and the following two facts hold: (i) the blamer's faults are isolated in the sense that they do not suggest in any way that this person cannot engage in all sorts of other unimpaired moral relationships to which the relevant greater faults are irrelevant, and (ii) the blamee's faults are much smaller when considered on their own, but are tied to a whole range of other faults in a way that suggests they cannot engage in all sorts of other unimpaired moral relationships. A person who steals from their parents has acted in a way that is much less blameworthy than a person who has stolen much more, and much more often, from the parents of others.[50] Intuitively, the latter is not in a position to blame the former for stealing. Yet Scanlon's account seems to suggest otherwise because, arguably, the theft of cash from one's own parents impairs all personal relationships with the agent because of what it indicates about them, whereas stealing from strangers does not indicate any comparatively severe impairment of the agent's ability to enter normal relationships with others. Hence, if the

---

[48] Accordingly, I suspect Scanlon's account fits the wrongfulness of blame that can be dismissed on tu quoque grounds better than hypocritical blame (see Section 4.2).

[49] In response, it might be suggested that the wrongfulness results from implying a claim that the blamer should believe is false even if they do not.

[50] Even more problematic are cases where the greater faults are indicative of their possessor being a more trustworthy participant in normal moral relationships.

thief who has committed many more wrongful thefts here blames the thief
who has only committed one wrongful theft (against their own parents), the
blaming thief implies no false claims about what impairs their relationship.

Third, Scanlon's account is hard to square with the absence of moral inappropriateness in publicly praising someone for their lesser virtues (see
Chapter 4).[51] Suppose that you have gone way beyond the call of duty to help
me and suppose that later I do you a minor favor at no real cost to myself. You
express gratitude to me, thereby indicating that it alters our relationship in
such a way that, given the symmetrical nature of our relations, we now have
stronger obligations to assist one another. On a natural extension of the falsehood account, it follows that, by praising me, you thereby imply something
false: namely, that it is my willingness to help you that enhances (the positive correlate of impairing) our moral relationship.[52] Hence, if what explains
the moral wrongfulness of hypocritical blaming is that the hypocritical
blamer implies a false claim about what alters one's moral relationship to the
blamee, and if, in otherwise comparable situations, one were implying a false
claim about what alters one's moral relationship to the praisee by praising
them, then the positive correlate of blame should similarly be undermined.
But intuitively it is not (see Section 5.5).[53] I conclude that what makes incoherent blame morally wrongful, when it is indeed so, cannot simply be that
it implies a false claim about what alters the blamer's and the blamee's moral
relationship.[54]

---

[51] By "praising" I mean the positive Scanlonian correlate of blame (Scanlon 2008, 151) (see
Section 5.2).

[52] The natural extension says: hypercritical praising is wrongful because it involves the suggestion
of a false claim; to wit, that the praiser's and praisee's moral relationship is improved because of the
praisee's merits, not the praiser's much greater merits (see Section 5.2).

[53] For a further criticism, see Wallace (2010, 339–341): "[I]t is important to be clear that there are,
on Scanlon's account, two values potentially at stake in any instance of blameworthy conduct. There
is, first, the value of relating to people in accordance with basic moral requirements, a value that we
have seen to be monadic, insofar as it is not contingent on the attitudes of others. Second, there is the
value that is realized through the nonobligatory attitudes of good will, helpfulness, and a readiness
to enter into trust-based relationships, a value that does seem to be contingent on some degree of
reciprocation. We might call the first value respect, and the second value good will." Wallace objects
that according to Scanlon the requirements of respect are unconditional, so that when I violate
requirements of respect in relation to another person, I do not impair my relation to that person—
this person is under the same requirements of respect to me as they were before (cf. Sections 7.4–7.5).
Hence, if I hypocritically blame this person for violating these requirements, then Scanlon's account
seems inapplicable since my prior (and no less bad) violations of requirements of respect did not
impair our relation. Yet such a case intuitively qualifies as a case of morally objectionable address,
Wallace thinks (plausibly).

[54] The case in which the lesser sinner ignores the much greater faults of another and blames themself, thus falsely implying that it is their own lesser faults that impair their relationship, supports
the same conclusion. The falsehood account could be revised to address these problems through an
amendment to the effect that the implied falsehood casts a negative light on the blamee/praisee.

3.9. A Clash with Moral Equality

In this section, I turn to what I think is the most promising blamer-blamee-relation-based—indeed, the most promising *sans phrase*—account of the wrongfulness of hypocritical blame, i.e., the moral equality account. Let me first note the strong intuitive force of the moral equality account. One of the most common things people say in response to hypocritical blame is, "Who are you to judge me?" thus implying that the hypocritical blamer is making a claim to an elevated position from which they can judge the blamee, their own faults not being a relevant matter for the interchange (cf. Section 7).

At least two prominent recent accounts of the wrongfulness of hypocritical standing are moral equality accounts. First, in an influential article, R. J. Wallace (2010) argues that the core of the wrongness of hypocritical blame lies in the blamer not treating the interests of different persons as being equally morally important.[55] A hypocritical blamer fails to do so in two ways. First, they treat their own basic interest in avoiding blame as more important than the similar basic interest of their blamee. My complex stance when I blame hypocritically "attaches to my interests greater importance than it ascribes to yours, affording my interests a higher standard of protection and consideration than it affords yours. This offends against a presumption in favour of the equal moral standing of persons that I take to be fundamental to moral thought" (Wallace 2010, 328). Second, a hypocritical blamer treats the victim of their own wrongdoing's interest in not being subjected to the relevant wrongdoing as less important, morally speaking, than the interest of the victim of the blamee's wrongful action in not being subjected to the relevant wrongdoing. Because persons have equal moral status and because equal moral status implies that, presumptively at least, the equally important interests of people are equally morally important, in effect the hypocritical blamer is committed to impermissibly denying the moral equality of persons, by virtue of which the hypocritical blaming is wrong (Lippert-Rasmussen 2018, 73–80).

Second, as we saw in Chapter 1, Fritz and Miller believe that hypocritical blame involves "making an unjustified exception of oneself. This

---

[55] Or, as Wallace puts it: the objection to hypocrisy is "grounded . . . in the victim's interest in equal consideration and regard, an interest that is both second-order and essentially comparative in nature" (2010, 332). Wallace connects this concern with a "system of social sanction and constraint that essentially involves the distribution of esteem and disregard" (2010, 333), thus connecting what it is to treat one another as equals with the distributive concern about the social goods of "esteem and disregard" (cf. Section 3.2).

exception-making involves a rejection of the impartiality of morality and thereby a rejection of the equality of persons" (2018, 118). While their avowed argumentative aim is to explain what undermines standing to blame, in providing that explanation they also take themselves to be explaining what makes hypocritical blame wrongful. This is so because, on their view, the fact that blame is standingless "is a consideration that weighs heavily against the [moral] appropriateness" of the blame in question (Fritz and Miller 2018, 119).

While there are differences between Wallace's and Fritz and Miller's accounts, e.g., in terms of why they think a hypocritical blamer denies moral equality, and for that matter between their accounts and the version of the moral equality account that I propose below, we can summarize the moral equality account as follows:

> *The moral equality account*: hypocritical blaming is pro tanto wrongful because it involves the blamer relating to the blamee as if the blamee were inferior.[56]

The way I have stated the account here accommodates the case of the hypercritical blamer introduced in Section 2.8, who I argued neither lacks standing to blame nor, so I would add here, engages in wrongful blaming when they are disproportionately harsh on themself. Perhaps we have an impersonal reason to affirm the moral equality of everyone, ourselves included, but the specific personal wrong of hypocritical blaming is, so I contend, absent in the case of the hypercritical blamer. Hence, while this twist is absent in Wallace's and Fritz and Miller's accounts, they should be amended to accommodate this issue for reasons like those indicated in Section 2.8. Accordingly, I shall not spend more time elaborating the issue of the wrongness of hypocritical blame considering the issue of hypercritics. Instead, I will say something about the way in which hypocritical blamers treat their blamees as inferiors, building on Wallace's and Fritz and Miller's accounts, and then proceed to discuss two kinds of challenges to the moral equality account, i.e., the challenge that there are cases of wrongful hypocritical blame that do not involve

---

[56] Unlike Fritz and Miller's account, my focus is on treating someone as an inferior rather than denying that this person is an equal, though ascribing to the blamee an inferior moral status in the way that they would consider denying moral equality is a way of relating to the blamee as an inferior. Also, I give an account different from Wallace's of how the hypocritical blamer treats the blamee as an inferior. Finally, the "pro tanto" qualification application applies, but is not stated, in relation to the previous accounts as well.

treating the blamee as an inferior and the challenge that there are cases of nonwrongful hypocritical blame that involve treating the blamee as an inferior.

In what way does hypocritical blame involving treating the blamee as an inferior? On Wallace's account the answer lies in how the blamer treats some people's interests—their own victims' and their blamee's interests—as being less important than other people's interests. While there is something to the egalitarian element in Wallace's account, the focus on interests in avoiding blame etc.—even broadly construed—is too narrow. There are at least three reasons why this is so.

First, it is not the case that hypocritical blamers fail to treat people as moral equals because they treat the victim of their own wrongdoing's interest in not being subjected to the relevant wrongdoing as less important than the interest of the victim of the blamee's wrongful action in not being subjected to the relevant wrongdoing. This is so for the simple reason that the victim of the hypocritical blamer and the victim of the blamee could be one and the same person.[57] This means that it is the first way in which Wallace contends that a hypocritical blamer fails to treat people as moral equals that is crucial to his account. Hence, let us focus on the alleged treatment of the blamee's interests as being morally less significant than the blamer's interests.

Second, while most people have an interest in avoiding blame, it is also true that at least some people have an interest in not blaming others. After all, many people report that their lives improve when they stop blaming others. There are several reasons why this is so (cf. Brunning and Milam 2018, 148–150). While some of these reasons might apply mostly to private blame—harboring a grudge can be emotionally very costly—other reasons might primarily apply to expressed blame—expressed blame can often prevent one from entering valuable social relations with one's blamee. Consider a hypocritical blamer whose interests are set back by blaming in proportion to how blaming sets back the interests of their blamee. Suppose this blamer is also aware of the fact that this is so, such that by blaming hypocritically the blamer is simply making everyone worse off to an equal degree—leveling down blame, we can label it. This might be morally objectionable, all

---

[57] Upadhyaya (2020) argues that it is not as if a hypocritical blamer whose victim is different from that of the blamee acts more wrongly, or blames with less standing, than a hypocritical blamer whose victim is identical to that of the blamee's, as one would expect if Wallace were right and that the distinctive wrongness of hypocrisy is an additive function of the two wrong-making features of hypocrisy that Wallace identifies.

things considered, as well as morally objectionable qua hypocritical blame. However, the hypocritical blamer is not treating the blamee's interests as if they were less important than their own.[58] Accordingly, Wallace's account cannot explain the wrongfulness of this hypocritical blamer's hypocritical blame.[59]

Third, consider a case where, generally, I am a self-effacing person who gives the interests of others greater weight than my own interests. Hence, even if on this occasion I give greater weight to my interest in avoiding blame than I do to that of my blamee, considering the wider context, it is not true in general that I give greater weight to my interests than I do to the interests of my blamee. Indeed, it might be true that, overall, I give greater weight to the interests of others. Still, my blaming could be wrongfully objectionable, in which case we must reject Wallace's account or refine it such that it becomes instance-relative; i.e., we should on each occasion treat people's interests as equally important. Such an account, however, might not be very plausible, since presumably, whether in each instance I treat another as an equal is in part determined by my pattern of actions in general.

In view of these criticisms of Wallace's account, I suggest that we broaden our perspective to account for the fact that, just as persons are interest-bearers, they are also attitude-bearers; i.e., they hold beliefs and emotions and do so in part in response to reasons. Arguably, in hypocritical blame one does not respect persons equally as attitude-bearers, whether or not one respects them equally as interest-bearers. For instance, one blames someone, thus implying that the person now has a reason to provide one with a certain response to one's blame, ignoring that one has, or would have in the presence of others' equally justified blame, similar or even stronger reasons for providing the same uptake. In effect, doing so amounts to subordinating the perspective of the other attitude-bearer in hypocritical blame (cf. Frick 2016, 246). In short, I propose:

---

[58] A similar implication follows if we assume that blamers believe that they have an interest in being blamed, e.g., to be better able to reform and to thus uphold and form valuable relations with other people. For a view along these lines, see Dover (2019).

[59] The case similarly points to how Wallace's account fails to account for the standing to blame even if, unlike Wallace, we think having the standing to blame is not simply a matter of (a particular kind of) lack of wrongfulness of blame. If the blamee refuses to be blamed in the case I have described, surely, the rejoinder on the part of the blamer—"But look, my interests are harmed just as much as yours by my blaming you"—does not show that the blamer does have the standing to blame after all (see Lippert-Rasmussen 2018, 94–120).

The subordination claim: hypocritical blaming involves relating to the blamee as inferior by virtue of involving a subordination of the perspective of the blamee.[60]

When coupled with the subordination claim, the moral equality account appears able to accommodate all three objections to Wallace's account. First, it can accommodate the case where the victim of the hypocritical blamer's and the blamee's wrongdoing is one and the same person. Surely, in that case, from the perspective of the blamee, the blamer has just as much to answer for as does their blamee.[61] Second, the blamer whose interests are set back similarly subordinates their blamee by ignoring the fact that, from the perspective of their blamee, there is an equally strong reason why the blamer should address their own wrongdoing (were the blamee to blame the blamer—see Section 1.3).[62] Finally, the self-effacing person who hypocritically blames does, in the particular instance in question, subordinate the perspective of their blamee even if it is not true of the blamer that they routinely subordinate the perspective of others. To engage in wrongful hypocritical blaming, one need not have the character of a hypocrite (cf. Rossi 2020, 103).

By way of further support for the suggestion that the wrongness of hypocritical blame is not narrowly tied to how the hypocritical blamer treats others' interests, consider an analogous situation involving disrespect for people as knowers because of the subordination of the perspectives of others. Suppose that you and I agree that one of us should do the cleaning today and that the person who should do it is the person who did not clean the house last time around. However, we have different recollections of who this person is—you seem to recall that you did it last time around, while I seem to recall that I did. Neither of us can offer the other reasons why their memory of the

---

[60] One important challenge to a version of the moral equality account that locates the wrongness of hypocritical blame in the failure to relate as equals notes that states can wrongfully blame individuals for violating norms that the state violates on a much grander scale, and yet it is unclear what it means for states and persons to relate as equals. The subordination version of the moral equality account is immune to that objection because it makes sense to say that a state subordinates an individual's perspective to that of its own and in that sense can relate to an individual as an inferior. You can say that even though you do not think that states and persons can relate as people with equal moral standing—something that seems dubious for the simple reason that, arguably, states have no moral standing.

[61] If the blamer is a self-blaming hypercrite, who blames themself when addressing others, arguably the addressees act wrongly by not distancing themselves from or, more plausibly, by participating in the blamee's self-inflicted subordination.

[62] The parenthesis accommodates my view that by being blamed one acquires an additional reason to respond.

matter is more reliable than the other's, and no issue of strategic misrepresentation of memories is at stake. If you nevertheless proceed to declare that since you did the cleaning last time around, now it is my turn, you treat me disrespectfully as a knower.[63] The only way in which I could accept your argument for why I should do the cleaning requires that I disregard my own status as a knower—one who happens to disagree with you—and simply take your word for what the matters of fact are.[64]

Something analogous takes place in the case of hypocritical blame. When I blame you hypocritically, in effect, I treat you disrespectfully as someone who forms attitudes about how you should respond to others on the basis of reason.[65] That is, I know that since I have a similar or even worse fault than the one that I blame you for, from your perspective it is no less fitting that you hold me to account than that I hold you to account. Hence, in demanding the uptake that follows from accepted blame, I ignore that from your perspective, it is equally reasonable for you to make the same demand against me.

At this point you might ask where relating to one another as equals comes into the picture (cf. Frankfurt 1999, 146–154; Raz 1986, 217–244). Could we not simply say that justice requires that we respect each other as reasons-responsive bearers of attitudes and that the requirement of equality is a by-product in the sense that since we are all reasons-responsive persons, if we all treat each other as reasons-responsive persons, it follows that we treat all in the same way and, thus, arguably relate as equals? I do not think so. The inequality is a necessary part of what makes the relevant hypocritical blame or the ignoring of your standing as a knower disrespectful. In my example involving conflicting memories, if I ignore not only your recollection, but my own as well, I might disrespect you as a knower, but I do so in a different and, to my mind, less objectionable way than if I simply ignored *your* recollection. Similarly, if I invite a group of sinners to hypocritically blame someone else, I disrespect their status as reasons-responsive persons, since I simply presume that they accept my invitation to unreasonably exonerate themselves from blame. While this might be disrespectful, in a way it is disrespectful in a different and less objectionable way than in the case where I blame someone

---

[63] Things would be no different regarding relating as epistemic equals, if we both recall that the other did the cleaning last and you proceed to declare that, since I did the cleaning last time around, you will do it this time around.

[64] In accepting your decision and its motivation I both treat and, if my treatment reflects how I regard you, regard you as my epistemic superior.

[65] This might not be the case when I know that you do not know that I am no less of a sinner myself. Here my hypocritical blame might be wrong for other reasons, e.g., the way in which I deceive you.

despite my being no less of a sinner. It is less disrespectful because it does not involve my treating them as less than an equal.

This is what I have to say by way of exposition of my favored version of the moral equality account. In closing, I will address the challenge that there exist cases of wrongful hypocritical blame that do not involve treating the blamee as an inferior. Perhaps the clearest example of such a case is one in which two persons consent to their hypocritically blaming each other and one of them then hypocritically blames the other. Such an instance of blame might still be hypocritical in the sense that the blamer knows that their own faults are relevantly similar or worse.[66] Yet it might not be wrongful.

I think this is the right and intuitive way of looking at such a case. The blamee cannot plausibly indignantly say, "Who are you to judge me?" After all, they have consented to becoming the object of hypocritical blame from their blamer, while acquiring the corresponding liberty regarding their blamer. Precisely for that reason, though, this is an exceptional case where the blamee—perhaps as opposed to the blamee's perspective—is not being subordinated through hypocritical blame from the relevant blamer. Accordingly, the moral equality account is immune to the strongest version of the first sort of challenge.

3.10. Conclusion

In Chapters 1 and 2 I offered a definition of hypocritical blame and of what having standing to blame involves. There I defended a commitment account of standing to blame according to which standing to blame, understood as either having the liberty right against one's addressee to blame or the claim on one's addressee—in paradigmatic cases: one's blamee—to provide an uptake to one's blame, depends on one being serious about the norm to which one appeals in one's blame. Lack of commitment, however, is not what explains the wrongfulness of hypocritical blame.

In this chapter I have critically surveyed seven, in my view, flawed or quite restricted accounts of the wrongfulness of hypocritical blame, to wit, the desert, commitment, wrong attention, moral authority, reciprocity, community,

---

[66] The blamer might think consent justifies their blame, in which case it does not count as hypocritical on the definition proposed in Section 1.2. To avoid this complication, we can simply imagine that the blamer does not think of consent as a justification.

and falsehood accounts. More constructively, I have defended a particular version of the moral equality account, according to which hypocritical blame is wrongful because it involves subordinating the blamee by subordinating their perspective to the blamer's. I have not argued that all instances of wrongful blaming involve such subordination, but I have argued that those instances of wrongful blaming that are wrongful because of the blame being standingless involve this form of subordination and are wrongful because of their having this feature. However, two qualifications to this account are important.

First, it does not imply that no instance of standingless blame is wrongful for one or more of the other reasons identified by the seven other accounts surveyed here (or for that matter for other reasons, e.g., that it is harmful to the blamee to be subjected to hypocritical blame). Perhaps some instances of wrongful standingless blaming are also wrongful because of how they result in an unfair distribution of moral esteem or because of how they violate norms of reciprocity.

Second, while I have denied that lack of commitment to the norm underpinning one's blame is not itself what renders one's blame wrongful even though this is what undermines standing to blame, that does not mean that lack of commitment (or for that matter lack of standing) is irrelevant to the moral wrongfulness of hypocritical blaming. Arguably, the subordination involved in wrongful, standingless blame might result, in part, from the blamer's lack of serious commitment to the norm that the blamer appeals to.

With these accounts of the nature and wrongfulness of hypocritical blame in place, it is now time to broaden our perspective and look at blame that for reasons other than hypocrisy is standingless and perhaps also for that reason wrongful. Specifically, it is time to see whether some of our analyses of standingless hypocritical blame and its wrongfulness can be extrapolated to forms of blame other than hypocritical blame. This is the task that I turn to in Chapter 4.

4

Other Ways of Not Having a Standing to Blame

4.1. Introduction

Up to this point we have looked at one way in which blamees might deflect blame. But factors other than hypocrisy might result in lack of standing to blame and, thus, other ways in which a blamee might justifiably indirectly dismiss blame. In this chapter I survey five such ways: the blamer has the same fault as the blamee (tu quoque—Section 4.2); the blamer is complicit in that for which the blamer blames the blamee (Section 4.3); that which the blamee is blamed for is none of the blamer's business (Section 4.4); the blamer lacks understanding of the action for which they blame the blamee (Section 4.5); and, finally, the blamer does not accept the principle to which they appeal (Section 4.6). While each of these additional ways of engaging in standingless blame can coexist with hypocrisy (and for that matter with each of the four additional ways for blame to be standingless), for the sake of simplicity I shall focus on cases where standing to blame is undermined in the absence of hypocrisy. Further, while these five ways of lacking standing to blame—together with the charge of hypocrisy—comprise the most discussed ways in which one can lack standing to blame, as I indicate in the conclusion (Section 4.7), I do not mean the list to be exhaustive.

My aim in this chapter is to analyze the nature and wrongness of each of these forms of standingless blame, while drawing on insights from the previous three chapters. One main claim in this chapter is that the six ways of lacking standing to blame that I have introduced in this book, when we get to Section 4.6, are distinct and cannot be reduced to one basic form of lacking standing to blame. One central claim, which manifests this pluralist view, is that the commitment account of why the hypocritical blamer lacks standing to blame cannot be extended to cover all five forms of standingless blame discussed in this chapter; e.g., it cannot be extended to cover dismissal of meddlesome blame. Another, and related, claim is that the different kinds of

The Beam and the Mote. Kasper Lippert-Rasmussen, Oxford University Press. © Oxford University Press 2024.
DOI: 10.1093/oso/9780197544594.003.0005

standingless blame are wrong for different reasons. Specifically, I shall argue that the moral equality account of the wrongfulness of hypocritical blame that I proposed in Chapter 3 cannot explain the wrongness of all of the forms of standingless blame that I discuss in this chapter; e.g., it is not true that in all cases what explains the wrongfulness of your blaming someone for something that is none of your business is that you are thereby relating to that person as an inferior (which is not to say that in no case of meddlesome blame is the blamer treating the blamee as an inferior).

4.2. Tu Quoque

As I have already suggested, often it is taken for granted that a blamer who is vulnerable to the tu quoque reply is ipso facto vulnerable to the charge of being hypocritical and vice versa. However, on my view, the condition that underlies the tu quoque response is objective; i.e., it depends on whether the blamer has a fault relevantly similar to that for which the blamer blames the blamee. This is unlike the condition that underlies the charge of hypocrisy. That condition is subjective; i.e., it depends on whether the blamer believes or ought to believe that they have a fault relevantly similar to that for which the blamer blames someone else (recall the incoherence condition; see Section 1.2 and specifically Section 1.2.2).[1] It might well be the case that, generally, blamers believe, or have evidence available to them to justify believing, that they have the faults they have, and in such cases their blame can possibly be dismissed both on hypocrisy and tu quoque grounds. However, in some cases these two grounds come apart. For instance, a blamer might have honestly forgotten about their own past faults (and about the evidence based on which they could know about these faults as well) and, thus, be vulnerable to a tu quoque reply but not to a hypocrisy reply.[2] Conversely, in some cases blamers might unjustifiably believe that they have certain faults that they do

---

[1] Suppose "hypocrisy" and the "you, too" charges, as they are used in ordinary language, are simply not determinate regarding whether they cover both the subjective and the objective conditions or one but not the other. In that case, the distinction I point to exists even so, and I think we have reasons in that case for rendering our language more precise in the relevant respect. One reason why is that different moral faults are at stake in the two cases.

[2] By "innocently" here I mean, inter alia, that the person's memory is not biased in their own favor.

not have. If so, their blame can be dismissed as hypocritical, but not on tu quoque grounds.[3]

Because this is the central difference between hypocritical blame and blame vulnerable to the tu quoque charge, it is also easy to see how the analysis of hypocritical blame offered in Section 1.2 should be modified to capture blame that is vulnerable to the tu quoque charge:

X blames$_p$ Y for ϕ-ing in a way that is vulnerable to the tu quoque reply if, and only if
(1) X blames$_p$ Y for ϕ-ing;
(2*) X themself has done (or would have done) something that is both relevantly similar to ϕ-ing and also contextually relevant.[4]

There are two crucial differences between hypocritical blame and blame that is vulnerable to the tu quoque reply. First, (2*) in the definition of blame vulnerable to the tu quoque charge differs from (2) in the definition of hypocrisy in that (2*) concerns what, in fact, the blamer has done or would have done, not the blamer's beliefs about this matter.[5] This difference also explains why a blamer whose blame initially cannot be dismissed on grounds of hypocrisy changes in that respect once it is met with a tu quoque reply and the blamer accepts the factual presupposition of that reply; to wit, that the blamer is guilty of a similar fault themself. Second, there is no counterpart to (3) and (4)—see Section 1.2—in the definition of blame vulnerable to the tu quoque reply. What is crucial to that dismissal of blame is not whether, say, the blamer believes—perhaps for good reasons—that there is a morally relevant difference between their own conduct and that of their blamee that justifies blaming the latter while refraining from blaming themself (cf. (4)), or whether the blamer would accept being subjected to blame if they were to become aware of the fact that they have a similar fault. The crucial thing is whether, in fact, there is such a moral difference between the faults

---

[3] Unless perhaps the blamee knows that the blamer in fact does not have the fault in question—in such a case perhaps the blamee can deny that the blamer has a belief-relative liberty right to blame, but the blamee might still think that they are under a duty to provide an uptake to the blame.

[4] As with the definition of hypocritical blame, the "would have done" bit is motivated by the possibility of circumstantial luck; i.e., if I would have done worse had I been in my blamee's situation, but simply had the luck not to end up there, the blamee can dismiss my blame.

[5] As with hypocrisy, it would be too simple only to focus on whether the blamer at some point in their life has committed the same wrong as the blamee. Perhaps the blamer has reformed and repented, received an appropriate amount of blame, or the like, and now fully restored their standing to blame.

in question; e.g., if the blamer can successfully show that there is, they might be able to defuse the blamee's attempt to dismiss their blame on tu quoque grounds.[6] Both differences reflect the fact that the tu quoque charge is an objective matter in a way that the hypocrisy charge is not.

Why does a blamer who is faulty in the same way as their blamee lack the standing to blame? Given that commitment is a subjective matter and given that the tu quoque issue is a purely objective one, the explanation for this hardly can be what explains why the hypocritical blamer has no standing to blame defended in Section 2.8; to wit, that the hypocritical blamer is not sufficiently committed to the norm to which they appeal.[7] The tu quoque blamer might be very serious about the norm in question, as serious as one can be—it is just that they have innocently forgotten about their own similar (or even worse) violations of that norm. However, the tu quoque blamer lacks the standing to blame even before the blamee points out to them that they are at fault themself, at which point in a certain way they would manifest themself to be unserious, because hypocritical, about the norm in question if they were to proceed with blaming and refuse to be blamed themself.

There are two aspects to the blamer's lack of standing. The first aspect is that the blamee is under no duty to respond to their blamer.[8] What undermines such a duty (relative to a normal interaction) is the fact that the blamer has a fault relevantly similar to their own, e.g., because they have a similar kind of fault that is at least as bad as the blamee's or because they have a different kind of fault that, while different, is no less bad given the normative consideration underlying what makes the former fault a fault. Thus, if the faults of the blamee ground a duty to respond to blame from the blamer, then so do the blamer's faults ground a duty of the blamer to the blamee to address the blamer's fault, e.g., apologizing and laying plans for avoiding wrongdoing in the future. Thus, it cannot be that the blamee is under a one-sided duty to the blamer, in which case the blamer does not have the standing to blame.[9]

---

[6] It might still be the case that the initial instance of blame could be dismissed on tu quoque grounds, while the more enlightened blame, i.e., one that is partially motivated by the relevant moral difference, that this transforms into in light of the blamee's dismissal cannot be so dismissed.

[7] Though, admittedly, the blamer's own forgotten fault—perhaps in addition to the fact about forgetfulness—can indicate lack of commitment.

[8] By denying the latter, the blamee is in effect affirming that they have a Hohfeldian immunity toward the blamer; i.e., the blamer has no moral power to change their duties regarding the blamee's addressing their blameworthy action.

[9] Cf. the reciprocity and the community accounts of the wrongness of hypocritical blame (see Sections 3.6–3.7).

The second aspect is that the blamer has no liberty right against the blamee to (unilaterally) blame the blamee.[10] What undermines this liberty right is simply the fact that the blamer has a similar or worse fault themself (for some complications, recall Section 2.6).[11]

Assuming that the relation between hypocritical blame and tu quoque–vulnerable blame is as described, we can now ask whether the latter kind of blame is wrongful—assuming it is wrongful—for a reason like why hypocritical blame is wrongful. Given the view I defended in Chapter 3 specifically, the question is whether the wrongfulness of blame that is vulnerable to the tu quoque reply involves the blamer treating the blamee as an inferior by subordinating the blamee's perspective.

Basically, there are two ways to go here. Either we can say that since, as a matter of fact, the blamer is guilty of the same fault for which they criticize the blamee, they fail to treat their blamee as an equal and they subordinate their perspective. This is so even if the blamer is innocently unaware of their own similar faults and, thus, is unaware of how they subordinate the perspective of the blamee. If we take this route, we can say that blame that is standingless because of how it is vulnerable to the tu quoque objection is wrongful whether or not it also involves being hypocritical.

Alternatively, we can say that since the blamer was innocently unaware of their own fault, they did not wrong the blamee in blaming them. Specifically, they did not do so by treating the blamee as an inferior, since they did not know that they themself had something similar to answer for. If we take this route, we can say that blame that is standingless because of how it is vulnerable to the tu quoque objection is not in itself wrongful. On this view, if I blame someone, innocently unaware of my own faults, and then either retract my blame or adequately address my own faults in response to my blamee pulling the tu quoque card, then no wronging of my blamee has taken place.[12] Often tu quoque–vulnerable blame is hypocritical and for that reason wrong, but being tu quoque–vulnerable is not in itself a wrong-making feature of blame.

In my view, the latter is correct. On this view, the wrong in hypocritical blame lies in the way in which the blamer relates to the blamee in a way that manifests an objectionable view of the blamee. However, no such flaw is

---

[10] Assume here that the addressee is the blamee.

[11] Or more precisely: what undermines X's liberty right to blame Y without blaming themself to an appropriate degree is the fact that their own faults are no smaller than Y's.

[12] There could be cases of pure negligence, where the blamer ought to have known of their own relevantly similar fault, but where that fault is not of such a nature that the accusation of hypocrisy is warranted.

manifested in the case of pure tu quoque–vulnerable blame. We can compare such blame with a case in which someone innocently says something
to someone that in fact is insulting. In such a case, we do not believe that any
wrong has taken place.[13] True, often we expect the insulter to apologize in
such cases, but the apology here should not be taken as an acknowledgment
of wrongdoing—not even some kind of epistemic negligence—as opposed
to an expression of regret over the harm, or the like, caused.[14] Indeed, we
would consider it inappropriate for the insultee to resent the insulter in such
a case. Similarly, it would be inappropriate for a blamee to resent a blamer involved in pure tu quoque blaming for their blaming and demand an apology
from the blamer once the blamer's own similar fault is pointed out. Hence, an
apology is likely not an acknowledgment of wrongdoing.

I conclude that blame that is vulnerable to the tu quoque charge is the objective correlative of hypocritical blame and that, unlike such blame, it is not
wrong because of how the blamer relates to the blamee as an inferior.[15] In
short, tu quoque–vulnerable blame is a form of nonwrongful standingless
blame, though, once pointed out to the blamer, it easily transforms into
wrongful hypocritical blame.

4.3. Complicity

Another way that we often indirectly dismiss blame is by pointing to the
fact that the blamer has contributed to making it the case that we did what
we are blamed for.[16] For instance, Gary Watson thinks that serious injustice

---

[13] Some might be skeptical of this view on the following ground: surely, making a racist utterance might be wrongful even if one is innocently unaware that it is racist; e.g., this would follow
on Hellman's (2008) objective meaning account of the wrong of discrimination. If so, why cannot
blaming someone in a way that is vulnerable to the tu quoque reply similarly be wrongful even if the
blamer is innocently unaware of their own similar fault? One thing one can say in response is that
blaming the blamee would in some sense be appropriate if we bracket the blamer's own fault—what
the blamer has done is blameworthy. There is no analogous way in which the racist utterance would
in some sense be appropriate if we somehow bracket some fact about the utterer. Perhaps therefore
the wrong of blaming in a way that is vulnerable to the tu quoque reply cannot result simply from
the objective meaning of the blame and independently of the blamer's mental states. I thank Andrei
Poama for pressing me on this matter.

[14] Similarly, I would not say that I wrong someone when I stand on their feet nonculpably, not
knowing that they were where they were.

[15] The four remaining ways of lacking standing to blame also come in subjective and corresponding
objective versions; e.g., believing one is involved in blamee's blameworthy action is different from
simply being involved in it.

[16] Possibly, there are also cases where the blamer did not contribute to making the agent perform
the blameworthy action, but rather made the action blameworthy. I know that a third party is about
to give their car to you and that you're going to take it whether they give it to you or not. I persuade

resulting in offenders committing crimes means that the state allowing these injustices might not be in a position to punish them: "The defendant's complaint to the criminal law . . . is that it has no authority to hold him answerable for a crime for which it shares responsibility" (2015, 178; see also Duff 2010; Tadros 2011). Call blame that merits such a response *complicitous blame*:

X blames Y for φ-ing in a complicitous way if, and only if

(3) X blames Y for φ-ing;

(4) X is involved in Y's φ-ing;[17]

(5) X does not to a suitable degree or in a suitable way blame themself for contributing to Y's φ-ing;[18]

(6) it is not the case that there are morally relevant differences between contributing in a significant way to someone's φ-ing, on the one hand, and Y's φ-ing, on the other hand, that justify blaming Y for φ-ing and not blaming being involved in Y's φ-ing.

Many accept the following:

The complicity condition on having the standing to blame: X is in a position to blame Y for φ-ing only if X is not involved in Y's φ-ing.[19]

---

the third party not to give the car to you and then blame you for taking the third party's car. Arguably, you can dismiss my blame, not on the ground that I made you do it, but on the ground that I made your action blameworthy. While you did take the car and I am not complicit in that, I made it the case that your act of taking the car was also your act of stealing it, and in that I am complicit. While this does not fall under the category of complicitous blame, as it is normally defined, I take it to be a special case, which, strictly speaking, a definition of complicitous blame should be amended to include, but which I shall nevertheless ignore.

[17] One important way of contributing to others' blameworthy action is by informing them that we condone their acting in the relevant way or even encouraging them to do so. However, suppose that I encourage you to steal. My encouragements have no effect on you. Nevertheless, you have reasons independent of my encouragements to steal and do so. In this case, I seem not to be in a position to blame you, even though you cannot dismiss my blame by retorting, "You made me do it." In short, the mere fact that I condoned or even encouraged your action prior to your acting seems to undercut my standing to blame you. Or perhaps this is a case where, arguably like the "You only blame me because . . ." deflection, the indirect dismissal is not a dismissal of the fact that the wrongdoer has something to answer for, but a request for a broader agenda, which also includes the blamer's previous encouragement to act wrongfully. In short, the category of complicitous blame is quite heterogeneous in a way that deserves further analytical attention.

[18] This condition and (6) do not bear on whether the blame is complicitous, but on whether it is complicitous in a way that undermines standing to blame.

[19] The "You don't know what it's like" reply (see Section 4.5) in some versions might imply—given the view that understanding requires involvement (at least)—that you can blame only for types of actions that you are involved in. Incidentally, this could be abused to immunize oneself against blame—standing to blame requires understanding, understanding requires involvement (at least), but involvement undermines standing to blame. Thus, no one can have the standing to blame one.

The person who, say, drove the bank robber to the bank and waited for them outside in the car to drive them away is not in position to blame them once the bank robber is back in the car and the driver accelerates to let them escape.

One crucial question in relation to the complicity condition is what exactly it means to be involved in the wrongful act that one blames someone for; i.e., what sort of cases Condition (4) covers.[20] G. A. Cohen suggests that standing-undermining involvement can take various forms. In Patrick Todd's helpful (though seemingly incomplete) list, such forms are brought out by the following responses in addition to "You forced me to do it": "You helped me to do it; You asked me to do it;[21] You gave me the means to do it; You commanded me to do it" (2019, 354).[22]

Todd doubts the coherence of the first indirect reply to blame—if X was forced to φ, then X was not morally responsible for φ-ing and pointing to the fact that X's blamer forced X to φ serves simply to bring this out (2019, 353).[23] But even if these doubts are unwarranted, he thinks that involvement by way of forcing, like the other involvements listed here, is relevant only as a sign of something else; to wit, the blamer's lack of seriousness in relation to the principles on which their blaming is based. This implies that whenever standing to blame is undermined and the blamer is involved in the action for which they blame the blamee, what is really doing the work is the hypocrisy of the blamer. Thus, Todd thinks we can reduce the complicity condition to the hypocrisy condition (and given Todd's view that "none of your business" [see Section 4.4] and the warrant constraints [see Section 4.5] on blame are not really constraints pertaining to standing to blame, we have a unified account of the standing to blame).[24]

---

[20] The same point that applies to "being involved in" applies to action verbs like "contributing to." See Lepore and Goodin (2015) for a helpful taxonomy of different kinds of complicity.

[21] I can ask you to do something, believing that my asking you to do it makes it less likely that you'll do it. Suppose that's what happened. Can I not then blame you for doing what I asked you to do? I think I can. I can point to a relevant difference between my seemingly wrongful action—that I asked you to do something wrongful—and your wrongful action; to wit, that my asking you to do it was something I did to cause you not to do it.

[22] I say "incomplete" because encouraging someone to do something also seems like a way of being complicit.

[23] I am not sure this indirect reply is incoherent. One can say: "What I did wasn't blameworthy because I was forced to do it. But even if it were, you would not be in a position to blame me for it, since it was you who forced me."

[24] The warrant constraint on blame says that the blamer's belief that the blamee's wrongdoing was blameworthy must be warranted.

I think Todd's point is partially correct, and will explain why below. I would put something like Todd's point like this:

The subspecies claim: complicitous blame is a subspecies of hypocritical blame, where the relevantly similar action performed by the blamer is whatever the blamer does to become complicitous in the blameworthy action.

On this view, complicitous blame is simply a version where

(2)   X themself believes or should believe that they themself have done (or would have done) something that is both relevantly similar to φ-ing and also contextually relevant.

On the definition of hypocritical blame this is true because the blamer engages in complicitous action and that action is relevantly like the blameworthy action for which they blame someone else and is contextually relevant, as it might be simply by virtue of its being connected to the very same (numerical-identity-speaking) action that the blamer blames the blamee for.[25]

Before defending the subspecies claim, I need to amend it. Not in all cases where blame can be dismissed as complicitous is it the case that the blamer is aware of their complicity. I agreed to drive you to the bank, wait for you outside, and then drive you away at high speed, not believing that you would rob the bank. In some such cases, I should have known what I was becoming complicit in, and in some, but not all, of these cases my failure to see that is of such a nature that blame on my part can be dismissed as hypocritical.[26] In the remaining cases, we have a case of pure negligence. Such cases are not a

[25] There is an interesting connection between this claim and the issue of quantity discussed in Section 2.6, i.e., the question of how large the blamer's faults must be in comparison to the faults of the blamee for the blamer to have no standing to blame. Often, assisting someone to perform a wrongful action is much less wrongful—and, so it seems, never more wrongful—than performing the action itself (though that judgment possibly relies on a one-sided diet of examples; e.g., if I assist X in insulting Y by feeding X some confidential, compromising information about Y and, unlike X, I am related family-wise to Y, possibly, my assisting X in their wrongful action is more wrongful than X's wrongful action itself). If in such a case complicitous blame is standingless, then lesser faults can undermine standing to blame (as I have suggested in Section 2.6).

[26] My failure to see what I would become complicit in might reflect negligence on my part, but it is negligence that is not so motivated as to make the charge of hypocrisy warranted; e.g., the negligence I display in this area is not motivated by my desire to make myself appear better than I am or to avoid myself being blamed.

subspecies of hypocritical blame, but of blame vulnerable to the tu quoque response, where

(2*) X themself has done (or would have done) something that is both relevantly similar to φ-ing and also contextually relevant

is true because the blamer is complicitous in the blameworthy action out of negligence. Finally, there might be cases where the blamer is innocently involved in the blameworthy action; e.g., they did something that enabled the wrongdoer to commit the blameworthy action, but it is not the case that they should have known that this is what they were doing. In such a case, standing to blame is intact. Suppose I lend you my car believing that you need it for driving to the beach on a hot summer day. I had no way of knowing that, in fact, you were going to use it to rob a bank, which you would not have been able to rob had I not lent you my car. I do not lose my standing to blame you simply by virtue of having lent you the car.[27] In fact, unlike in the tu quoque case, I retain my standing to blame you even when you alert me to the fact that, in the absence of my action, you could not have performed the blameworthy action in question. In view of that, my slightly more complex view on complicitous blame is captured by:

> *The amended subspecies claim*: complicitous blame is either a subspecies of hypocritical blame, *or* a subspecies of blame vulnerable to the tu quoque claim, where the relevant similar action performed by the blamer is whatever the blamer does to become complicitous in the blameworthy action in relation to the first disjunct, or noninnocently complicitous in the blameworthy action in relation to the second disjunct, where the blamer retains standing to blame.

Let us now return to the subspecies claim. What can we say in its defense? I think we can say two things at least. First, compare the following two cases:

> *Complicity*: John drives Joe to the bank, waits for him outside in the car to drive him away, and blames Joe for robbing the bank once Joe is back in the car. John accelerates to make sure that Joe escapes the police, who give chase.

---

[27] There is no strict liability condition in relation to standing to blame, as Göran Duus-Otterström helpfully suggested to me that one could put this point.

Relevantly similar noncomplicity: Jerry once did the same thing for Jill as John did for Joe. Jerry meets Joe on the street after his escape and starts blaming him for robbing the bank.

The question to ask here is whether the standing that John and Jerry have to blame Joe for robbing the bank is equivalent or not.[28] Intuitively, John has no standing to blame Joe—Joe might say, "Who are you to blame me for robbing the bank, when at this very moment you're assisting me in doing so and could have refrained from doing so at no cost [assume this is so] or difficulty?"—so the question is whether Jerry likewise has no standing to blame.

In my view, there is no real difference between John and Jerry as regards their standing to blame Joe. Admittedly, there might be a superficial, epistemic difference in that, in practice, because John was involved in assisting Joe in performing the very same bank robbery that he blames Joe for, while Jerry was not, Jerry—or, more precisely, people in Jerry's situation—typically will be able to contend that the bank robbery he assisted was somehow morally less bad than the bank robbery performed by Joe, whereas no such reply is available to John. However, once we stipulate that no such reply is available to Jerry—the bank robbery he assisted was in all morally relevant respects exactly as bad as Joe's—there is no difference standing-wise between the two blamers. This supports the subspecies thesis for the following reason. If the subspecies thesis were false, we should find that being complicit in the numerically identical action for which one blames the blamee in itself makes a difference to standing. Since it does not—John's and Jerry's blame is equally hypocritical and the fact that John is also complicitous of the wrong for which he blames the wrongdoer adds nothing to his lack of standing relative to Jerry's case—we can infer modus tollens that the subspecies thesis is true.

---

[28] Pedantically, you might distinguish between blaming someone for a particular robbing of a bank (a particular numerically distinguishable event) and blaming someone for bank robbing, i.e., for performing a numerically distinguishable event (which one does not matter) of a particular kind, and then suggest that whereas Jerry, unlike John, has standing to blame Joe for the particular bank robbery, neither of them has standing to blame Joe for bank robbing. However, I do not think this is how we think of standing to blame. If I blame you for a particular act that you did today and you retort that I have no standing to blame you, since I did the exact same thing yesterday, I cannot retort: "I agree that I did the exact same thing yesterday, but I am not blaming you for performing an action of a particular type. I am blaming you for performing this token action, which I am uninvolved in, and I am only concerned with that event." In this way, blame, I take it, is never blame just for tokens, but always also blame for instantiating types of action. One might speculate that this reflects that blaming is a reason-governed activity and that reason is not concerned with particulars per se.

I now turn to the second thing one can say in defense of the subspecies thesis. Consider a case where someone blames someone else for a blame-worthy action that the blamer is involved in, but where, including from the blamer's perspective, there is a justification (or an excuse) for the blamer's being complicit in the blameworthy action. Suppose that by driving Joe to the bank that Joe intends to rob, John earns money that enables him to do some-thing good, such that he is justified in offering his assistance. If that is the case, then John is not being hypocritical in blaming Joe because Condition (2) in the definition of hypocritical blame is not satisfied; i.e., John does not believe that his action is morally relevantly like Joe's in that his complici-tous action has a feature that justifies it, which Joe's robbing the bank does not have. Still, John *is* complicit. Hence, if the complicity condition states a condition for standing to blame that is not captured by a similar hypocrisy condition, then one would expect that John has no standing to blame Joe in such a case. Intuitively, however, John does have such a standing. If Joe dismisses John's blame in the car on grounds of his assisting him in robbing the bank, John can retort that he does have the requisite standing, since, un-like Joe, he has a justification for what he is doing. Indeed, John can point to Condition (6) above and say that there is a morally relevant difference be-tween his contributing in a significant way to Joe's robbing the bank, on the one hand, and Joe's robbing the bank, on the other hand, that justifies him in blaming Joe for robbing the bank while not addressing his own complicit ac-tion. I conclude that the subspecies claim is vindicated.

Before proceeding to discuss the moral wrongness of complicitous blame on this background, I want to address a certain complication that I think might be thought to give rise to a problem for the commitment account of standing to blame (see Section 2.8). Consider the following case:

> *Strongly committed blamer.* John helped, ordered, encouraged, etc. Joe to do something wrong. John thinks the relevant act is wrong and he is strongly committed to the norm in question; e.g., he entertains no doubts whether that kind of action is wrong, and he has never been in the slightest motivated to perform an action proscribed by the norm himself. However, he also thinks that while Joe's action is wrong, it is not wrongful to help, order, encourage, etc. others to perform an act of this kind. Accordingly, he blames Joe for his wrongful action.

If the commitment account of standing to blame is correct, then it seems John should have the standing to blame Joe. Yet, even if John is indeed very serious about the norm proscribing Joe's action, intuitively he nevertheless lacks standing to blame him for it (if commitment to a certain norm does not depend on having a certain substantive moral view about helping, ordering, encouraging, etc. others to perform actions that violate this norm). That is a problem for the commitment account.

Also, John is not being a hypocrite since on his—innocently, we can assume—mistaken view he has performed no relevantly similar action in helping, ordering, or encouraging John to perform the relevant wrongful action. But since John lacks standing to blame, that seems like a counterexample to my subspecies claim as well. I concede this point but remind the reader that my real commitment in this relation is to the amended subspecies claim. The amended subspecies claim says that complicitous blame is *either* a subspecies of hypocritical blame *or* a subspecies of blame vulnerable to the tu quoque claim. I concede that John's blame is not hypocritical, but I also think that it is vulnerable to the tu quoque response, where what makes that response merited is the fact that helping, ordering, or encouraging John to perform the relevant wrongful action is relevantly morally similar to John's performing that action. Moreover, in response to the challenge to the commitment account of standing to blame, I suggest that the present challenge shows that the commitment account is best thought of as identifying a necessary, but not a sufficient, condition for having standing to blame.

I now turn to the question of the wrongfulness of complicitous blame. Given that I have argued that the wrongfulness of core cases of hypocritical blame can be accounted for by the moral equality account, and given that I have defended the claim that core cases of complicitous blame really form a subspecies of hypocritical blame, one would expect core cases of complicitous blame to involve treating blamees as inferiors.[29] In fact, I think they do. Complicitous blamers treat their blamees as inferiors in that they treat them as being under a duty to them to account for their wrongful action, whereas they themselves are under no similar duty to the blamees to account for their complicity in the relevant blameful actions. But, surely, from the perspective of blamees, if they are accountable to their blamers for their wrongful

---

[29] Admittedly, the amended subspecies claim was formulated disjunctively and the second disjunct said that complicitous blame was a subspecies of blame vulnerable to the tu quoque claim—see next paragraph.

actions, then so are their blamers accountable to them (as well as the victims of the relevant blameworthy actions) for their complicity. In that sense, complicitous blame subordinates the perspective of the blamee to that of the blamer. Hence, the moral equality account applies to complicitous blame.[30]

In response, it might be pointed out that the present line of argument only applies to complicitous blame that forms a subspecies of hypocritical blame, but that it follows from my discussion of the amended subspecies view that some forms of complicitous blame are not of that kind, but rather a subspecies of tu quoque–vulnerable blame. About that sort of complicitous blame, I will say something like what I said about blame vulnerable to the tu quoque charge; to wit, that the wrong in complicitous blame lies in the way in which the blamer relates to the blamee in a way that manifests an objectionable view of the blamee. Since no such objectionable view is manifested in complicitous blame that is a subspecies of tu quoque–vulnerable blame, this form of standingless blame is not wrongful.

The claim made in the previous sentence is worth elaborating, using the case I described of a blamer who is very serious about a norm proscribing a certain action while also believing that nothing follows from this norm or the values informing it to the effect that helping, ordering, encouraging, etc. people to perform such wrongful actions is wrongful. My claim here is that this person is not treating their blamee as inferior. After all, the blamer might not blame others who have helped, ordered, encouraged, etc. others to perform wrongful acts of which blamer was the victim. (If the blamer does blame such people, then, of course, that blame would be hypocritical and inegalitarian, and the blamer's own blame would no longer be an instance of blame that falls only under the tu quoque subspecies.) In short: the blamer's blame reflects a false view about morality, but it does not reflect an objectionable view of the blamee.

Is blame of the former sort wrongful even if it is not wrongful because of the view of the blamee that it manifests? One way to approach this question is to ask whether blaming someone for an action that one innocently believes to be wrongful but which in fact is not, is wrongful. Suppose I blame you for being partial toward your children, which I innocently and falsely believe to be wrongful. I certainly would wrong you if I were to physically prevent you from being partial in a way that you are entitled to, even if I innocently think

---

[30] The same is true of the complicity-focused analogue to the hypercritical blamer, e.g., one who is not upset about the wrongful action of the wrongdoer the hypercrite assisted but very much upset by their own complicity in that very wrongful action.

that preventing you is the right thing to do. If so, plausibly, I can also wrong you by blaming you for being partial toward your children, even if I innocently think this is wrongful. Perhaps not all forms of such blame—especially not milder forms—are wrongful; however, some might be (or perhaps they all are, even though some of them are only a tiny bit wrongful). So, similarly, perhaps some forms of complicitous blame of the tu quoque species can be wrongful as well. With this qualification of my embrace of the moral equality account in relation to the wrongness of complicitous blame, I now proceed to consider a third way in which one can lack the standing to blame—one that I think clearly cannot be accounted for, though it is consistent with and forms an important background to the application of the moral equality account.

4.4. None of Your Business

Suppose you have not been doing your part of the household chores. It so happens that through very roundabout ways, your bus driver has acquired knowledge of that regrettable fact about you (cf. Duff 2010, 125–126; McKiernan 2016, 145–151; Smith 2007, 478–480; cf. Nagel 1998). You are about to exit the bus when the bus driver, with whom you have never spoken before, starts blaming you. Most would think that the bus driver is in no position to blame you in this scenario. The bus driver has no liberty right to blame you to your face—perhaps they have a liberty right to blame you when the addressee is someone else, say, a colleague of theirs, but in the absence of special circumstances, they—a stranger—should not blame you to your face for this, and they owe it to you not to do so. They wrong you by blaming you, even if what you have done is indeed blameworthy.[31] You also have no duty to them to provide an uptake to their blame—you can simply ignore it without any wrongdoing on your part. This you can do even if your failing to do your bit of the household chores is blameworthy, and even if some others are in a

---

[31] At this point, one might draw a parallel to consent: "Consent is only possible within moral domains over which someone can wield normative powers" (Liberto 2021, 29). I can consent to my having a vaccination, but I cannot consent to my partner having one. Of course, I can say, "I consent to my partner having a vaccination," but my doing so does not affect the rights and duties of anyone regarding my partner receiving a vaccination. Similarly, one can blame others in relation to matters that are none of one's business, but when one does so, this does not affect the rights and duties of anyone regarding the blameworthy matter in question; e.g., the blamee has no obligation to provide me with an uptake to my blame.

position to blame you for it such that were your partner to do so, you would be under an obligation to them to provide an uptake to their blame.[32]

Call blame that can be dismissed on the ground that the blameworthy action is none of the blamer's business "meddlesome blame." We can define it as follows:

X blames Y for φ-ing in a meddlesome way if, and only if
(7) X blames Y for φ-ing;
(8) Y's φ-ing is none of X's business.[33]

This definition contains no condition like Condition (3) in the definition of hypocritical blame. This reflects that meddlesome blame is no less meddlesome, even if the blamer, say, is open to others similarly blaming them for things that are none of their business.[34] Meddlesome blame might be less wrongful in such a case—certainly, the meddlesome blamer would respect the moral equality of their blamees in such a case (see below in this section)—but it is no less meddlesome.

Similarly, this definition contains no condition like Condition (4) in the definition of hypocritical blame. This reflects a similar fact. If a blamer believes that there is a justification for blaming their blamee for something that, in the absence of this justification, undeniably would be none of this person's business, then the presence of the agent's belief in this justification does not turn the blame into nonmeddlesome blame—merely justified blame that also happens to be meddlesome.

This might ignore the special case where the blamer believes—and not entirely unreasonably so—that there is a reason for the blamer to regard the blameworthy action as being their business; e.g., the bus driver justifiably, but mistakenly, believes that the two of you are siblings. In such a case, we

---

[32] Could there be a blameworthy action such that it is no one's business to blame the agent for it? Perhaps. I do not think anything in what follows hinges on that question.

[33] Is this definition viciously circular because being meddlesome is simply to interfere in what is none of one's business? Arguably so. However, the present definition serves mostly a presentational point, and below I discuss a couple of views about when something is someone's business, e.g., the interest principle. Those views could be used to offer amended, noncircular versions of (8), where the relevant none-of-your-business-making facts can be substituted for "none of the blamer's business."

[34] Arguably, if the meddlesome blamer is not open to others blaming them for what they regard as something that is none of other people's business, perhaps they can deflect the blamer's blame for two reasons: that it is meddlesome and that the stance the blamer adopts (though perhaps not the particular content of their meddlesome blame—after all, they might be innocent of the specific wrong and similar ones that they blame for) is hypocritical—the blamer would not themself accept blame of a meddlesome kind.

might say that while the blame is meddlesome fact-relatively speaking, it is not meddlesome belief- or evidence-relatively speaking. The definition above captures the former kind of meddlesome blame. To capture the latter form, we need

> X blames Y for φ-ing in a meddlesome way, belief- or evidence-relatively speaking, if, and only if
> (9) X blames Y for φ-ing;
> (10) Y's φ-ing is none of X's business;
> (11) it is neither the case that X believes that (10) is true, nor that X has evidence warranting the belief that (10) is true.[35]

The distinction between belief- or evidence-relative meddlesome blame and fact-relative meddlesome blame corresponds to the distinction between blame that can be dismissed on grounds of hypocrisy and blame that is vulnerable to the tu quoque charge. In both distinctions, the first kind of blame is standingless by virtue of how things look from the perspective of the blamer, whereas in the second kind of blame in both distinctions, standing depends on what is in fact the case. In what follows, for simplicity I will focus on blame that is meddlesome in all three ways.

So much for the definition of meddlesome blame. I now turn to the question of when a certain blameworthy action is someone's business. Most accounts of meddlesome blame and blame that is standingless due to being meddlesome are informed by

> The nonuniversalist view: it is not the case that for any wrongful act, any person is in a position to blame the agent of that act for their wrongdoing (absent special contexts) (Radzik 2011, 2012; cf. the simple view in Section 3.1).[36]

---

[35] This leaves open the question of what to say about blamers who blame without any beliefs about whether the relevant object of blame is their business or not (and without any evidence suggesting that the relevant object of blame is their business). Perhaps there is a broader sense of meddlesome blame in which they too are meddlesome blamers.

[36] The none-of-your-business requirement easily applies to many illocutionary acts other than blaming. For instance, if it is not my business to blame someone for something in their private life, typically I also do not have the standing to comment upon it, at least not in such a way that this person acquires a duty to respond to my comment (cf. Section 5.6).

Given the right sort of context, people are answerable to one another. If I hurl unfounded insults at the bus driver on exiting the bus, accusing them of being lazy and exploiting their partner, then my failure to do my part of the household chores perhaps becomes their business—at least to the extent that they acquire the standing to blame me for that. However, in principle on the nonuniversalist view, there might be wrongs that are only the wrongdoer's own business (Radzik 2011, 575).[37] (This view might be particularly plausible if there are such things as duties to oneself.) However, the nonuniversalist view can accommodate some universalist intuitions about standing to blame. For instance, it is compatible with the following claim:

> *Restricted universalism*: for some wrongs, any person is in a position to blame the agent of that act for their wrongdoing.

It might be that anyone is in a position to blame any perpetrator of a crime against humanity for their wrongs; e.g., Stalin could not say, "None of your business" to a bus driver when getting off the bus in response to the bus driver's complaints about the Holodomor.

The alternative to the nonuniversalist view is uncommon:

> *The universalist view*: for any wrong, any person is in a position to blame the agent of that act for their wrongdoing.[38]

---

[37] McKiernan (2016, 149) appeals to Bernard Williams's internalism about reasons to explain the none-of-your-business reply. The explanation says that in cases where such a reply is appropriate, the blamer does "not have access to knowledge about the person or situation in question without prying or objectifying that person" (McKiernan 2016, 150). I do not think this provides an explanation of the right sort. Suppose I have permitted my psychoanalyst to share the information that they obtain during my sessions with others and to permit those others to share that information with others too. Somehow that information got to my bus driver, who, being a perceptive and thoughtful person—more so than I am—has knowledge of what I have reason to do—more so than I have—assuming an internalist view of reasons for action and motivational states. In my view these facts do nothing to undermine the appropriateness of my "mind your own business" reply. Discussing a case by Angela Smith where a stranger blames a husband for belittling the conversational contributions of his wife, McKiernan (2016, 151) also seems to want to defend the present standing condition on the ground that standingless blame can "reinforce, instead of prevent, relationship abuse." In my view, such considerations, while relevant to whether blame is justified all things considered, are not relevant to the standing to blame, even though they are relevant to whether it is good to exercise one's right to blame.

[38] To the extent that the standing to blame comes in degrees—something that, as indicated, I find plausible—the universalist view can accommodate the view that special relations matter for standing to blame, since it is compatible with saying that given that X has a certain special relation to Y, X has greater standing to blame Z since Z has no comparable special relation to Y. That such moderate universalism is more plausible than radical universalism comes out in the following situation: Y and Z blame X for X's flaws as a spouse. Y is X's spouse and Z is a stranger. X can only respond to one of these

According to Marilyn Friedman, Stephen Darwall is one who accepts, or at any rate is committed to, the universalist view. However, Friedman rejects the universalist view. On her view, responsible blaming satisfies a commitment requirement, which rules out hypocritical blame, for instance (Friedman 2013, 275). Similarly, given the universalist view, I cannot dismiss the bus driver's blame as being none of the bus driver's business. By virtue of their blaming me for my wrongdoing, I now have a reason to provide them with a certain uptake, e.g., an explanation of how I came to act in this way and an account of how I plan to avoid similar wrongdoing in the future. On the nonuniversalist view, this is not so. The bus driver case provides significant intuitive support for the nonuniversalist view—the mere fact that one is a person, where that involves having a certain amount of moral understanding, does not imply that one has the standing to blame anyone for any moral flaw of theirs (cf. Friedman 2013, 272; Todd 2019, 347).[39] It might be

two persons' blame. Surely, X should not flip a coin about whose blame to respond to, but should respond to their spouse's blame (cf. Upadhyaya 2020).

[39] Todd (2019, 350–351) believes that whereas "none of your business" concerns only the expression of blame, the complicity dismissal of blame concerns the standing to experience certain reactive emotions. I believe this interpretation is mistaken. First, it is unclear that hypocritically blaming someone in *foro interno* is really a matter of standing. Suppose I do so and my blamee learns about it. I have never let my hypocritical blame affect my conduct toward this person and have never expressed it (suppose they learned about it using a sophisticated brain scanner). At least, it is unclear that I have wronged the person I blame at heart (Sher 2021). True, my feelings toward them are inappropriate and my having them might manifest a character flaw on my part, but I am not sure that I wrong them (Section 7.5). Second, it is unclear to me that the "none of your business" complaint only pertains to public expressions of blame. Perhaps if I have illicitly obtained information about someone's private life that is none of my concern, my blaming them from what I have learned about them is something I do not have the standing (in Todd's sense) to do. At least some people think that the concerns underlying the right to privacy speak to which beliefs we should hold. If so, why should there not similarly be moral constraints on harboring private grudges against others, even if we never express them? Even setting these two points aside, one important issue—among other standing-related issues—is whether one can provide a unified account of the standing to publicly blame. Todd seems to allow that, at least by virtue of his views about meddlesome blame, one cannot provide a unified account of that issue. However, he thinks that the issue of standing in relation to reactive attitudes is the basic issue. He does not explain what he means by "basic." One suggestion is that his issue is the more basic one, because one has no standing to blame publicly only when one has no standing to experience blame and one has standing to blame publicly only when one has standing to experience blame (for support for an interpretation along these lines see Todd 2019, 350). If so, I do not think experiencing blame is the more basic issue, e.g., for reasons related to consenting to be (privately or publicly) blamed. (Todd also argues that the "none of your business" reply is of a kind different from the hypocrisy reply. Whereas the former is a response that points to lacking "the standing with morality" to blame someone, the latter response points to the fact that the blamer lacks "the standing with me [i.e., the recipient of the blame]" to blame them (Todd 2019, 349). To defend this point, Todd imagines two hypocritical blamers, one, and only one, of whom it is also true that the relevant matter is none of their business. I do not find this defense of the contrast convincing. To my mind, the latter blamer lacks the standing with the blamee in two ways: to wit, their own faults are no smaller and they do not have a suitable relation to the blamee. Of course, it is morality, or at least that part of it that regulates blaming, that determines that the hypocritical, noninvolved blamer lacks the

that a necessary condition for some wrongful action being my business is that I am a rational and free moral agent in Darwall's sense, but, intuitively, this is not a sufficient condition.

This point also brings out an important way in which the "none of your business" reply is different from all the other indirect dismissals of blame. These point to a certain feature by virtue of which one has lost the standing to blame, i.e., a standing that one had at the outset and would have retained but for one's, say, comparable faults or for one's complicity in the action in question. The "none of your business" reply is different in that it points to the putative fact that one never had the relevant standing at the outset (setting aside perhaps the case where the reply is directed to someone who has pledged not to stand in judgment over one in relation to certain issues where that person otherwise would have had a standing to blame one, but where this person has relinquished it).

Given that we adopt the nonuniversalist view, one crucial question to ask in relation to the dismissal of meddlesome blame is what features ground the standing to blame others in the first place—a question that is different from, but presumably intimately connected to, the question of what makes one lose that standing. One suggestion here is

> *The interest principle*: Y's φ-ing is none of X's business if, and only if, X's interests are unaffected by Y's φ-ing.

The interest principle is something like John Stuart Mill's harm principle, extended to acts of blaming, as it were (cf. Radzik 2011, 581).[40]

That suggestion immediately raises the question of what counts as an interest in the relevant sense. Assume that interests here mean the blamer's prudential interests such that one is in a position to blame another if and only if one's life, prudentially speaking, is affected by the blamee's wrongdoing. The interest principle on that interpretation cannot be right. One can be in a position to blame someone for wrongdoing that does not affect the quality of one's own life prudentially speaking; e.g., one can blame one's partner for

---

standing to blame their blamee. But the same is true of the hypocritical blamer whose business the relevant wrongdoing is.

[40] By "interference" Mill also had in mind social sanctions, and, of course, blame is—in addition to whatever else it is—a central social sanction, so this proposal here seems quite congenial to Mill's view.

their involvement with the Mafia even if that does not affect, or perhaps even promotes, one's interests. The partner cannot say: "None of your business" when you complain about their affiliation with the Mafia on the grounds that their involvement has made your life much better, e.g., no financial problems etc. Similarly, citizens can blame politicians for faults in personal matters, even if the politicians' relevant faults do not affect the interests of citizens. A politician cannot say: "True, I violated the law, but it never harmed any of you citizens, so it is none of your business." Citizens have a right to know and care about the moral quality of their representatives, in some areas of life at least, independently of how it will affect their lives prudentially speaking. And, finally, persons who might not stand in any particular close connection with one another but who have agreed to hold each other accountable in relation to some standard might be in a position to blame each other for actions that do not affect their interests.[41] In short: a blamer and blamee can be in such a relationship to one another that the blamee's faults are the blamer's business even if these do not affect the blamer's interests (relatively narrowly construed). Thus, the interest principle fails to state a sufficient condition for when something is not a particular person's business.

It also fails to state a necessary condition. There might be cases where one is not in a position to blame someone, even if their wrongdoing affects one's interests negatively to a significant degree. Suppose someone takes my car and drives over some bumpy terrain to rescue someone whom I have been trying to drown, thus forcing me to pay for an expensive repair of the car. Given my involvement in the situation, I am in no position to blame the rescuer for the negative effects on my interests. Similarly, if I have consented to the relative negative effects on my interests that follow from blamee's ϕ-ing, then blamee's ϕ-ing might be none of my business despite the fact that it affects my interests. In view of these two criticisms, I propose

---

[41] Consent plays an interesting role in relation to the "none of your business" reply. The basic picture being drawn here is that, setting aside special contextual factors, there are certain cases in which the "none of your business" reply is warranted and others where it is not. However, consent and pledges can modify this area. They can both expand and contract it. If I have given permission to others to comment on any of my faults, then I might never be in a position to dismiss blame on the ground that this is none of the blamer's business. Conversely, if I am in a position to comment on a certain range of flaws of a person with whom I am related in a certain way, I might lose the standing to blame that person, if I promise never to judge the person in those respects anymore. If I cannot resist the temptation to backtrack on my promise, the blamee might dismiss my blame as none of my business given my previous undertaking.

The relation and interest principle: Y's φ-ing is none of X's business if, and only if

(i) X and Y are not related in any special way such that Y's φ-ing is X's business by virtue of their relation and;

(ii) X's interests are either unaffected by Y's φ-ing, or affected by Y's φ-ing but X has either consented to their interests being affected in this way or has forfeited their right to have these interests protected or promoted.[42]

This principle seems roughly right. However, let me make two remarks on it. The first condition is a bit uninformative in that it does not say anything about what sort of nature a blamer and blamee's relation must have for the blamee's doings to be the blamer's business, even when they do not affect the blamer's interests. I say a bit more about this below. The second embodies the assumption that if the blamer's interests are affected, then the blamee's doings are the blamer's business at least as a point of departure, i.e., unless the blamer does something such that the blamee's relevant doings are no longer any of their business.[43]

Finally, I turn to the question of what makes meddlesome blame wrongful. Like with the other forms of standingless blame, the claim here is not that meddlesome blame is all things considered wrongful—indeed, sometimes meddlesome blame might be morally justified all things considered, because of its good effects. Rather, the claim is that there is something pro tanto wrongful about meddlesome blame.

Initially, it is natural to ask whether the egalitarian account, which I defended in Section 3.9 as providing a good account of the wrongfulness of hypocritical blame and have argued in this chapter can be extended to explain the wrongfulness of complicitous blame, applies to meddlesome blame too. In asking that question, cases immediately come to mind in which meddlesome blame does indeed involve an inegalitarian subordination of the blamee. If I treat a loose acquaintance as someone whose every blameworthy action I can hold them accountable for, while at the same time refusing to be held accountable by this acquaintance for a majority of my own conduct,

---

[42] Cf. "[W]hen it comes to expressing moral criticism, whether a person has a standing to do so or not will normally depend upon her relationship to the agent, and upon whether she has a relevant interest or stake in the matter" (Smith 2007, 478).

[43] What if the blamee's φ-ing affects the blamer's interests but only marginally so? In that case, I think the blamer might still correctly regard the blamee's φ-ing as their business, but only marginally so. The extent to which something is someone's business—or at least the properties on which this property supervenes—is a scalar matter.

which, despite my better judgment, I regard as a private matter in relation to this acquaintance and, thus, something for which I do not have to answer in relation to them, then in some sense I do treat this person as an inferior— intuitively and in a way that seems well accounted for by the moral equality account.

That being said, it seems equally clear that meddlesome blame can be wrongful, even when it involves no clash with moral equality; e.g., even if I would be open to my loose acquaintance holding me accountable for how I conduct myself in my most private, intimate relations with others, my meddlesome blaming of their conduct in their most private, intimate relations with others is pro tanto wrongful, just as the fact that I might be open to others manipulating me to achieve certain aims does not render my manipulating them to achieve similar aims in no way morally wrongful.[44] For the reason indicated here, the moral equality account seems unable to explain the wrongness of meddlesome blame, whether we restrict our attention to blame that is meddlesome in a belief- or an evidence-relative sense.

The commitment account of the wrong of hypocritical blame seems equally inapplicable in the context of meddlesome blame. Perhaps the clearest reason why this is so is that a meddlesome blamer might be a busybody precisely because they care intensely about the norm in question.

Assuming neither the moral equality nor the commitment accounts can be generalized to account for the wrongfulness of meddlesome blame, this raises a question of how we can explain this residual wrongness.[45] To do so, I propose

---

[44] Consent might make a difference morally here, but the mere fact that I am open to others blaming me in the way I blame them does not mean that I have consented to their doing so; e.g., I might not have communicated to them that I grant them permission to do so.

[45] Admittedly, what I have said so far does not imply that none of the last six of the altogether eight accounts discussed in Chapter 3 cannot be extrapolated to explain the wrongness of meddlesome blame. Hence, note that neither the reciprocity nor the moral account would seem to do the trick since meddlesome blame from someone who themself is open to being meddlesomely blamed still would be wrong. The falsehood account seems inapplicable because the meddlesome blamer need not be suggesting any falsehood about how the blamer's action has impaired their relation. Indeed, the meddlesome blamer might well be aware that they are only related qua both being persons with moral standing. The flaws with the wrong attention and the desert accounts identified in Chapter 3 would seem to apply even if the scope of these accounts were restricted to meddlesome blame only. Finally, the moral authority account comes close to the sovereignty account, but unlike the sovereignty account it is not the interference in another's legitimate sphere of moral sovereignty as such but the staking of a claim in something one does not have a claim to that generates the wrongness.

The sovereignty account: meddlesome blaming is wrongful because it involves the blamer failing to respect the blamee's sphere of moral sovereignty.[46]

There are (at least) two aspects that are relevant to a person's sphere of sovereignty.[47] First, persons have special relations—relations that are deeper than the relations one has to another simply by virtue of being free and moral rational agents—to others that are valuable; e.g., they relate as spouses, as parents and children, as family members, and as friends.[48] It is a constitutive part of the value of such relations (and, probably, for the greater part also a causal promoter of the realization of this value) that the relatees can hold each other to account for their conduct within the framework constituted by their special relation to a greater degree than "outsiders" can. When an outsider blames someone for something that is none of blamer's business, then the blamer fails to respect the value embodied in these special relations. Moreover, to the extent that the blamer succeeds in making the blamee provide an uptake to their blame, typically, that will undermine the special relations in question; e.g., my partner should not be happy that I am willing to enter a conversation with the bus driver about my misdemeanors in our relationship, since that would imply that I do not see myself as specifically accountable to her in relation to these matters. And, of course, if both the bus driver and my spouse are blaming me at the same time and I can only respond to one of them, my responding to the bus driver's blame would amount to my not relating properly to the value embodied in the special relationship I have with my partner.[49]

[46] Some might wonder why I do not appeal to moral autonomy instead. "Moral autonomy," however, can mean quite different things. For instance, it might refer to the sort of psychological properties that wantons lack. However, autonomy in that sense is hardly undermined by meddlesome blame. The sort of autonomy that does clash with meddlesome blame is, I suspect, something like what I describe as a matter of moral sovereignty.

[47] You might think that "the blamee's sphere of sovereignty" is just a pretentious expression for things that are not someone else's business. I agree, but the account below offers more than just the substitution of one synonymous expression for another.

[48] People who deny that special relations give rise to moral claims might for that reason be skeptical about whether we can dismiss blame as meddlesome. Admittedly, they might think that it has impersonal value that we dismiss meddlesome blame.

[49] There might be some analogies between this account of the wrongfulness of meddlesome blame and James Rachels's (1975) account of the value of privacy (cf. Smith 2007, 478 n. 18, who also mentions "rights of privacy"). On his account, privacy is valuable because of how it enables us to have intimate social relations—we reveal more information about ourselves to them than we do to strangers, and that differential pattern of information disclosure is part of what constitutes the difference between intimate and nonintimate relationships.

Second, persons have a special relationship to themselves, as it were. They make choices that affect themselves only or, since it is hard to imagine a choice that is literally only self-regarding in this sense, they make choices that affect themselves in a particularly deep way relative to how they affect others such that it holds value that, within certain constraints, they are not accountable to others for these choices; e.g., perhaps choices of lifestyle, career, and partners are like that. We can call this value the value of individuality, thus deliberately pointing in the direction of John Stuart Mill's classical exploration of the value of freedom. By holding someone accountable for self-regarding choices, we disrespect that person by disrespecting their individuality and, typically though not necessarily, we will also causally undermine that person's individuality to the extent that they might find it harder not to make the relevant self-regarding choices on the basis of a desire to avoid blame from others, thus typically resulting in a greater degree of conformity and less individuality. I conclude that blame can be standingless because meddlesome, and that what explains the wrongfulness of meddlesome blame is very different from what explains the wrongfulness of the other kinds of standingless blame that we have looked at so far. Hence, the argument so far leans in the direction of a pluralist account of the wrongfulness of standingless blame.

4.5. "You Don't Know What It's Like"

Sometimes when people act wrongly in complex and emotionally stressful situations; e.g., on the front lines in war, they reject blame for what they did in those situations from people who have not been in a relevantly similar situation (and from people who have been in such a situation but then have forgotten what it is like etc.). Sometimes the dismissal is direct; e.g., the blamee denies that what they did was wrongful or not excusable and points to the alleged fact that the blamer cannot see that. The blamee was scared to death in a way incomprehensible to those without relevant experience and because of that state, their wrongful action was excusable. On other occasions, the dismissal is indirect; i.e., the blamee concedes that what they did was or at least might be wrongful and blameworthy, but the blamee denies that the blamer has standing to blame people who did what they did in that situation. More specifically, the kind of indirect dismissal of blame that will concern us here is what I shall label *uninformed blame*:

X blames Y for φ-ing in an uninformed way if, and only if

(12) X blames Y for φ-ing;

(13) X is unaware of or ignores certain facts about Y's φ-ing;

(14) These facts bear on whether and in what way Y is blameworthy for φ-ing.[50]

Of these conditions, (13) and (14) require a bit of explanation. (13) implies that the blamer's uninformedness can concern not just the state of mind of the blamee when the blamee φ-ied, but might also pertain to other relevant facts, e.g., lack of the relevant kind of moral knowledge. In this section, however, I focus on blame that is uninformed because of the blamer's lack of understanding of how the agent experienced the situation they were in when they φ-ied.

(13) is consistent with the blamer being informed of the relevant facts if the blamer pays no proper attention to these facts. A person who once was desperately poor and who has later become exceedingly rich and now blames a poor person for stealing to survive might in some sense understand the agential situation the poor person was in but willfully ignore it when blaming.[51] Plausibly, this rich person has no more standing to blame the poor thief than a rich person who has never been poor and thus simply lacks the relevant information.[52]

Whether or not the blamer is aware of and properly attends to all (relevant) facts is a matter of degree. Arguably, no blamer is ever completely aware of and attentive to all (relevant) facts about their blamee's agential situation and yet, certainly, some people sometimes have standing to blame. Plausibly in response to these facts one might say—as I have done previously (Section 2.5)—that standing to blame is a matter of degree, strictly speaking. On such a view, we might say that even a slight degree of unawareness and lack of proper attention detract somewhat from standing to blame even if, almost

---

[50] For authors who have defended the view that one can lack standing to blame because one's blame is uninformed in the relevant sense, see Elster, forthcoming; Jones 1999; McKiernan 2016, 149–150; Misak 2008.

[51] As with the sincerity condition (see Section 4.6 below), the information condition thus does not just require that the blamer believe that the agent is blameworthy but also that the blamer believe this on the right ground and not, say, just because of wishful thinking of some sort.

[52] In fact, such blame might be more wrongful than blame that simply involves a nonculpable ignorance of the relevant facts about the blamee's agential situation. Such blame involves a subordination of the perspective of the blamer and, provided the blamer does not adopt a similar uninformed perspective when engaging in self-blame, i.e., they lack knowledge of or fail to attend to their own agential situation when blaming themself, their blame might be wrongfully inegalitarian.

always, such deficiencies do not mean that blamers do not have the standing to engage in the sort of blame that they engage in.

(14) says that the facts that the blamer either has no knowledge of or does not properly attend to are facts that bear on the blamee's blameworthiness in ϕ-ing. Thus, if the facts about the agent's agential situation do not bear on the blamee's blameworthiness in ϕ-ing, e.g., are not facts about the precise experiences involved in performing the relevant action in the relevant circumstances, then the blamer's lack of knowledge of those facts does not bear on the blamer's standing to blame. "Bears on" simply means that the facts are one factor among others that affect the blamee's blameworthiness. Basically, there are two ways in which this could be the case. First, there is the case where failure to take the relevant factors into account affects either whether the blamee is blameworthy at all or affects the degree to which or the way in which the blamee is blameworthy. For instance, the blamee might concede that they are indeed blameworthy even when the relevant ignored facts are considered, but submit that they are less blameworthy or should be blamed in a different way in light of the relevant facts. This also means that the indirect dismissal of blame in a dialogical context, rather than taking the form of a flat-out refusal to be blamed, sometimes will take the form of a refusal to be blamed in the absence of the blamer attending to the relevant facts—which sometimes, but not always, the blamer can do post hoc in the exchange—and, thus, a willingness to be subjected to blame provided the blamer improves their understanding of the blamee's agential situation.[53]

Second, suppose the blamer fails to take the relevant factors into account, but that the irrelevant factors that the blamer does consider lead the blamer to determine correctly whether the blamee is blameworthy and to what degree. The error made by the blamer in such a case is like that of someone making an error in the calculations and nevertheless getting the right result, or, perhaps more relevant to the case at hand, a judge reaching the right verdict but on the basis of a mistaken view about the evidence in the case. Some might doubt that a blamer has no standing to blame if (14) is true for that reason in the relevant case of blame. After all, if the blamer were instead to attend to the relevant facts, this would make no difference to the blamer's blame. Suppose the blamee dismisses being blamed by saying: "In blaming me you fail to understand the situation I was in. True, if you were to acquire

---

[53] This is analogous to how someone subjected to hypocritical blame might refuse to be blamed unless the blamer addresses their own similar or even worse flaws.

such an understanding this should neither make any difference to your view regarding my blameworthiness, nor the degree to or the way in which I am worthy of being blamed. All the same, I refuse to be blamed by you." Such a dismissal might seem to lack force.[54] However, on my view it is a sound dismissal of the blamer's particular instance of blame. What one should distinguish between here is proper deflection of a particular instance of blame—here: blamer's uninformed blame—and deflection of being blamed by the blamer as such—here: the blame that the blamer could possibly subject the blamee to once the blamer's ill-informedness is corrected.[55] What makes the indicated reply from the blamee seem odd is that in deflecting the particular instance of uninformed blame, in effect the blamee might be conceding that what they did was blameworthy and offering the real reasons why it is. Hence, in principle the blamer could take the supplied information on board and continue blaming—now being well informed.[56] However, like in the case of punishment, it matters to us not just that people blame us when, and only when, we are blameworthy and to a proportionate degree. It also matters to us that blame is based on sound deliberations.

There is a further feature of (14) that deserves attention. Suppose a blamer blames their blamee for ϕ-ing based on an assumption that the blamee saw their own agential situation in a much more complex and nuanced way than the blamee in fact did. The blamee should have understood their agential situation in that way but, being insensitive, they did not. In short, the blamer is too charitable and misunderstands the blamee's agential situation by seeing nuances, complications, etc. to which the blamee was insensitive themself. As above, there are two cases to consider here: cases where the blamer's being overcharitable leads the blamer to blame the blamee less severely than the blamee should be blamed, and cases where it does not affect the degree to which or the way in which the blamer subjects the blamee to blame, but only the soundness of the deliberations based on which they do so. Can the blamee dismiss being blamed in either of these cases on the grounds that the blamer "does not know what it was like" to act in that situation?

---

[54] Cf. Coates (2016, 459) on the last resort of the scoundrel.

[55] Hence, I am taking a more demanding view on standing to blame than the view suggested by Coates's epistemic norm (setting aside that this norm is not proposed as a norm regulating standing to blame, as opposed to appropriateness of blaming): "It is inappropriate (absent special justification) for A to blame B for x-ing if it is not reasonable for A to believe that B is morally responsible for x-ing" (Coates 2016, 458).

[56] Sometimes the blamee does not possess the relevant information, despite being able to show that the blamer's blame is ill informed, or the blamer cannot take the supplied information on board, in which case the blamee can persist in dismissing blame.

I think so. Consider the case where a blamer subjects their blamee to milder blame based on a too-charitable understanding of the blamee's agential situation given what the blamee knows to be the correct understanding. In such a situation, it is crucial to have in mind the distinction I drew between dismissing a particular token of blame, on the one hand, and dismissing being subjected to blame, on the other. The blamee can dismiss the token of ill-informed and disproportionately mild blame. However, in the very course of doing so, the blamee might appeal to the facts that warrant subjecting them to more severe blame, thus in effect conceding that it would be justified to subject them to more severe blame than the blamer does. Hence, I conclude that the facts not attended to by the blamer need not bear on whether and in what way the blamee is blameworthy for ϕ-ing. This is a negative way, as it were, for this to render the concrete instance of blame dismissible.[57]

So much for the nature of uninformed blame. I now turn to the question of why the fact that one's blame is uninformed undermines one's standing to blame. Obviously, this question presupposes that uninformedness undermines standing to blame, and some deny that it does. So before offering my answer to the question, I want to address this skepticism about the question's presupposition.

Todd thinks that, in relation to blame, something like the condition of being informed is an "important condition on something" (2019, 350). This is so whether we are concerned with private or public blame. Violating the condition might well manifest the vice of judgmentalism.[58] However, he thinks that the warrant condition, as he calls it, is not a condition on the moral standing to blame: "I take it that lacking the moral standing to blame is never merely a matter of not being justified in believing (or not knowing) that a person is indeed blameworthy: it is a condition such that, if one lacks it, one would still lack it even if one knew that the target agent is really blameworthy" (Todd 2019, 351). Note, however, that these two sentences make different claims. If one thinks that one needs a certain level of warrant in

---

[57] An interesting question here is whether the same point applies to uninformed praise, i.e., that it is only when the uninformed praiser is uninformed in a "negative way," i.e., the praiser underestimates how difficult it was to perform the praiseworthy act in the relevant agential situation, that the praisee can dismiss the praise as uninformed, or whether the praisee can also do so in cases of praise when the praiser is uninformed in a "positive way" (see Chapter 5).

[58] Violating the warrant condition need not reflect judgmentalism. It could be very hard to understand the situation the agent was in, and someone who blames the agent could for that reason be one who is very cautious with whom they blame even if, in this case, they fail to understand, say, all of the factors that bear on the blamee's blameworthiness.

order to be morally justified in blaming someone, then one might reject the first claim—it is not merely a matter of epistemic justification, since it is also a matter of moral justification, which, however, is partly determined by the level of warrant (cf. Coates 2016)—even if the second claim is true—if there were sufficient warrant, then the blamer might be morally justified in blaming. In any case, if we define the topic of the moral standing to blame relying on the second claim, then I might simply say that my topic is different, because more general, and includes other issues relating to standing to blame. However, I do not see the motivation for wanting to delimit the topic of standing in this narrower way (other than that it makes a reductionist account of standing to blame of the sort Todd canvasses easier to justify), so I shall persist in treating being sufficiently informed as a condition on standing to blame.[59]

Let us return to the question of why an uninformed blamer lacks standing to blame. One answer to that question that clearly will not do is the answer that I gave to the question of why a hypocritical blamer has no standing to blame; to wit, that they are not serious about the norm to which they appeal in blaming the blamee. Clearly, an uninformed blamer might be dead serious about the norm to which they appeal in their blame. Indeed, their insensitivity to the blamee's agential situation might be the causal result of their being so serious about the relevant norm that they fail to pay attention to psychological details that might, as it were, bend the beam of light that the relevant norm in question casts on the pertinent blameworthy action. If this is right and if Todd's view that matters of being informed do not bear on standing to blame is false, then we need a pluralist account of what undermines standing to blame.

Another answer sometimes proposed in relation to the question of what undermines the hypocrite's standing to blame is the moral equality account. Like the commitment account, however, it too seems like one that does not easily lend itself to explaining the uninformed blamer's lack of standing to blame. This is easily seen if we consider someone who is equally uninformed

---

[59] Todd notes that "if one's moral standing has been challenged . . . one can never meet this challenge merely by citing one's evidence that the person really is blameworthy" (2019, 351). However, something like the following interchange can indeed take place. A blamer blames their blamee for what they did on the battlefield. The blamee retorts that the blamer has no standing to blame them, because the blamer does not know what it is like to be on a battlefield. The blamer retorts that they do indeed know that—they have been on a battlefield many times, so the blamee does owe them a response to their blame. Of course, Todd might stipulate that "standing" in his sense is not at stake here, but if so then his sense strikes me as unhelpfully stipulative.

when it comes to self- and other-blame, whoever the other person is. While such a uniformly uninformed blamer might be unusual, at least they act in a way that in no way clashes with moral equality.

If neither lack of seriousness nor a clash with moral equality is what undermines the uninformed blamer's lack of standing to blame, then what does? I propose

> *The accuracy account*: X has the standing to blame Y for φ-ing only if X is informed of and properly influenced by the facts that are relevant to Y's blameworthiness for φ-ing.

The accuracy account does not in itself imply that uninformed blame in the present sense is standingless blame. That only follows when we add

> *The relevance claim*: facts about the agential situation Y was in when Y φ-ied are relevant to Y's blameworthiness for φ-ing.

The relevance claim is plausible to my mind. Unlike moral wrongness, moral blameworthiness is internal to the agent's perspective. That is, whether an agent is blameworthy depends on the agent's perspective, where that includes the evidence accessible to them, which might warrant views other than those they have and fail to revise in light of the evidence available to them.

Why does standing to blame require being well informed? I believe this reflects the fact that when blaming someone, one makes a demand on that person and, generally, before making demands on others one should be informed about facts that bear on those demands and their justifiability. This requirement is not one that follows from reciprocity or from moral equality. An agent who blames others while uninformed about their agential situations can be open to blame from uninformed others, thus respecting both reciprocity and moral equality, and yet the agent's blamees can correctly deny that the agent has standing to blame them.[60]

What makes uninformed blame morally wrong when it is? Before answering this question substantively, I need to explain the qualification "when it is." The motivation for this qualification is like why complicitous blame that is a subspecies of tu quoque–vulnerable blame (Section 4.3) and meddlesome

---

[60] In this way, blaming and punishing are analogous. When courts hand out sentences, we expect them to be well informed about the crimes on the basis of which they punish.

blame where the blamer innocently believes that the relevant matter is their business (Section 4.4) are not wrongful. If the blamer is innocently unaware of relevant facts about the blamee's agential situation, arguably, there is nothing wrongful about uninformed blame since it reflects no disrespectful attitude toward the blamee. This is not to say that uninformed blame cannot be wrongful for other reasons; e.g., it might have very bad consequences for the blamee, who is fragile; but again, this is a contingent fact about certain instances of innocently uninformed blame and not a very common, let alone necessary, feature of such blame. Thus, let us focus on culpably uninformed blame, and why it is wrongful.

One reason why such blame is wrongful and that is often implied when blamees dismiss culpably uninformed blame is that the relevant blameworthy action is traumatic for the blamee and that in light of the fact that the blamee has already suffered for doing what they did—sufferings to which the culpably uninformed blamer is insensitive—it is somehow unfair that they now have to suffer further by being blamed.

While the desire to avoid such a situation might be part of the reason why we are reluctant to blame people for wrongful actions we do not really comprehend, it cannot be all of it. Suppose that our blamee who performed a blameworthy action in an agential situation that we do not really understand is psychologically robust and has suffered no trauma or other kinds of harm because of performing the wrongful act. In my view, our blame could be wrongful—though of course it must be less wrongful than if the blamer would suffer from our blaming them—even so.

Another reason that is also often implied when blame is dismissed as culpably uninformed is that the blamer is not relating to the blamee as an equal, because the blamer would not themself accept being subjected to uninformed blame by anyone. While this complaint might indeed typically be warranted and add to the wrongness of culpably uninformed blame in those cases, it does not go to the heart of the matter for a reason already indicated; to wit, that the blamer might be open themself to being subjected to uninformed blame, in which case they are not relating to the blamee as an inferior. Yet such uninformed blame might be wrongful.[61] In view of this, I suggest

---

[61] In my view, the seven other accounts of the wrongness of hypocritical blame that I discussed in Chapter 3 for similar or different reasons do not apply to uninformed blame. For instance, while uninformed blame might be more likely to result in a distribution of esteem that does not fit desert, in some cases it will not. Similarly, even uninformed blamers might sometimes imply correctly what has impaired the relationship between blamer and blamee.

Epistemic duty: culpably uninformed blaming is wrongful because certain interferences with other people involve a duty to be suitably informed about their relevant circumstances. Blaming a wrongdoer is interference in that person's life. Hence, uninformed blame sometimes involves a violation of a duty to be suitably informed about the relevant circumstances.[62]

Epistemic duty explains why certain instances of uninformed blame are wrongful (even irrespective of its harmful consequences for the blamee and for others). Moreover, it involves more than simply a claim to the effect that blamees have a right that their blamers are as well informed about their agential situation as one could reasonably demand, since this duty derives from a more general duty pertaining to interferences in other people's lives and, thus, gains support from the fact that such a duty is plausible in these areas as well. Consider paternalism. Plausibly, if we compare two instances of paternalism that are similar in all relevant respects except for the fact that one paternalizer is well informed about the recipient's situation, whereas the other is culpably ignorant but happens to get it right (as does the well-informed paternalizer), then the recipient has a complaint against the uninformed paternalizer that they do not have against the well-informed one. When one interferes with other people's lives, one has a duty to be as well informed about their situation as circumstances permit, and the uninformed paternalizer violated that duty.

Epistemic Duty supports the pluralistic conclusion already defended in Section 4.4, i.e., that different forms of standingless blame are wrongful (when they are) for different reasons. More generally, I submit that blame can be standingless in a way that is like how hypocritical and other forms of blame can be standingless, because it is uninformed. What this amounts to is that the blamer has no liberty right to blame or that the blamee has no duty to provide an uptake to the blame.

---

[62] Since it might be very difficult to comprehend the agential situation of the wrongdoer, being innocently ignorant of their agential situation might involve very little knowledge of that situation. Note also that, on this account, blaming someone to a bystander is not covered by the epistemic duty, assuming that one's blame does not amount to an interference in the blamee's life (because one's addressee will not interfere with the blamee's life either). To the extent that such uninformed blame is wrongful as well, e.g., because one can wrong someone simply by believing (Section 7.5), or expressing the belief, that they are blameworthy in a way and to a degree to which they are not, epistemic duty needs to be amended.

4.6. "You Don't Accept That Principle Yourself"

Sometimes people blame others for acting in a way that is wrongful according to a moral principle that they do not themselves accept; e.g., a religious extremist who is prevented from making political statements complains that the preventer violates their human right to freedom of expression.[63] The religious extremist themself thinks that the notion of human rights is bogus, so while they might think that they should not be prevented from making their political statements, the way in which they blame their silencer does not express their true complaint that, say, those who speak religious truth such as they themself, but certainly not those human beings who are nonbelievers, should not be prevented from expressing their views. We might think, even if we accept the human right to freedom of expression to which the religious extremist insincerely appeals, that we can dismiss blame coming from the religious extremist as standingless.[64] This case illustrates the fifth kind of standingless blame I shall discuss in this chapter:

> *Uncommitted blame*: X blames Y for ϕ-ing in an uncommitted way if, and only if
> (15) X blames Y for ϕ-ing;
> (16) In so doing X appeals to principle P as the moral principle in light of which Y's
> ϕ-ing is blameworthy;
> (17) X does not accept P.

(16) reflects that of any act it is true that if it is blameworthy then it is blameworthy in light of a certain moral principle—it cannot be the case that an action is blameworthy and yet there is no moral principle in light of which it is blameworthy.[65] (16) also implies that it is the instance of blaming that is uncommitted. In this way it differs from the other forms of standingless

---

[63] For a related discussion, see Aspeitia 2020. Aspeitia thinks that many "whataboutism" objections, e.g., to blame, articulate the objector's suspicion that the blamer does not really accept the principle they appeal to.

[64] A similar claim applies to cases where the blamer and the blamee accept the same principles but where they disagree about what the principles imply regarding the specific case at hand and where the blamer blames the blamee even though the blamer, unlike the blamee, thinks that the relevant principles do not condemn the blamee's actions. For simplicity, I set aside this case.

[65] Perhaps moral particularists deny this claim. However, even they must concede that (16) is true if "moral principle" is understood in a very thin sense; e.g., a principle to the effect that any act that is identical in all relevant aspects is blameworthy too.

blame that we have discussed. If the blamer accepts another moral principle in light of which their blamee's φ-ing is blameworthy, the blamer might have the standing to blame the blamee appealing to *that* principle. Thus, in a sense standingless uncommitted blame does not reflect that the blamer as such has no standing to blame. The blamer has no standing to blame *appealing to the specific moral principle to which the blamer appeals*. This is unlike, say, typical instances of hypocritical blame, where the hypocrite has the exact same flaw as the blamee and, thus, has no standing to blame the blamee for that flaw (in the absence of suitably addressing their own faults).[66]

Another interesting difference between hypocritical blame and uncommitted blame is that proportional self-blame works differently in the two cases. In the case of hypocritical blame, if the hypocritical blamer engages in proportional self-blame, their blame loses its hypocritical nature, and the blamer regains their standing to blame. In the case of blame that appeals to principles that the blamer does not accept, the blamer cannot regain standing to blame by engaging in what will then be insincere self-blame. The blamee can dismiss being blamed even so.[67]

Generally, we see ourselves as being entitled to indirectly dismiss uncommitted blame:

The commitment constraint on standing to blame: X has the standing to blame Y for φ-ing in light of P only if X is committed to P.[68]

Thus, we can dismiss blame from the religious extremist even if we ourselves accept the human right to freedom of expression to which they appeal.[69]

---

[66] This is also why uncommitted blame is not a form of hypocritical blame in my sense. The uncommitted blamer might justifiably and correctly think that their own record assessed in light of the principle to which they appeal in their blame and that she does not accept is spotless. This is not to deny that in a broader sense of "hypocrisy," uncommitted blame typically is hypocritical, e.g., because it involves deceiving one's blamee and others about one's true moral commitments, typically with the aim of appearing better in their eyes.

[67] This has the interesting implication that attempts to provide a unified account of standing to blame, e.g., Todd's, fail, because if the two ways of lacking the standing to blame can be restored in different ways, then it follows that the grounds for lacking the standing to blame that they involve must be different. A blamee can dismiss the hypocritical blamer who does not even accept the moral principle on which their blame rests on an additional ground in comparison with a blamee who is subjected to otherwise identical blame from a hypocritical blamer who does, however, sincerely accept the moral principle to which their blame appeals.

[68] Which principles people are committed to typically changes over their lifetime. Possibly setting aside weird cases, standing to blame requires that the blamer accept the principle to which they appeal in their blame at the time of their blaming.

[69] For obvious reasons, i.e., that the blamer acts strategically when blaming the blamee and, thus, wants to appeal to a principle that the blamee accepts or, at least, is forced to be seen as if they accept, typically the moral principle appealed to is one that the blamee accepts. In such cases, e.g., the

To repeat what I said elsewhere, this does not imply that we are not under a moral obligation to take seriously the content of the blame. However, we have no duty *to the blamer* to provide an uptake. Also, consistently with denying that, we can think that it is morally important that the blamer has a legal right to complain about any curtailment of their freedom of expression.

If we accept the commitment constraint on standing to blame, then a question arises as to whether one should embrace an even stronger commitment constraint on standing to blame (as well). Suppose one accepts a certain principle and blames others for violating it. However, one is not really upset about their violating the principle and one's motivating reason for blaming is the desire to achieve a certain aim that is completely unrelated to that principle, e.g., to appear better than in fact one is.[70]

One could object that one's mental states do not matter to one's standing to blame and, thus, that what motivates one to blame someone is irrelevant to whether one has the standing to blame. However, that objection is not available to someone who believes that acceptance of a principle is a precondition of having the standing to blame, given that acceptance of a principle is a mental state. If we find this view attractive, we might subscribe to

The strong commitment constraint on standing to blame: X has the standing to blame Y for ϕ-ing in light of P only if
(i) X accepts P and

religious extremist might say: "True, I do not think that there are any human rights. But *you* do and nevertheless you do what on your view amounts to a human right violation." But if that is the real complaint, the content of the blame shifts; i.e., it is not the violation of the right to freedom of expression, but the failure to treat others in accordance with principles that one accepts and often proudly espouses that is the allegedly blameworthy action. Presumably, both the religious extremist and the intervener accept that such a failure is wrongful and blameworthy and, because of the former's commitment to *that* principle, the blame is not uncommitted. Hence, I want to set aside this complication, where the content of the blame really is not acting in accordance with the principle that the blamer does not actually accept, though it captures an important fallback position that blamers who are accused of not being committed to the principle to which they appeal resort to.

[70] Arguably this is related to a view defended by Daniel Statman (2023). He thinks that one can lose standing to blame if one's blame has the wrong sort of motivation. Consider a case in which I blame you for violating a particular duty, but it is obvious that while you have violated this duty and are blameworthy for having done so, what motivates me to blame you is the fact that, say, I am jealous of you for some reason. In that case, you can say: "You're only blaming me because you're jealous," thus deflecting my blame. One response here might be that while this reply brings an extra topic to the table, so to speak, it does not show that the blamer has no standing to blame. They might still have a liberty right to do so and the blamee might still have a duty to respond to the blame rather than simply ignore it; i.e., the person pressing the "You say this just because" reply still cannot dismiss the blame. The "You're only saying this because" reply is a demand for an extended agenda, not necessarily a dismissal of blame on this view.

(ii) X's motivating reason, to a sufficiently high degree, for blaming Y for
φ-ing is X's acceptance of P.[71]

Like the commitment constraint, the strong commitment constraint does
not imply that a blamer who violates it is in no position to blame the blamee
full stop. It does not even imply that the blamer is in no position to blame appealing to the very same principle to which they appeal. All it takes to blame
with standing is that their motivating reason for blaming changes.

Setting aside whether we should embrace the strong commitment constraint or the commitment constraint (if we should accept the former, then
we should accept the latter, but not the other way around), why does not
accepting a principle undermine one's standing to blame others in light of
it? (After all, the principle might be correct and one's blamees might accept
it.) From the perspective of the analysis of having the standing to blame that
I offered in Section 1.3, to blame is to make a certain demand on the blamee,
and to have the standing to blame is to have the moral power to impose a
duty on the blamee to provide an uptake to the blame. So, from this perspective, the question is this: Why does one not have the moral power to impose
a certain duty on someone else to apologize, lay plans to prevent violating a
certain moral principle in the future etc., when one does not think that what
the other person has done is something blameworthy or, at least, one does
not think so for the reasons that one offers them when blaming them?

There are two cases to consider here: (1) cases where the blamer thinks
that what the blamee does is blameworthy, though in light of principles other
than the ones to which they appeal (like the religious extremist who dislikes
lack of integrity whom I mentioned in the opening example in this section)
and (2) instances where it is not the case that the blamer thinks that what the
blamee has done is blameworthy at all. In the former case, the blamer thinks
the blamee does have a reason—though a different one from the one implied by the blamer—to apologize etc., whereas in the second case the blamer
might think that the blamee has no such reason. Nevertheless, both forms of

---

[71] The "to a sufficient degree" bit indicates that there could be an even stronger commitment
constraint—one that demands purity of heart in the sense that the blamer's motivating reason for
blaming the blamee is solely the blamer's acceptance of P (or perhaps some other moral principles as
well). Additionally, the strong commitment constraint probably must be weakened to accommodate
cases where the blamer appeals to P when blaming, accepts P, but where their motivating reason for
blaming is their acceptance of another moral principle. Arguably, such blame cannot be dismissed as
uncommitted even if the blame is a moral rationalization (as opposed to a self-serving rationalization). Or perhaps it can be so dismissed even though, in dismissing it, the blamee will typically have
to concede that the blamer has standing to blame on other grounds.

standingless blame are rooted in a norm pertaining to the constraining of our exercise of moral authority over others:

The openness and sincerity constraint: X has the standing to blame Y for φ-ing only if X exercises the moral authority that this standing involves in an open and sincere way.

Basically, the rationale for this constraint lies in the fact that while we are entitled to hold each other accountable, we are also independent, rational beings, and the openness and sincerity constraint provides us with normative protection against another's arbitrary and nontransparent exercise of their moral powers over us; i.e., a blamer's blaming of their blamee does not give the blamee a reason to respond if the blamer either believes that the blamee is not blameworthy or believes that the blamee is but for different reasons. The openness and sincerity constraint embodies respect for moral agents as rational beings. This picture seems intuitive; e.g., if a blamer and blamee both blame a third party on the grounds of their violation of P and the third party knows that while the blamer accepts P, the blamee does not, it seems intuitive that the third party sees no reason to respond to the blamee, but thinks they now have a reason to provide the blamer with an uptake. In a sense, if the openness and sincerity constraint did not apply, our moral authority to impose duties to respond to blame would be arbitrary—we can create duties for others even if we think such duties are not grounded in moral duties they have—and unconstrained by our moral beliefs.

Let me finally turn to the question of why standingless uncommitted blame is morally wrongful. Here I think there is an obvious answer, which is that uncommitted blame is manipulative, and manipulation is morally wrongful. Typically, when I blame someone appealing to a certain moral principle that I do not myself accept, then I do so because I want to achieve some aim of mine that I am not stating openly and that I think I would achieve less well if I only appealed to moral principles that I accept myself—principles according to which what my blamee did might not be blameworthy at all.[72]

While, typically, uncommitted blame is manipulative and, for that reason, wrongful, it need not be. Suppose I blame you, appealing to a moral principle that I do not accept. I am indifferent to how you respond to the blame. I am

---

[72] Moreover, typically I would not myself be open to uncommitted blame and, thus, in subjecting others to that form of blame I am not relating to them as equals.

simply being paid to blame you for violating that principle, and I blame you for doing so simply to get the money. Arguably, I am not manipulating you in this case—I am not trying to make you do certain things that I want you to do. Moreover, I might be open about my motivation, since you might have no doubt that I do not accept the principle to which I appeal, and I may make no attempt to deceive you into thinking otherwise.[73] Even so, I think there is something wrongful about uncommitted blame in this case:

> *The sovereignty account*: uncommitted blaming is wrongful because it involves the blamer making a claim to moral authority over the blamee that, by the blamer's own lights, the blamer does not have.[74]

This, I take it, is a wrong-making feature that is common to all forms of uncommitted blaming. Uncommitted blaming is wrongful because it involves demanding that the blamee act in a way that the blamer does not think the blamee has any reason to act—at least not for the reason implied by the blamer's blame. If respecting someone involves respecting their status as a rational being, then demanding that someone act in a way that one does not think they have any reason to act is, if anything ever is, not to respect to their status as rational beings. Moreover, it is a wrong that, arguably, is not committed in some of the other forms of standingless blame that I have addressed in this chapter; e.g., it is not the case in blame that is vulnerable to a tu quoque reply that, by the lights of the blamer, they are making a claim to a moral authority that they do not have.

4.7. Conclusion

It is time to zoom out and briefly describe the big picture that emerges from this chapter. As announced in the introduction, two main claims were

---

[73] In such a case, it is also hard to see how an extended version of the falsehood account applies. After all, given that it is clear to both blamer and blamee that blamer does not accept the principle to which they appeal, arguably, blamer is not implying any falsehood about what impaired the relation in question.

[74] The sovereignty account is related to, but different from, the moral authority account of the wrongness of hypocritical blame that I discussed in Section 3.5. One reason is that the former principle is about the wrongness of blame involving an appeal to a moral principle that the blamer does not accept and not the wrongness of hypocritical blame. Another reason is that the moral authority account appeals to what moral authority the blamer in fact has, whereas the sovereignty account appeals to the moral authority that the blamer has by their own lights.

developed. First, blame can be standingless for reasons other than hypocrisy. Specifically, it is not the case that lack of commitment, which I argued
in Section 2.8 undermines the hypocrite's standing to blame, is what explains
why the other forms of blame that I have discussed are standingless. Second,
the different kinds of standingless blame are wrong for different reasons and
in quite different ways. Specifically, they are wrong for reasons other than the
wrong-making feature of much hypocritical blame; to wit, that it involves the
blamer relating to the blamee as a superior. The picture that emerges is pluralist and complex.

One natural question to ask at this point is whether the present list of ways
of lacking standing to blame is exhaustive or whether the full picture is even
more complex. I think it is the latter. Here is another way of not being in a
position to blame that I have not addressed so far. Suppose Ann, Burt, and
Carla live together in a collective. Ann steals money from the collective and
Burt blames Ann. The next day Burt starts blaming Ann again for the theft
and Ann accepts blame. This continues. My contention is that at some point
in time, Ann can deny that Burt is in a position to blame her. Before Burt
started blaming Ann, he was in a position to do so. However, by repeatedly
blaming Ann Burt has, as it were, exercised to exhaustion his right to blame
Ann—his blame has become excessive blame, and in so doing he has lost the
right to continue to blame. The right to blame is, to use a metaphor, a ticket
without a full day of travel. You can blame when you like (though perhaps
there can be moral constraints on the time at which you exercise your right
as well, just as some open tickets state that you cannot travel on Sundays and
perhaps the ticket has an expiry date), but there is a limit to how many times
you can use your ticket. Carla, of course, can still blame Ann, even though
Carla might not have anything new to add to what Burt has already said.
Specifically, Ann cannot dismiss blame from Carla on the grounds that she
has already apologized to Burt and that this was a painful experience for Ann
and, thus, that she has no duty to apologize to Carla also (which is not to say
considerations such as these might not imply that it would be wrong of Carla
to exercise her right to blame Ann).

The reason for bringing up blame that is standingless because excessive
here in closing is not an ambition to say something very definitive about
why excessive blaming is standingless and wrongful (I think it is). My ambition is simply to lend support to the pluralistic and complex picture already
defended, and to the conjecture that it—despite already being complex—
might not even be the whole story. However, the present chapter completes

my defense of this view. In Chapter 5, we shall see how blaming is not the only illocutionary act that an agent can either have or lack the standing to engage in. Indeed, we can have or lack the standing to engage in the positive complement to blame, i.e., praise (in a certain partly technical sense to be explained shortly).

5

Praising

5.1. Introduction

In a recent edition of Fox News' *The Five*, the hosts praised Donald Trump for meeting with Kim Jong-un without preconditions while laughingly conceding that had their political adversaries met with him, they would have criticized them for doing so.[1] Awkward, but not uncommon, moments such as this make one wonder: Can one have the standing to praise hypocritically?[2] As we have seen in Chapters 1–4, many philosophers have asked the same question about blame. So far we have argued that (a) a blamer can lack the standing to blame an agent for an act even if that act is blameworthy; (b) standingless hypocritical blame is pro tanto morally wrongful; (c) several factors other than hypocrisy can undermine standing to blame and render blame pro tanto wrong.[3]

In this chapter, I defend two claims. The first is the *conditional claim* that *if* (a)–(c) are true, *then* so are (a*)–(c*).[4] The latter are (a*) a praiser can lack the standing to praise someone for an act even if that act is praiseworthy; e.g., the Fox News hosts do not really have the standing to praise Trump for meeting with Kim Jong-un (whether or not doing that is praiseworthy); (b*) standingless hypocritical praise is pro tanto morally wrongful; e.g., there is

---

[1] https://www.mediamatters.org/donald-trump/fox-hosts-laugh-about-their-hypocritical-praise-trump-meeting-dictators-admit-theyd (accessed May 4, 2020).

[2] Some theorists might say that since the hosts are not praising themselves, they are not praising hypocritically even if they are praising unfairly. (Similarly, some theorists—probably the same—would say that in blaming one's enemies for minor faults while passing over the greater faults of one's friends, one is blaming unfairly but not hypocritically.) While, ultimately, the difference between these theorists and me might come down to a terminological difference, I do think that in ordinary language, hypocrisy can focus on differential treatment of different third parties, some of whom one sympathizes with and others whom one does not sympathize with.

[3] See Cohen 2013, 115–142; Dworkin 2000, 182–188; Fritz and Miller 2018, 2019a, 2019b; Herstein 2017; Isserow and Klein 2017; McKiernan 2016; Piovarchy 2023; Radzik 2011; Roadevin 2018; Rossi 2018, 2020; Smith 2007; Statman 2023; Todd 2019; Wallace 2010.

[4] I would affirm the biconditional that (a)–(c) are true if, and only if, (a*)–(c*) are. However, since a large part of the argumentative strategy in this chapter consists in showing that the reasons offered in defense of (a)–(c) apply mutatis mutandis to (a*)–(c*) as well, and since as of yet philosophers have offered very little, if anything, in defense of (a*)–(c*), I shall not defend the biconditional claim here.

The Beam and the Mote. Kasper Lippert-Rasmussen, Oxford University Press. © Oxford University Press 2024.
DOI: 10.1093/oso/9780197544594.003.0006

something pro tanto wrongful about praising one's political heroes for doing the exact same thing that one would blame one's political enemies for doing; (c*) several factors other than hypocrisy can undermine standing to praise e.g., meddlesome praise can be dismissed in the same way as meddlesome blame.[5] The second claim I defend in this chapter is the *unconditional claim* that (a*)–(c*) *are* true.

The first two sections provide some analytical groundwork. Section 5.2 identifies the concept of praising that is the analysandum of this chapter. Section 5.3 proposes a disjunctive analysis of what it is to dismiss praise on the ground that the praiser has no standing to praise (see Section 1.3). Section 5.4 defines hypocritical praise. It also shows that such praise is standingless, and that the reasons that have been offered for the view that hypocritical blame is standingless support, mutatis mutandis, a similar view of hypocritical praise, thus strengthening (a*). Based on the definition proposed in Section 5.4, I argue in Section 5.5 that hypocritical praise—like hypocritical blame—is wrongful because it involves subordinating the perspective of the addressee of the praise to that of the praiser, thus defending (b*). I also argue that the conditional claim is robust because even if one of the four competing accounts of the wrongfulness of hypocritical blame in the recent literature I consider were true instead, it would still be the case that hypocritical praise is wrongful for reasons similar to wrongful blame. Section 5.6 establishes (c*) by running through four reasons other than hypocrisy why blame may be groundless, and showing that these apply in the case of praise as well (cf. Chapter 4). Section 5.7 argues that, ultimately, the aim of our analysis of standing should be even more general. It should apply to holding people responsible, where that includes blaming, praising, *and* a neutral, intermediate form of holding people responsible, for which I have needed to coin a new term: "praming."[6] Section 5.8 concludes.

---

[5] Several philosophers have noted that we can praise hypocritically (e.g., Isserow and Klein 2017, 203; Fritz and Miller 2018, 123; Lippert-Rasmussen 2013, 307–308). However, to my knowledge none has offered any extended analysis of standingless praise. Possibly, this asymmetric focus reflects the—in my view, misleading—conception that "blaming tends to be a much more serious affair" than praising (Watson 2004, 283). For other pathologies of praise, see Jeppsson and Brandenburg (2022) and Holroyd (2021).

[6] As noted, some philosophers are skeptical of the notion of standing to blame (Bell 2013; Dover 2019; King 2019; see Section 2.7). Their arguments can also threaten the notion of standing to praise (and prame). Here I do not attempt to rebut these arguments. While skeptics about standing must reject my unconditional claim, they are not qua skeptics about standing (to blame) committed to denying my conditional claim. Indeed, they might attempt (erroneously, in my view) to enlist the conditional claim in a novel argument against standing to blame, reasoning that if there is such a thing as standing to blame, then there is also such a thing as standing to praise, and that since the latter is illusory, the former must be too.

5.2. What Is Praising?

In developing the following account of praise, my aim is to construct an explicative concept of praising that is the positive equivalent of a particular kind of blaming.[7] Basically, there are two hurdles here. First, "praising," as it is often used in ordinary language, is not an exact positive equivalent of "blaming." As Thomas Scanlon (2013, 85; see also Scanlon 2008, 151–152) puts it: "One natural interpretation of blame is that to blame someone is just to have a negative assessment of what he has done and the character this reflects. This interpretation is suggested by the frequent pairing of blame with praise. Since praise is a (positive) evaluation, blame would also be purely evaluative if it were simply the negative correlate of praise." Scanlon thinks—correctly in my view—that blaming involves more than the mere expression of a negative evaluation, and thus he infers that, as it is commonly understood, praise is not the positive equivalent of blame.[8] However, this does not prevent us from identifying a subspecies of praise that, like blame, involves more than the mere expression of an evaluation. The subspecies will involve features similar to those that distinguish blame from the mere negative evaluation of actions and the kind of character they reflect, and in an important range of cases I believe it captures what people do when they praise (cf. Watson 1996, 242).[9]

The second hurdle is that blame is multifarious, and one sort may have features lacking in others. Consider the distinction between blaming someone publicly and blaming someone privately. Philosophers take different views on which of these kinds of blame is at stake when we discuss standing to blame. This matters because they do appear to be quite different. For instance, it may be possible to blame someone publicly without harboring any negative reactive emotions toward them, although one cannot blame someone privately without experiencing such emotions.

---

[7] By "explicative" I mean to signal that the definition offered below is not intended as a lexical definition of praise. While my definition does capture important aspects of ordinary language use of the term, it also deviates from some such uses in the interest of theoretical purposes.

[8] "In the case of second-personal prescriptives, we rarely utter them for the mere purpose of declaring a truth.... Rather, we speak in order to call that person's [i.e., the addressee of the second-personal prescriptive: author] attention to the norm that binds him" (Kukla and Lance 2009, 107). This captures well the distinction between mere negative evaluation and blame in relation to what I below call the second-person case (albeit in relation to praise).

[9] As noted above, there are various accounts of what blame involves in addition to a negative evaluation of the object of blame, e.g., Section 1.2.1; Coates and Tognazzini 2013, 7–17; McKenna 2013, 119–120; Scanlon 2008, 123–153; Sher 2006, 112; Smith 2013, 29–33; Wallace 1994, 75; 2010, 318–319.

To overcome these two hurdles, I have taken as my analysandum in this chapter the *speech act* of praising[10]—something that, like other speech acts, is necessarily public and dialogical.[11] Accordingly, I take the conditional claim to assert that if (a)–(c) are true of speech acts of blaming, then (a*)–(c*) are true of speech acts of praising. This claim also informs my view of what it is that praising (and, for that matter, blaming) involves beyond the expression of an evaluation. Extrapolating from Herstein's (2017, 2020) analysis of blaming, I contend that a speech act of praising, in my sense, involves the praiser "directing" a particular kind of "uptake" from the recipient of the praise (see Macnamara 2013b, 895; Mason 2019, 107–112).

Quite what that uptake is varies with context. Taking these in turn, we can say that directives are speech acts that govern and guide or at least are intended to guide the addressee's action. They include orders, demands, and commands, but they are not limited to imperatives (Herstein 2017, 3315; see also Macnamara 2013a, 158–159). Examples of nonimperative directives include requests, urgings, suggestions, recommendations, and even encouragement. One contrast between praising and blaming is that in the latter the relevant uptake is often demanded, whereas in the former it generally is not. Riedener notes: "In expressing resentment or indignation to another person, you standardly demand that she acknowledge her fault to you, or more generally, that she enter an exchange with you that constitutes her being held accountable by you or her giving account to you" (Riedener 2019, 186–187). In praising someone you do not normally demand that they acknowledge the virtuousness of their deed and demand that they enter into an exchange with you about the steps they could take to ensure that they continue to act praiseworthily (Section 1.2.1; Macnamara 2013a, 151–154; 2013b, 903).[12] This is

---

[10] Roughly, an act is a speech act (e.g., an act of promising, commanding, or apologizing) if it is performed through the uttering of a sentence (Austin 1962, 6–7). The utterance of a sentence, however, is not necessary for the performance of a speech act. Clapping one's hands can be a speech act of praising. For other attempts to analyze blame and praise drawing on speech act theory, see Beardsley (1970, 1979), Darwall (2006, 52–54, 120), and Macnamara (2011, 2013a, 2113b). Austin (1962, 83–84) thinks blame is an impure performative, since we can sensibly ask, "But did he really blame him?" when we are in no doubt about what was said and what it means, but are in doubt as to what mental state the utterance reflects. Here I discuss "blame" and "praise" understood as pure performatives—i.e., in the case of blame, a reproof. Pure performatives "*constitute* new truths . . . by instituting a new state of affairs *in and through the very act of their utterance*" (Kukla and Lance 2009, 88).

[11] Some are skeptical about the possibility of private praise (Coates and Tognazzini 2013, 5). I do not share this skepticism. I also think praise can be monological: I can praise myself without an audience, in other words. In any case, the skepticism, were it warranted, would not present a problem for me given my focus on public, dialogical praise.

[12] This is reflected in my definition of praise below being broader than my definition of blame in this dimension.

not to deny that praisers often invite praisees to express some kind of gratitude for, or acknowledgment of, the praise they are receiving, and often encourage, and perhaps even urge, praisees to continue their admirable deeds.

These contrasts are not conceptual. Self-praisers can praise themselves in a way that amounts to a demand for uptake (an example is the Mafia boss insisting on unalloyed loyalty), and sometimes blamers merely encourage blamees to recognize the relevant wrongs.

Consider next the direct uptake of praise. Notionally, we can distinguish the person doing the praising, the person being addressed, and the person being praised. In this chapter, I use the letters P (praiser), A (addressee), and R (recipient) as placeholders for each of these person types. We now have three scenarios. In cases of *first-person* praise, e.g., boasting, P and R are the same person, and A is another person. The uptake typically demanded of A is either an expression of gratitude (where the action benefited or was intended to benefit A) or participation in the praising ("Yes, what you did is really amazing") (see Kukla and Lance 2009, 90; Macnamara 2011, 90). In cases of *second-person* praise, R and A are the same person, and P is another person. The uptake typically demanded of A is an expression of gratitude ("Thanks, that's very generous of you") (see Darwall 2006, 85–86). Last, in cases of *third-party* praise, P, R, and A are three different individuals, and the uptake typically demanded of A is the expression of a view on the matter and participation in the praising ("Yes, I too admire Trump's wise foreign policy moves").

In sum, then, I analyze the speech act of praising as follows (cf. the definition of blaming in Section 1.2.1):

P praises R for φ-ing to A if, and only if[13]
(1) P communicates to A that they believe R's φ-ing is praiseworthy;
(2) P communicates to A that in doing 1) they direct suitable uptake from A in response.[14]

---

[13] Whereas actions, or at least items somehow affected by the blamee's actions, are the typical objects of blaming, there is nothing awkward about praising someone for something that is unaffected by their actions, say, their being naturally good looking. It would be incoherent to blame someone for their "natural" bad looks. Since my technical notion of praising is restricted to praising someone for what they do, this is an additional way in which my notion of "praising" is a technical one.

[14] Mason (2019, 109) too thinks the "praiser is asking for something." However, what is asked for on her account is "for the praisee to respond with pleasure." There is a form of hypocritical praise that is not praise of anyone in particular, but simply the praising of certain kinds of acts, objects, etc. Isserow and Klein (2017, 203; see also Beardsley 1970, 164) mention "the environmentalist who praises fuel-efficient cars while driving a Hummer" as an example. My definition here, and my

The corresponding definition of blame simply replaces "praise" and its cognates with "blame" and its cognates.

Before I discuss what is involved in dismissing someone's standing to praise in the present sense, I want to say two things to address the worry that by focusing on speech acts of praising, my analysis becomes too narrow.[15] First, while not all praising takes the form of speech acts, it surely is important to understand what undermines standing to praise in cases, like that of the hosts of *The Five* praising Trump for meeting unconditionally with a dictator, where praising *does* take this form. Such cases are quite common.[16]

Second, even if this narrower topic were uninteresting in itself, and the only interesting question is about what undermines standing to praise generally, whatever form it takes, my narrow account might have instrumental value. For it may be that it can be extrapolated to acts of praising that do not take the form of speech acts (see Riedener 2019, 205–207).[17] For reasons of space I cannot explore this possibility here. But plausibly, even when they are privately praising someone, the praiser must believe that if, say, they were to express their praise to its recipient, that recipient would then have a reason to uptake the act of praising in an appropriate way.[18] Generally, the interpersonal quality of the communicative act means that these are regulated by moral norms.[19] Perhaps this explains why we criticize people for having

account of hypocritical praise in Section 5.4, are easily extended to cover such cases. One can give different accounts of what exactly "suitable uptake" amounts to. For present purposes, however, which of these accounts is correct does not matter. Thus, one can assess the commitment and moral equality accounts of standing discussed below independently of settling the present issue.

[15] This worry is largely analogous to the similar worry about my speech-act definition of blame that I addressed above, e.g., Sections 1.2.1 and 2.2.

[16] Cf. the strategy adopted in (McKenna 2013, 120). It may even be true of some speech acts of praising that they do not involve making demands, e.g., even if for some reason I have promised you never to praise you, it seems I can still praise you—say I am taken aback by your athletic excellence— despite my recognition that in doing so I exercise no moral authority and, thus, lack standing to make any demands for uptake (see Macnamara 2013a, 151–154). My response, again, is to say that analyzing standing to blame and praise in ways that involve demands (as opposed to, say, "weaker directives" like urgings or invitations) is an important topic in itself, and one that might generate insights into other forms of blame and praise as well. In any case, the appropriateness of restrictions of the scope of the present exploration such as this one must be judged on the basis that holding responsible is an exceedingly complex phenomenon.

[17] Some philosophers believe that public blaming is, fundamentally, the sort of public holding responsible that is involved in speech acts of blaming (or praising) (Darwall 2006, 120; McKenna 2012, 176; 2013, 121, 126; Smith 2013, 39; cf. Driver 2016; Macnamara 2013a, 151–156). I am suggesting that perhaps public praising relates to other forms of praising in the same way.

[18] Admittedly, this suggestion does not square well with the possibility of monological self-praise (cf. Section 2.2). However, monological self-blame gives rise to similar challenges; see Shoemaker (2022).

[19] It is less clear that adopting an attitude has an interpersonal character.

reactive attitudes, like those involving praise and blame, when they lack standing to have those attitudes, even if, strictly speaking, it makes no sense to talk about the standing to harbor an emotion—e.g., because one cannot directly obey a command to have, or eschew, a certain emotion (Macnamara 2013a, 156; see also Section 7.3).

5.3. Standing to Praise

One can dismiss blame directly or indirectly (Section 1.3; Cohen 2013, 119). The same goes for praise. When the dismissal is direct, one rejects the normative, evaluative, or aretaic judgment that is part of blaming or praising.[20] One does so because one denies that the agent performed the act; or that the act in question is morally wrong(/bad) or morally good;[21] or that the act is morally blame- or praiseworthy, e.g., because the agent had a valid excuse (although, perhaps, one agrees that it is morally wrong/bad or good and that the agent performed it).[22]

Alternatively, one can dismiss praise (or blame) indirectly: "indirectly" because one's reason for dismissing the praise is not that one denies the evaluation expressed in the praise (which, of course, one might do as well). Rather, one dismisses the praise by, say, giving no deliberative weight to the praiser's praising one's action. As with blame, the appropriateness of the dismissal here is agent- and patient-relative—perhaps the praiser has the standing to praise others for similar acts, and perhaps other praisers have the standing to praise the recipient for the very same act. It is also object-relative—perhaps the praiser has standing to praise the recipient for acts other than the praiseworthy act in question.

---

[20] Some philosophers tie blaming narrowly to the deontic judgment that the agent has acted wrongly. Others think blame might also extend to negative evaluative or aretaic judgments—e.g., the judgment that the agent has acted in a way that is morally bad (even though it might be a morally permissible act) or reflects the fact that the agent lacks moral worth. For present purposes, I can remain neutral on this topic.

[21] It might be said that merely good, as opposed to supererogatory, actions cannot be praiseworthy, and hence that the denial in question must be a denial that the action is supererogatory. For a decisive counterexample to this view (i.e., that morally good actions that are morally required cannot be praiseworthy), see Driver (1992, 286–288).

[22] Oddly, there is no word for the negative version of an excuse—i.e., for agreeing that what one did was morally very good, yet conceding that it was not praiseworthy, e.g., because any normal person would have done the same in these circumstances.

Following Herstein's (2017, 2020; see also Riedener 2019, 187) exclusion model of the structure of dismissals of directives on grounds of standinglessness, I propose the following:

A dismisses P's praising of R's φ-ing if, and only if, A decides not to see P's praising as reason-giving (cf. Section 1.3 on dismissing blame).[23]

Herstein focuses on blame, but his model is easily adapted to praising. Suppose that in praising their own φ-ing, P directs A to acknowledge their virtuousness and encourages A to φ themself. Suppose also that P is known for never having φ-ed before, despite often having had the opportunity to do so at little cost or inconvenience to themself, unlike A, who has often φ-ed in the past, generally at significant cost to themself. Here, A might decide—and correctly so—not to see P's invitation and encouragement as giving them any reason to praise P.[24] Of course, A could have plenty of other reasons to acknowledge that P's φ-ing is praiseworthy, and to φ herself. But, in a contrast with the situation where P has the standing to praise herself, in this situation A can choose to disregard the reason for doing those things that P is directing, and thus deliberate about what to do while ignoring it.

On Herstein's (2017, 3129) analysis the pertinent norms of standing are exclusionary, permissive norms. That is, they are second-order norms—"reasons that relate to reasons (not to actions, beliefs or feelings)"—permitting the agent in question to either regard or, more to the present point, disregard certain first-order reasons.

I cannot do justice to the richness of Herstein's exclusion model here. The bare essentials of it will have to suffice. One important clarification is, however, in order. It is sometimes said that agents can have moral duties both to subject others to and be subjected by others to standingless blame. This observation is sometimes taken to cast doubt on the very idea of standing to blame, and clearly a similar point can be made about standingless praise. However, given the present analysis of what it is to dismiss standingless praise, it is clear

---

[23] There are at least two ways in which P's praising can fail to be reason-giving, e.g., because P lacks a liberty right to praise or because A has no duty to respond to P's praise. Hence, to dismiss praise as standingless can be analyzed, in part at least, along the lines suggested by the disjunctive account of indirect blame dismissal (Section 1.3). I write "in part at least" because praise is not in the same way as blame naturally interpreted to involve a demand as opposed to some weaker kind of directive, e.g., an invitation.

[24] It is crucial to Herstein (2017, 3130) that A might also, without any form of unreasonableness, decide to see P's directive as a reason. This possibility is one that some of the alternatives to his exclusion model (e.g., the invalidation, competition, and alteration models) are unable to explain.

why this view is incorrect. The Hersteinian account I am employing is compatible with its being the case both that the addressee rightfully disregards the praiser's praise in their deliberations about what they should do and that the praiser is nonetheless morally required to praise (e.g., because exceedingly good consequences will result from that standingless praise).[25] In a rather different kind of case, the addressee of praise from a certain potential praiser could be required to see the praise as reason-giving even though that potential praiser is morally required to refrain from praising (e.g., because the praising would give the praisee a seriously inflated conception of their own importance). Hence, on the present account one can indirectly dismiss praise as standingless, or deny that the praiser has standing to praise, and at the same time accept that the praise in question is morally permitted. One might even agree that the praise is morally required. The conditions under which praise is morally permitted, or required, all things considered, merit investigation, certainly, but this question will not be taken up here.[26]

5.4. Hypocritical Praise

Can praise, as construed above, be dismissed as standingless?[27] Since standingless blame has been discussed mostly in relation to hypocrisy, to establish claims (a)–(c), I will need to show that praise can be hypocritical and for that reason dismissed as standingless. With this, my main aim in the present section, in mind, I propose the following (conjunctive) account of hypocritical praise:

P hypocritically praises R_1 for ϕ-ing to A if, and only if
(3) P praises R_1 for ϕ-ing to A;
(4) P believes, or should believe, that R_2 (an "equally or more deserving" potential recipient) has (or would have) done something ϕ^* that is relevantly similar to ϕ-ing and contextually relevant (e.g., because R_2 and A are identical);

---

[25] This is compatible with its being the case that, typically, because of the features from which the standinglessness results, the praise will not have good results.
[26] My account can accommodate the idea that whether the praiser has standing is just one factor among many that determines whether the praise in question is morally permitted, or required, all things considered (cf. Cohen 2013, 119 n. 8; Telech and Tierney 2019, 37).
[27] Cf. Mason (2019, 110) on the delicacy of peer praise.

(5) noncoincidentally, P does not (to a suitable degree, in a suitable way) praise R_2, or accept R_2 being praised, for ϕ^*-ing;[28]

(6) *either* P does not believe there are morally relevant differences between R_1's ϕ-ing and R_2's (actual or potential) ϕ^*-ing that justify their praising R_1 for ϕ-ing while not praising R_2 for ϕ^*-ing, *or*, if P has this belief, this is for reasons they can, or should be able to, see are not sufficient reasons.

This account is structurally similar to an analysis of hypocritical blame I presented in Section 1.2. (3) reflects that, arguably trivially, to praise someone hypocritically, one must praise them. (4) implies that hypocrisy is subjective in a way that praise and blame that are vulnerable to a tu quoque reply are not (see Section 5.6). This vulnerability depends on the virtues and vices that the agents in question in fact have, not the praiser's beliefs about what these are. (5) recognizes that randomly incoherent praise is not hypocritical (Fritz and Miller 2018, 122; cf. Rossi 2020, 103). It also imposes a standard of relevance. Although this is left unexplained, it is essential. If I praise a colleague for intervening to prevent a staff meeting from becoming nasty, you cannot out of the blue accuse me of being hypocritical for not in the same breath praising Gandhi much more for preventing more serious hostilities (Lippert-Rasmussen 2013, 308).[29] Finally, in its first disjunct, (6) adds that praisers are not behaving hypocritically when they ignore the greater and relevant virtues of another provided they believe that there is a moral justification for praising in a way that is disproportionate given the differential virtues involved (e.g., because the character of the agent performing the less praiseworthy act will improve much more as a result of being praised). With the second disjunct, (6) accommodates hypocrites who display a lack of sensitivity to the evidence because they "see" self-serving moral differences that "justify" differential inclinations to praise where no such differences exist.

I shall offer two arguments for the view that, on my account of it, hypocritical praise is standingless. The first appeals to our intuitions about two examples of praise that qualify as hypocritical on my account.[30] Consider Fox News' *The Five* again. But this time imagine that both Obama and Trump

---

[28] Perhaps "noncoincidentally" should be read so as to include cases where P can be excused for not praising R_2; e.g., P is just about to do so, but then something excusably distracts P's attention from the need to praise R_2. I thank Kartik Upadhyaya for alerting me to this complication.

[29] Assume we all know that we all admire Gandhi and that he was not mentioned at the meeting.

[30] These two examples not only support that praising can be standingless, but also that the grounds of its being so are identical to those for why blaming can be standingless.

were invited to the studio, and that the presenters praised Trump for his willingness to meet dictators without preconditions, while blaming Obama for his (past) willingness to do the same, without pointing to any morally relevant difference between the dispositions of the two men.[31] Surely, it would be odd to suppose that Obama could dismiss the blame as standingless but could not similarly dismiss the praise lavished upon Trump. Indeed, if Trump himself joined in *The Five*'s praising of him while blaming Obama to his face (not that unlikely), what would make it the case that while Obama is entitled to interrupt and ignore Trump's blame, he is not entitled to interrupt and ignore Trump's self-praise?

At this point, some might object along the lines I described above when explaining my focus on self-praise. They might say that while Trump's hypothetical self-praise involves a certain kind of inconsistent application of normative standards, it does not amount to hypocrisy. Consider hypocritical blame. That involves exception-seeking for *oneself* of some kind; it involves failure to judge oneself negatively by the normative standard one is applying in blaming another (Fritz and Miller 2018, 121–122).[32] No such thing is going on in the Trump case. This challenge misconstrues the nature of hypocrisy. It confines hypocrisy to exception-seeking for oneself, and in one's own favor, of a *specific* kind, when actually, beyond that restriction, other types of exception-seeking for oneself and in one's own favor can qualify as hypocritical. In particular, exception-seeking consisting in not judging others favorably by the standard one appeals to in praising oneself involves hypocritical exception-seeking favoring oneself. The exception here is that one is lavishing praise upon oneself when the standards, or normative principles, one is appealing to make praise for others also appropriate. Presumably, one thing that people usually find objectionable about hypocritical exception-seeking for oneself in cases of blame is the unfairness of blaming others while remaining silent about one's own faults. But fairness norms apply to praising

---

[31] Unlike Trump, Obama never met with Kim Jong-un. All the same, Fox News gave him a hard time for suggesting a willingness to meet with dictators.

[32] Fritz and Miller (2018, 131–138) distinguish between two kinds of inconsistent but nonhypocritical blamer: the former refrains from blaming specific others for violations of N but blames themself and others, while the latter is just erratic in the way they blame. They think the first kind, unlike the second, lacks standing to blame, because they alone have a differential blaming disposition (more on this below) and thus implicitly deny moral equality. Todd (2019, 368–371) sees it as a liability of Fritz and Miller's account that the nonerratically inconsistent but nonhypocritical blamer has no standing to blame. Todd thinks this blamer does have the standing to blame even if they exercise it unfairly (see also Telech and Tierney 2019, 27–27 n. 5). By restricting attention to hypocritical blame and praise, I can bypass this issue.

too. It is not uncommon for someone to object, on grounds of unfairness, when one person unfairly praises somebody while declining to praise the similar or greater virtues of another. For this reason, it is unsurprising that exception-seeking for oneself can undermine standing to praise in much the same way that exception-seeking for oneself can undermine standing to blame.[33]

The Simpsons provides another fictional, but brilliant, example of standingless hypocritical third-person praise. Bart urgently needs to warn some people about impending danger. Unable to figure out how to do it, he comes up with the idea of asking Lisa to solve the problem, and, being intelligent and resourceful, Lisa solves it. Being a sexist, Homer praises Bart for hitting on the idea of asking Lisa, while Lisa quietly remarks: "Don't I deserve some of the praise?" Surely, this is funny because Lisa's action is much more praiseworthy than Bart's, and because Homer's praise is for that reason standingless. Plausibly and setting aside some complications similar to those discussed in relation to blame in Section 2.5, Lisa is entitled to silence Homer's hypocritical praise of Bart and entitled also to (courteously?) refuse to join in with the praising of Bart (at least, in the absence of her demand for a suitable and broader agenda being met).[34] The case seems fully analogous to one in which Homer blames Lisa for a minor misdemeanor while completely ignoring Bart's much greater misdeed in the presence of them both.

Appeals to intuition can be controversial. It can be disputed, e.g., that the intuitions are universally shared. This is where my second argument enters the picture. In presenting this, I look at the moral equality and the commitment accounts of the way hypocrisy undermines standing to blame and explain that these accounts apply in a parallel way to cases of praise. My argument is that, if either of these accounts is correct, we have no more reason to think that hypocritical blame is standingless than we do to think that hypocritical praise is too. Consider first

---

[33] In my view, hypocrisy is not limited to exception-seeking for oneself (see Section 2.4). People are quite often accused of hypocrisy when they blame others they dislike for doing something that they see as blameless in people they like. While hypocrisy can take the form of exception-seeking for others whom one favors, exception-seeking for oneself is arguably the clearest and most uncontroversial case of it. For the purpose of arguing that hypocritical praise can be standingless (and pro tanto wrong), one could leave praise involving exception-seeking for others one favors for another day.

[34] See the last paragraph of Section 5.3.

> *The commitment account of lack of standing*: what deprives the (potential) blamer of their standing to blame R for φ-ing on the grounds that φ-ing violates norm N is their inadequate commitment to N (Section 2.7).[35]

The intuitive core of the commitment account seems clear and correct. If one blames others for acting in certain blameworthy ways, but ignores the equal or even greater comparable faults of oneself, (generally) one shows oneself to lack a serious commitment to the norm in question relative to a person who is also willing to submit themself to blame for acting in these ways.[36] The uncommitted blamer appeals to a norm when it serves their purposes and otherwise ignores it, and this surely undermines the duties others have to provide uptake to this person's blame-involving appeals to the norm, or indeed to tolerantly refrain from interrupting their appeals to it.

But something similar is true of standing and hypocritical praise. If I hardly ever do what I praise myself for having done on this particular occasion, despite often having had the opportunity to do so, that is a strong indicator that my commitment to the norm to which I appeal in my self-praise is inadequate.[37] Similarly, if I hardly ever praise others for acting out of respect for, or in accordance with, the norm to which I appeal in my self-praise—even when their doing so is more praiseworthy than my single act of compliance—the natural conclusion is that my commitment to the norm in question is inadequate.[38] The selective praise suggests that my commitment to the norm is so flakey (perhaps because it is subordinate to strategic thoughts about my self-image) that I have no standing to communicatively praise myself. Thus, if insufficient commitment undermines standing to blame, it is plausible to hold that it undermines standing to praise as well. True, this does not strictly follow, but it is a reasonable inference given the analysis of what is involved

---

[35] One might be sufficiently committed to a particular norm, e.g., inasmuch as one is normally very alert to violations of it, including one's own, even if on a particular occasion one fails to manifest this commitment.

[36] In the remainder of this section, I focus on first-person hypocritical blame and praise. However, my argument readily generalizes to second- and third-person hypocritical blame and praise. Possibly, I need the qualification "generally" to accommodate cases where the blamer refrains from addressing their own faults because they are so ashamed of them. In one sense at least, my differential pattern of blame seems to reflect a strong commitment to the norm in question, so this case needs further discussion.

[37] I realize that things might well be more complicated here when we have praise for supererogatory acts in mind.

[38] It is not the hypocrisy of the hypocritical praising(/blaming) that undermines the praiser's(/blamer's) standing. The hypocrisy indicates lack of commitment, and *that* undermines standing to praise.

in dismissing blame on grounds of lack of standing offered in Section 5.3 and given, also, that there is no obvious reason why unwelcome blaming of others and unwelcome praising of oneself should differ.[39]

We should note that the conclusion sought here about self-praise (and, if this is the focus, praising in general) need not be established via a comparison with blame. After all, praising oneself for acting out of respect for, and in accordance with, N, and then adding, "By the way, I don't care about N myself! It's a silly norm," has the air of a Moorean paradox: the last part of the utterance seems to seriously threaten the idea that the praise was indeed praise.[40]

In my view, something like lack of commitment provides the best basis on which to understand what undermines standing to hold people responsible. However, in relation to blame an alternative approach has been canvassed in which it is the affirming (or at least not denying) of moral equality that grounds standing to blame (at least in part):

The moral equality account of lack of standing: what deprives the hypocrite of their standing to blame others is the fact that by virtue of their own fault, the hypocrite's blaming the blamee involves relating as people with unequal moral status, e.g., by implicitly denying the blamee's equal moral status (see Fritz and Miller 2018, 125; Wallace 2010, 335; see also Section 2.7).

For present purposes I need not seek to adjudicate between the commitment and the moral equality accounts, though recall that in Section 2.8 I defended the commitment account over the moral equality account.[41] Rather, I will show that on the moral equality account one can lack the standing to praise for the same reason as one can lack the standing to blame, because in praising hypocritically one implicitly denies the moral equality of persons. Hence,

---

[39] One possible difference between blaming and praising, which the qualification "unwelcome" allows me to sidetrack, is that standingless praise might less often be unwelcome than standingless blame is.

[40] Incidentally, mutatis mutandis, that is one of the reasons (i.e., that if you blame someone "you can't cancel the suggestion that you take the pertinent norm seriously yourself" [Riedener 2019, 201]) that Riedener gives in support of something quite like the commitment account (2019, 184).

[41] In Section 2.8 I argued that this account of standing to blame fails. I appealed, inter alia, to the notion of hypercrisy, i.e., disproportionately severe blaming of oneself while ignoring the much greater faults of others. I shall label the praise-related antonym to hypercrisy "hypereulogy." A hypereulogical person is insufficiently attentive to their own superior virtues while overly appreciative of the lesser virtues of others. Hypereulogy can disfigure praise in the same way that hypercritical blame can. Also, just as being hypercritical does not undermine one's standing to blame, being hypereulogical does not undermine one's standing to praise.

whether or not the commitment or the moral equality account is correct, it follows that there is such a thing as standing to praise.

Consider the following two lines of argument offered by subscribers to the moral equality account. First, R. J. Wallace submits that we have an interest in not being blamed (recall Section 1.4). Accordingly, a hypocritical blamer who remains silent on their own faults treats their interest in avoiding blame as more morally weighty than the similar interests of those they hypocritically blame (Wallace 2010, 332). Affirming (implicitly) that one's own interests carry greater moral weight than the similar interests of others is one way of denying (implicitly) that others and oneself are morally equal. Thus, the hypocritical blamer denies moral equality.

Whatever the force of this argument, an analog argument pertaining to praise is no less convincing. Just as people have a negative interest in not being blamed, they have a positive interest in being praised.[42] For most people, being blamed is an unpleasant experience, reducing the esteem one has in the eyes of others. Likewise, being praised is usually a pleasant experience. Even among philosophers, cravings for praise are not unheard of. Generally, praise boosts the esteem one has in the eyes of others. Hence, if the hypocritical blamer takes their own interests to have greater moral weight than the interests of those they blame, then surely the hypocritical self-praiser treats their positive interests in being praised as carrying greater moral weight than the same interests of others. From there, Wallace's reasoning takes us to the conclusion that the hypocritical praiser denies moral equality. Since there is no reason to think that standing to blame presupposes nondenial of moral equality while standing to praise does not—at any rate, with suitable adjustments the intuitions Wallace mobilizes in support of the former claim support the latter as well—it follows that the hypocritical praiser has no standing to praise.

Consider next Kyle G. Fritz and Daniel Miller's defense of a similar, but subtly different, moral equality account of lack of standing. In their view, we only have an interest in avoiding *public* blame. This creates a difficulty because "even private hypocritical blame is morally objectionable" (Fritz and

---

[42] It might be said that we also have an interest in being blamed for our wrongdoing, since it helps us see that we have acted wrongly and avoid future wrongdoing. If so, something similar is true of praising us for our morally praiseworthy actions; i.e., it helps us realize that we have done well and motivates us to continue to do so. It might be suggested that our negative interest in avoiding blame is stronger than our positive interest in being praised even when the blame and praise are of the same magnitude, as it were. I would question this asymmetry. Even if it is real, it is unclear why this is a problem for my argument to the effect that hypocritical praise can be standingless.

Miller 2018, 124). To address this problem, they propose that hypocritical blame involves an unfair differential blaming disposition (DBD): "The hypocrite is disposed to blame others for violations of N, but she is not disposed to blame herself for violation of N, and she has no justifiable reason for this difference" (Fritz and Miller 2018, 122). The disposition is inconsistent with impartiality of morality (with regard to N) and therefore involves a denial of the moral equality of persons. The moral equality of persons, however, is what grounds the right to blame, so by virtue of her DBD, the hypocrite "forfeits the right to blame" (Fritz and Miller 2018, 125).

Again, my aim here is not to assess this argument (see Section 2.7) but to argue that a similar one pertaining to praise is no less convincing. The hypocritical praiser has an unfair differential *praising* disposition. As Fritz and Miller might have said, the hypocrite is disposed to praise herself (or people with whom she sympathizes) for acting out of respect for and in compliance with N, but she is not disposed to praise others for acting out of respect for and in compliance with N, and she has no justifiable reason for this difference. According to Fritz and Miller (2018, 123), the hypocritical blamer's DBD "unfairly contravenes the equality of persons." Strikingly, to support this point they appeal to the case of Max, who has an unfair differential praising disposition, and whose unfairness "stems from the fact that Max is disposed to praise his mother in conjunction with the fact that he lacks the disposition to praise his [equally praiseworthy] father" (Fritz and Miller 2018, 123). They then proceed to note: "A similar kind of unfairness can obtain in cases of blame" (123)!

The point is not just that Fritz and Miller seem sympathetic to an important part of the argument here given their use of a case of unfair differential praise to support the idea that differential blame can be unfair. By the lights of their own wider commitments, this is how it should be. To explain the unfairness of the hypocrite's DBD, they offer the following reasoning:

> Morality demands that persons be regarded equally if there is no morally relevant difference between them. If R ought to regard S in some way, then, if there are no morally relevant differences between S and some other person T, R also ought to regard T in this way. Because there is no justifiable basis for this difference in the hypocrite's blaming disposition, the hypocrite's DBD unfairly contravenes the equality of persons. (Fritz and Miller 2018, 122–123)[43]

---

[43] We can run an argument demonstrating why hypocritical praisers have no standing to praise similar to the one that Fritz and Miller (2018, 125) offer showing why the hypocritical blamer has no

On the safe assumption that if blaming R is regarding R in some way, then so is praising R, it follows that the hypocrite's DPD "contravenes the equality of persons" too.[44]

Fritz and Miller might reply as follows (though I have little reason to think they would want to resist the overall line of argument I am developing here). We need a right to blame others when they are blameworthy for violations of moral norms. This right is grounded in moral equality and forfeited when we deny its grounding (Fritz and Miller 2018, 127). However, we have a liberty right to praise independently of whether we are moral equals. Given this, the hypocritical praiser does not implicitly deny moral equality.

In response, we can note first that it is unclear why one needs a right to blame but not to praise.[45] Fritz and Miller think that private, hypocritical blame can be wrong. If one needs a right to engage in such blame, then we cannot say that one does not need a right to praise because praise does not affect the interests of others negatively. After all, that is true of private, hypocritical blame as well. Second, in at least a number of cases of communicative hypocritical self-praise where the similar or greater virtues of others are rendered invisible, I find it hard to see why we do not need a liberty right to engage in such praise, and why such a right cannot be grounded in moral equality—at least, if the right to blame is, and if rights are tied to interests in the way implied by the present challenge. Certainly, such cases might involve harm to the addressee's interests. This concludes my defense of the claims

standing to blame. Its first premise says: "If R is hypocritical with respect to instances of acting from respect for and in compliance with N, then R has a DPD with respect to instances of acting from respect for and in compliance with N." In the four remaining premises and the conclusion of Fritz and Miller's argument we simply substitute "instances of acting from respect for and in compliance with N" for "violations of N" and "DPD" for "DBD."

[44] If we understand praise communicatively in the way I have done, there is another potential problem here. Fritz and Miller focus on the way in which the hypocritical blamer's attitude is morally objectionable. They believe this objectionableness somehow transfers to expressions of the objectionable attitude (Fritz and Miller 2018, 123). However, this is a relatively minor issue because, plausibly, the presumption in favor of equality to which they appeal in relation to how persons should be regarded also applies to the ways in which people are treated, and thus to communicative praising that might not express any attitudes of praise. Incidentally, I doubt it follows from the fact that a blaming attitude is morally objectionable that all public manifestations of the attitude are also morally objectionable. My attitude of blaming you for not paying enough attention to my complaints about my day at work might be morally objectionable even if my decision to inform you of (manifest) my attitude is unobjectionable because I previously promised you I would tell you whenever I had an attitude of blame toward you.

[45] Quoting R. J. Wallace (1994, 54), Telech and Tierney (2019, 30) suggest that this need is due to the fact that "there is a more than accidental connection between blame and harm. Blame is characteristically manifested in negative modes of expression and treatment, like 'avoidance, reproach, scolding, denunciation, remonstration, and (at the limit) punishment.'"

that hypocritical praise is standingless—or, to be more precise, that it is so *if* hypocritical blame is standingless.

5.5. The Wrongfulness of Hypocritical Praise

If hypocritical praise can be standingless, as I have argued, we must ask whether it is *wrongful*. Hence, I now turn to the defense of (b*), and to a defense of the claim that hypocritical praise is wrongful *if* hypocritical blame is. My defense of the latter claim will consist of an explanation of why four of the main contending accounts of the wrongfulness of hypocritical blame imply that hypocritical praise has the same features by virtue of which hypocritical blame is thought to be wrongful.

Consider first the moral equality account of the wrongfulness of hypocritical blame:

> *The moral equality account of the wrongfulness of hypocritical blame*: hypocritical blame is pro tanto wrongful because it involves the blamer relating to the blamee as inferior, e.g., by either (implicitly) denying or acting in ways that are incompatible with the moral equality of persons.

Above I argued that this is a plausible account of *a* wrong-making feature of hypocritical blame (Section 3.9). When, to take one of the stock examples from the literature, I blame my partner for being late for a meeting, completely ignoring my own greater lateness for many past meetings, what makes my hypocritical blaming pro tanto wrongful is precisely *either* that I subject her to disadvantageous treatment that I have forfeited my right to subject her to by implicitly denying our moral equality (Fritz and Miller 2018, 125) *or* that I fail to treat her interest in avoiding idle waiting time as less important than my own (Wallace 2010, 335).[46]

Whether or not this is correct, it seems—as in effect I argued in Section 5.4—that hypocritical praise has the wrong-making feature identified here.[47]

---

[46] Another way to explain this, specifically regarding the blame-focused equivalent of the uptake condition, is to say that the hypocritical blamer treats the addressee as someone who falls under the blamer's moral authority more readily than the blamer falls under the addressee's moral authority.

[47] Above I discussed the case of "hypercrites," i.e., those who are disproportionately hard on their own faults and easy on the faults of others (Section 2.7; Lippert-Rasmussen 2020; Tierney 2021). Arguably, the analogous case of the hypereulogical person—see footnote 47—shows that the moral equality account of the wrongness of hypocritical praise, in both Fritz and Miller's and Wallace's

In my hypothetical example it would seem that Trump, in praising himself for something he blames Obama for, implicitly denies (in the Fritz and Miller manner) moral equality. Hypocritical self-praise is unfair for the same reason as hypocritical other-blame: one treats oneself better than others even though there are no moral differences between oneself and them, so that one's conduct "unfairly contravenes the equality of persons" (Fritz and Miller 2018, 123). Similarly, in praising himself Trump treats his own interest in being the object of praise as more important than the interest of Obama in being the object of praise, and that, according to Wallace, amounts to acting in a way that clashes with the basic moral equality of persons.

Lines of argument of the sort presented here cohere well with other parts of the literature, too. Telech and Tierney (2019, 29 n. 9) suggest, but do not assert, that comparative fairness norms govern not just blame but also praise. They submit that given "the inherently social character of moral responsibility . . . it is unsurprising that we care . . . about the way others blame us relative to their blame of similar agents" (Telech and Tierney 2019, 39). In view of the fact that praising is a way of holding people responsible in a broad sense, which, like blaming, has an "inherently social character," it is similarly unsurprising that we care about the comparative fairness of praise and, more to the point, the comparative unfairness of hypocritical self-praise.

Consider next the desert account of the wrongfulness of hypocritical blaming:

The desert account of the wrongfulness of hypocritical blame: hypocritical blaming is wrongful because it involves trying to acquire (or actually acquiring) more esteem in the eyes of others than one deserves (Section 3.2).

If this is correct, so is the equivalent account of hypocritical self-praise:

The desert account of the wrongfulness of hypocritical praise: hypocritical praising of oneself is wrongful because it involves trying to acquire (or actually acquiring) more esteem in the eyes of others than one deserves.

One can deserve praise in a way that is quite analogous to the way one deserves blame. If I praise myself for a minor virtue, ignoring your much

versions, could be problematic. Because my concern is not with the merits of the moral equality account of wrongness of standingless blame or praise as such, I set this problem aside here.

greater virtue, it is likely that I will receive more esteem than I deserve (both absolutely and comparatively). Admittedly, when one praises oneself, one does not always believe that one will acquire more esteem than one deserves, or thinks one deserves. However, the same is true of blaming. Hence, if the desert account is correct, then hypocritical praising can be wrongful for the same reason as hypocritical blaming.

Third, consider:

The reciprocity account of hypocritical blame: hypocritical blaming is wrongful because it involves a failure to reciprocate to the blamee on part of the blamer, i.e., the blamer demands something from the blamee, but rejects a relevantly similar demand from the blamee (Section 3.6).

A similar failure of reciprocity can be detected in the case of hypocritical self-praise. The act of praising oneself for one's lesser virtues, thus demanding an uptake from those in the presence of whom one praises oneself and displaying disproportionately little attention to their similar or greater virtues, amounts to a failure of reciprocity that is relevantly similar to the failure involved in hypocritical blaming. One expects others to participate in the praising of oneself on account of one's own virtues, and one does so without honoring the expectation that one will reciprocate by praising others for their similar or greater virtues. Hence, from the perspective of a concern for reciprocity, hypocritical praise and blame are wrongful on the same grounds.

Consider, finally:

The falsehood account of hypocritical blaming: hypocritical blaming is wrongful because it involves the suggestion of a false claim, i.e., that the blamer's and blamee's moral relationship is impaired as a result of the blamee's, not the blamer's, faults (Section 3.8).

Again, if this account is correct, a similar account of hypocritical self-praising also appears to be sound (cf. Smith 2013, 37–41; Wallace 2010, 317–323, 339–341):

The falsehood account of hypocritical praising: hypocritical praising is wrongful because it involves the suggestion of a false claim, i.e., that the praiser's and praisee's moral relationship is improved as a result of the praiser's, not the other person's, virtues.

By an "improved moral relationship" I have in mind changes in the relationship between two persons that, as it were, are the reverse of those involved in Scanlonian impairment. Two impairments that Scanlon mentions are withdrawal of goodwill and the reduction of trust. With reference to these, I suggest that strengthening of goodwill and the building of trust are *improvements* of a moral relationship. In, say, hypocritically praising myself for the relatively minor ways in which I have helped you, I falsely imply that it is by virtue of my actions that stronger relations of goodwill and mutual trust now characterize, or ought to characterize, our relationship. Hence, if we accept Scanlon's account of the wrongfulness of hypocritical blame, we should also accept that hypocritical praise is wrongful.

So much for my support for the claim that hypocritical praising is wrongful, and is so for the same reason as hypocritical blaming is. Obviously, I have not shown that there could not be an account of the wrongfulness of hypocritical blaming implying that hypocritical blame is wrongful while hypocritical praise is not.[48] However, I have covered four leading accounts of the wrongfulness of hypocritical blame, and thus my defense of (b*) is robust.

5.6. Other Forms of Standingless Praise

As we saw in Chapter 4, blame can be standingless in ways other than by being hypocritical and thus, rightly, indirectly dismissed. I believe praising can be standingless, mutatis mutandis, in these ways, too. To support (c*), I will now go over four sources of standinglessness other than hypocrisy and show that, like blame, praise can be standingless in these ways as well.

First, as argued in Section 4.2, blame can be standingless because the blamer has done something similar to that for which they blame the recipient, in which case the addressee can indirectly dismiss the blame, exclaiming, "Tu quoque" or some vernacular equivalent (Cohen 2013, 118–125; Section 4.2). Praise, too, can be indirectly dismissed in the tu quoque mode. Suppose I am addressing you in the presence of someone who I believe is a fellow Hummer

---

[48] However, I do believe that (b*) is also robust across the remaining accounts of what makes hypocritical blame wrong examined in Chapter 3, i.e., the lack of commitment, the wrong attention, the moral authority, and the moral community accounts. I have not argued, and need not claim for present purposes, that there are no respects in which hypocritical blaming is typically morally more objectionable than hypocritical praising—e.g., perhaps, generally, people are harmed more by being subjected to hypocritical blame than otherwise comparable cases of their equal or greater virtues being ignored by praisers who hypocritically praise themselves.

fan, but who happens to be Greta Thunberg. I praise myself to the skies for using public transportation a few times instead of driving around alone in my Hummer. In this case you can properly dismiss my self-praise in one of the two ways involved in the disjunctive account, pointing to Thunberg's much greater virtues where climate change is concerned. The indirect dismissal would be *Illa quoque*, but it has the same substantive structure as the tu quoque reply.

Second, blame from a complicit blamer can be indirectly dismissed as standingless (Cohen 2013, 125–131; cf. Todd 2019, 354; Section 4.3). I do not have the standing to blame you for robbing a bank if I assist you by handing you the gun that you use. Consider the (curiously unnamed) positive equivalent of complicity, where someone knowingly assists another to perform a praiseworthy act.[49] Imagine someone who is assisted in this way praising themself in the presence of the positively complicit person, completely ignoring that person's contribution. (The contribution may be more praiseworthy than the action itself: to take my earlier example from the Simpsons, Bart might praise himself in the presence of Lisa for being the messenger who delivered Lisa's solution to the problem, neglecting to praise Lisa for solving the problem.) In this kind of case, the person who is assisted, or some relevantly involved third party, can properly dismiss the praise as standingless. They can do so even if the self-praiser's action is indeed praiseworthy, and even if the self-praiser, on account of that, might have the standing to praise themself in the presence of, say, a mere bystander to the praiseworthy action (e.g., someone who in a similar situation failed to do their small praiseworthy bit).

Third, most philosophers who agree that blame can be indirectly dismissed as standingless think that one ground for the dismissal is that the blameworthy action is none of the blamer's business (McKiernan 2016, 141–151; Radzik 2011; Smith 2007, 478–480; see also Kukla and Lance 2009, 108; Section 4.4). Suppose that, from a talkative customer who also happens to be a close friend of mine, my taxi driver, with whom I have no relationship other than the present commercial transaction, has learned about my blameworthy unfriendliness at early family breakfasts. The taxi driver starts rebuking me for this. Surely, I am entitled to stop them, or ignore the blaming, and tell them to mind their own business. The appropriateness of this reply, however,

---

[49] Most antonyms of "complicity" listed by dictionaries designate cases where the agent assists wrongdoing unknowingly.

is not narrowly tied to blame. It can be extended to praising situations as well. Suppose that through the same source the taxi driver has also learned about the eloquence of my love letters to my partner, and that, to relax the tense atmosphere following our previous exchange, they start praising me for the aesthetic qualities of these letters. Surely, this is none of their business either. Even if (justifiably or not) I accept their evaluation of the letters, I am entitled to interrupt their praise, or at least have no conversational duty to respond to it.[50] My partner is differently placed. She is the addressee of my love letters, so their quality is *her* business, and in the absence of other standing defeaters *she* has the standing to praise that quality. I, or for that matter a third party, cannot dismiss (not even at the morning table . . .) her praise by telling her to "mind her own business" (though the third party *would* be entitled to ignore it, saying, "It is none of my business").

Finally, blamers who appeal to standards they themselves do not accept can be indirectly dismissed (Section 4.6). Even an addressee who *does* accept those standards can dismiss the blame.[51] Such a blame dismisser will accept that the act is blameworthy. What they will deny is that *the blamer* (unlike others with whom the blame dismisser shares a commitment to the relevant norm) has any entitlement to blame the blamee, or that the blame dismisser should join in with the blaming. In this respect, praise is the same. If, to return to the Fox News example, I praise Trump by appealing to a foreign policy principle to which I am not committed (as the fact that I blame Obama for compliance with that principle shows), I am not praising in good faith, and my addressee has no obligation to provide me with a response. Similarly, if I praise myself in your presence by appealing to standards that you know (and I know you know) I do not endorse myself, and by which your conduct might even look deficient, you are under no conversational

[50] It might be suggested that the reason why it is none of your business to praise the aesthetic qualities of my love letters is that my love letters, period, are none of your business. Hence, even if you do not praise them, but simply express the view that their aesthetic qualities are high, you are expressing a view about something that is none of your business to express (to me at least) or perhaps even forming a belief about that is none of your business to hold beliefs about (cf. Section 5.2; Tognazzini, forthcoming, 4. Whatever the merits of this suggestion, it has no force in the present argumentative context, since a similar view in relation to blame—i.e., the matter over which one is blaming someone is "none of one's business" because in simply expressing the associated negative evaluation one is meddling in something that is none of one's business—is no less plausible. Accordingly, the present objection does not warrant asymmetric analysis of blame and praise.

[51] There is a sense of hypocrisy in which such blame will typically be hypocritical, i.e., typically the blamer will pretend to accept those standards even if in fact they do not. However, the pretense, or deception, that this involves is not the most basic ground for rejection. This is shown by the fact that we can dismiss such blame even if the blamer makes no secret of the fact that they themself reject the principles to which they are appealing (Wallace 2010, 314–317).

obligation to provide uptake to my self-praise. Indeed, you can silence me without wronging me.

I conclude that the defeaters of standing to blame other than hypocrisy—similar faults, complicity, meddlesomeness, and noncommitment to principles relied on—apply in relation to praise, too.[52] This supports my conditional claim. And since they do seem to defeat standing to blame and (as I have argued in this section, appealing to a range of cases) praise, and since I do not see how blame and praise differ in other relevant respects, they support my unconditional claim too.

5.7. Standing to Prame

In this section I briefly generalize my claims further. As I have noted, praise, in the sense defined in Section 5.2, is the positive equivalent of blame. However, praise and blame as I have defined them do not exhaust the logical space of holding people responsible. Between them there lies the following: expressing the judgment that someone has done something that is neither blameworthy nor praiseworthy; and, in doing so, doing something analogous to whatever extra is needed for one's speech act to qualify as an instance of blaming or praising (beyond expressing one's judgment that the relevant act, or whatever, is blameworthy or praiseworthy). Drawing on the view I defended in Section 5.2, and with the help of an inelegant neologism, I therefore propose the following analysis of "praming":

P_n (the pramer) prames R for ϕ-ing to A if, and only if

(7) P_n communicates to A that P_n believes that R's ϕ-ing is neither blame-nor praiseworthy;[53]

(8) P_n communicates to A that in doing 7) P_n directs a suitable uptake from A in response.

Together, praming (to be illustrated two paragraphs below), blaming, and praising exhaust the logical space of holding people responsible. Praming

---

[52] I have not shown that praise can be dismissed on the ground that the praiser does not know what it is like to be in the situation in which the praisee performed the praiseworthy action ("Any minimally decent person would have done this"). However, I think that praise likewise can be indirectly dismissed on these grounds.

[53] Hence, one does not prame another simply because one neither blames, nor praises someone for an action.

falls between blame and praise, because a prameworthy action is one that merits a neutral (not negative or positive) response. It also differs from merely expressing the evaluation that the action in question merits neither blame nor praise, because it involves a demand for a certain uptake—e.g., if I prame myself for something I have done, I might demand that you express your moral indifference to my action as well.

Even if my account of what blaming, praising, and now praming involve, in addition to the mere expression of an evaluation, is rejected, on at least some of the alternative accounts of that extra element something like the concept of praming is needed. Thus, suppose we accept Scanlon's account of blaming. Earlier on, I suggested that, using that account, we can introduce a slightly technical notion of "praising" that is the positive equivalent of blaming: an account of cases where that extra element consists in the fact that the praiser's and the recipient of praise's moral relationship has improved as a result of the praiseworthy action. Similarly, based on Scanlon's account we can define praming as involving, in addition to the expression of a neutral evaluation, the suggestion that the prameworthy action in question leaves the moral relation between pramer and the recipient of the prame unchanged.

Suppose that holding responsible comprises blaming, praising, and praming. The question then arises: Can one lack the standing to prame? Here is an example of praming showing that one can. Suppose that on countless previous occasions I have morally praised myself for acting in ways that are in fact neither blameworthy nor praiseworthy, e.g., when choosing which among a wide range of great novels to read. Now you act in a similar way. I respond by emphatically praming you for your act: I communicate to you that, morally, your act deserves neither blame nor praise, and in doing this I demand that you concede that this is true. Plausibly, just as hypocritical blame and praise can be indirectly dismissed as standingless, in this case you can indirectly dismiss my prame as standingless. You can do that even if, completely reasonably, you agree that your choosing Tolstoy over Dostoyevsky should be neither blamed nor praised, morally speaking. In light of my own previous self-praise for relevantly similar acts, I have no standing to prame you for it. If, incredibly, I nevertheless do so, I am being hypocritical, and my hypocrisy undermines my standing to prame as surely as it undermined standing to praise and to blame in the similar cases I have described. In short, you can interrupt my praming of you (and, for that matter, my praising of myself for choosing the great novel I chose the next time that happens), and you have no conversational duty to respond to it.

In my view, then, although philosophers have tended to focus on standing to blame, the features of that standing that they identify are features of all three forms of holding people responsible that I have identified—blaming, praising, and praming. One can lack standing to blame, and in very closely analogous ways one can lack standing to praise and to prame.

5.8. Conclusion

In this chapter I have offered an account of what it is to have standing to praise and what indirectly dismissing praise amounts to that builds on the work in the previous four chapters. I have argued that praising in the form of a speech act is something one can lack standing to do in the same way that one can lack standing to blame (see Chapters 1, 2, and 4). Proper analysis of standing to praise can restore praise to the place it deserves in the exploration of what we are doing when we hold people responsible. As Coleen Macnamara (2011, 89) puts it: "Praise is, after all, just as much a form of moral appraisal as blame" (and I would add: so is praming).[54]

Specifically, I have argued that praise can be hypocritical in the same way blame sometimes is. Both involve a lack of commitment to a norm—the norm being appealed to (see Chapter 2). I have also defended the claim that standingless praise can be morally wrongful in the same ways blame can be (see Chapter 3). I have argued that sources identical or similar to those that can undermine standing to blame other than hypocrisy (e.g., meddlesomeness and complicity) can also undermine standing to praise (Chapter 4). Finally, I have tentatively suggested that the features of standing we can see in cases of blaming and praising are actually detectable in all cases of holding people responsible, where that includes, in addition to blaming and praising, what I called praming.

If they are sound, my arguments suggest that philosophers working on the standing to blame should, at least for some important argumentative purposes, shift their focus to the more general explanandum of standing to hold people responsible.[55] In particular, it suggests a degree of skepticism about the foundationalist view that there is nothing to be said about *why*

---

[54] Praise need not appeal to moral standards. In the quoted passage, Macnamara has in mind praise that does that.

[55] Cf. Wallace's narrow focus on resentment and indignation in his account of holding responsible (1994, 18–82).

hypocrisy deprives one of the standing to blame—it just is a basic, unexplainable fact that it does so. Given that exactly the same applies to praise and prame, arguably, there is a story to be told about the feature that is common to all three speech acts by virtue of which each can be standingless.[56] In the next chapter, I will accordingly explore another aspect of holding people responsible; namely, to forgive people. Finally, and more straightforwardly, the arguments in this chapter vindicate the uneasiness we might feel about hypocritical praise such as that on display in the clip from Fox News' *The Five* mentioned in my opening sentence.

---

[56] Admittedly, for all I have said here there might be nothing more fundamental that explains why *that* feature undermines standing to blame.

6

Forgiving

6.1. Introduction

Relationship therapists report that when partners are confronted with evidence of their infidelity, they sometimes go on the offensive and start to blame those they have deceived for, say, having been unjustifiably neglectful in ways that partly explain their affairs.[1] Sometimes there is something to the counteraccusation. Imagine you are the deceived party in one of these cases. And imagine that, after pointing a finger at your past blameworthy neglect, and without having addressed the issue of their own infidelity, your partner magnanimously states that they forgive you, suggesting that—after the appropriate expression of gratitude, on your part, for your partner's magnanimity—this is a suitable point at which to end the conversation and move on. Very probably, you would want to continue the conversation, pressing *your* points, even if you accept—and even if you *say* that you accept—that your past neglect was blameworthy. Would you accept the forgiveness being offered? I think most of us would dismiss it as an offer your partner has no standing to make, given that the wrong they have committed against you is much greater—as we will suppose—than yours. In this chapter, I want to support the idea that there is such a thing as (not) having the standing to forgive, and I shall try to make some sense of what is going on when people dismiss forgiveness *despite* conceding that they have wronged the other party in the way for which they are being offered forgiveness.

As noted in previous chapters (e.g., Section 1.3), forgiveness can be dismissed in two ways (cf. Cohen 2013, 119). You *directly* dismiss it if you deny that you did what you are being forgiven for; concede that you did it, but deny that it was wrongful; concede that what you did was wrongful, but claim that you have a valid excuse for it; or, finally, concede that your action was wrongful and inexcusable, but submit that it is such that, by its very nature, it is

[1] https://www.news.com.au/why-cheaters-blame-their-innocent-partners/news-story/6b56c157ba66540524925d640565f0bb.

unforgiveable.[2] In my opening example, none of these bases of direct dismissal captures your reason for dismissing the forgiveness of your past neglect. Your dismissal is *indirect*, because you are neither, as it were, challenging the truth of the claim about blameworthiness that the forgiveness presupposes, nor challenging whether, in principle, your act is forgivable. Your dismissal is indirect, because what you are submitting is that, by virtue of facts about the forgiver, or the forgiver's relation to you, the forgiver has no standing (a notion I explain in Section 6.3) to forgive you for your blameworthy action.

In this chapter, my focus is on indirect dismissals of forgiveness, and I explore these dismissals in light of indirect dismissals of blame. Forgiving and blaming are closely connected—most obviously, because forgiving simply is ceasing to blame in the right way (Khoury 2022). Hence, if one lacks standing to blame, one also lacks standing to forgive. Or so I shall argue. Call this inference the *simple argument*. While the simple argument is one important thought underlying this chapter, it far from summarizes it. For instance, while the simple argument might make it reasonable to expect that the norms regulating blame regulate forgiveness as well, it does not establish this. Perhaps standingless forgiveness is morally wrongful for reasons other than standingless blame, or, unlike standingless blame, not wrongful at all. Additionally, some of the arguments offered in this chapter in defense, for example, of the claim that hypocritical forgiveness can be standingless make no claims about standingless blame at all. The first of the two arguments presented in Section 6.4, for instance, simply appeals directly to freestanding intuitions about standingless forgiveness.

As we have seen in Chapters 1–4, many philosophers argue that (a) a blamer can lack standing to blame for an act even if that act is blameworthy; (b) standingless hypocritical blame is pro tanto morally wrongful; and (c) factors other than hypocrisy can undermine one's standing to blame.[3] I shall defend analogous claims about forgiving: (a*) a forgiver can lack standing to forgive someone else for an act even if that act is forgivable (henceforth: the *standinglessness claim*); (b*) standingless hypocritical

---

[2] It is uncommon for recipients of forgiveness to dismiss it on this last ground, since normally wrongdoers want to be forgiven. However, it does happen (as my examples suggest, I hope) and, in any case, it is conceptually possible. Some deny that there are any actions that are in their very nature unforgiveable. I take no stand on this issue. My point is that *if* you (perhaps mistakenly) dismiss forgiveness on this ground, you dismiss it directly.

[3] Cohen 2013, 115–142; Dworkin 2000, 182–188; Fritz and Miller 2018, 2019a, 2019b; Herstein 2017; Isserow and Klein 2017; McKiernan 2016; Piovarchy 2023; Radzik 2011; Roadevin 2018; Rossi 2018, 2020; Smith 2007; Statman, forthcoming; Todd 2019; Wallace 2010.

forgiveness—like that manifested in my opening example—is pro tanto morally wrongful (henceforth: the *wrongness claim*); (c*) factors other than hypocrisy can undermine someone's standing to forgive (henceforth: the *plurality claim*). I also try to defend the more cautious *conditional claim* that, for each of (a)–(c), if that claim is true, then so is the corresponding claim about forgiveness, i.e., (a*)–(c*). I am not aware of any previous discussions tying standing to forgive to standing to blame, so this chapter is exploratory. On the other hand, in the philosophical literature on forgiveness, the question of whether standing to forgive a wrong requires one to be the victim of that wrong is familiar (Hughes and Warmke 2017, Section 4; Russell 2019, 2–3; Zaragoza 2012, 612–619).[4] This question is peripheral to my concerns. However, it is worth noting that many philosophers are inclined to answer it affirmatively, suggesting that the concept of standing to forgive is intelligible.

Section 6.2 identifies the sense of the term "forgive" at stake in this chapter, and Section 6.3 defines the relevant notion of indirect dismissal of forgiveness. Section 6.4 defines hypocritical forgiveness and argues that the hypocritical forgiver lacks standing to forgive, thus supporting the standinglessness claim. Section 6.5 explains why the hypocrite's standing to forgive is annulled. It appeals to the idea that hypocritical forgivers display insufficient, or deficient, commitment to the norms whose violation they are forgiving. Section 6.6 defends the wrongness claim, submitting that, like hypocritical blame, hypocritical forgiveness is wrongful because it involves relating to the recipient (person being forgiven) as an inferior. Section 6.7 defends the plurality claim by showing that three widely acknowledged sources of the standinglessness of blame—tu quoque, complicity, and meddlesomeness—also undermine standing to forgive. Section 6.8 introduces a negative equivalent of forgiving that, for want of a better word, I call "fromtaking." Like forgiving, fromtaking is a matter of the discretionary exercise of one's normative power to hold responsible, in this case, rather differently, by praising. Like forgiving, fromtaking, too, can be standingless, suggesting that an account of standing to forgive should be broad: it should explain our standing to exercise discretionary powers in relation to holding people responsible more generally. Section 6.9 concludes. The Appendix explores the notion of standing to apologize. This is relevant in the present context given that apologizing is the wrongdoer side of a wrong, while forgiving is the victim side of a wrong, as it were. Obviously, the structure of this chapter is very similar to that of

---

[4] See my discussion of Condition (4) in Section 6.2 below.

Chapter 5. This reflects the fact that the argumentative aims in this and the previous chapter are structurally similar.

6.2. What Is It to Forgive?

Forgiveness is a complex and varied phenomenon. However, my discussion examines the following communicative notion of forgiveness:

F (the forgiver) forgives W (the wrongdoer) for ϕ-ing if, and only if

(1) F communicates to W that F believes that W's ϕ-ing was blameworthy;

(2) F communicates to W that, henceforth, F *either* releases W from some or all of the duties to F that W has acquired, by ϕ-ing, to respond to the blame for ϕ-ing from F (i.e., F exercises their normative power to change wrongdoer norms); *or* renounces whatever liberty rights F has acquired against W to blame W for W's ϕ-ing (i.e., F exercises their normative power to change victim norms);[5]

(3) the setting of F's communicative act is of the right sort;

(4) F is either the victim of the wrongdoing or suitably related to the victim of the wrongdoing; and W is either the person who wronged F by ϕ-ing or suitably related to the wrongdoer (see Section 1.2.2 and Section 5.2).[6]

---

[5] See Nelkin 2013, 175–183; Pettigrove 2012, 9–12; Warmke 2016, 688, 697–699; cf. Allais 2008, 47–50. Condition (2), in conjunction with the rest of the definition, implies that one can forgive and still insist on, say, compensation for the harm caused by the wrong just as one can see one's relation to the wrongdoer as impaired. Relinquishing one's liberty right to blame or one's claim right to a response to one's blame is irreversible (though perhaps there are deviant cases of probationary forgiveness); i.e., one cannot forgive and then at some later point in time say: "Now I don't forgive you anymore. Hence, you owe me an apology." Such a demand can be dismissed by referring to the earlier act of forgiveness. Hence, the forgiver also relinquishes their normative power to change the wrongdoer's rights and duties and the recipient of forgiveness acquires immunity against the forgiver retracting forgiveness. I thank Ludvig Beckman for clarification of this point.

[6] Forgiving, in my sense, does not require any uptake by the recipient: being forgiven does not require that the "gift" is accepted (but see Fricker 2016, 172, on how the illocutionary act of blaming cannot be "fully successfully performed without the uptake of the hearer"; see also Brunning and Milam 2018, 15–157). Additionally, (4) is consistent with its being the case that the only person who is suitably related to the victim(/wrongdoer) is the victim(/wrongdoer) themself. One plausible way to look at (4) is to see it as a condition on having forgiven. If I say: "I forgive Tomás de Torquemada for wrongs he committed during the Spanish Inquisition," there is a sense in which I have not performed an act of forgiveness even though I use the verb "forgive" and even though it might be true that prior to saying that I blamed Torquemada for his deeds but that after my utterance I no longer harbor any hostile feelings toward him. Because of (4), "to forgive" has a stronger claim than "to blame" to be regarded as a success verb (as opposed to a try verb [Ryle 1954]; see also Fritz and Miller 2022).

On this definition, to forgive is to perform a speech act.[7] However, the extension of "forgiving" is broader than that. Specifically, there is a sense of forgiving where "forgiveness centrally concerns how you feel about the wrongdoer as a person" (Allais 2008, 49; Adams 1991, 294; Murphy and Hampton 1988, 21). While one might never have communicated forgiveness to the person who has wronged one, one might have forgiven this person in one's heart—i.e., one might completely "dissociate her wrongdoing from the way [one feels] about her" (Allais 2008, 57; see also Brunning and Milam 2018, 155). Conversely, one can perform the speech act of forgiving someone and nonetheless continue to resent one's wrongdoer for what she did.

This dual reference of "forgiving" explains why we can sometimes say, of those who have forgiven in the communicative sense, that they have forgiven insincerely. We mean that their thoughts about the wrongdoer are still very much shaped by their wrongdoing.[8] Forgiving is an impure performative (Austin 1962, 83–84; see also Warmke 2016, 694–698). When you say, "I forgive you," I can intelligibly have a skeptical thought: "You *say* you've forgiven me, but have you *really*?" In this chapter, I am exclusively interested in the pure performative sense of forgiving (just as, in the previous chapters, I have been exclusively interested in the pure performative senses of blaming and praising). By stipulation, the question "But did you *really* forgive me?" makes no sense: you have uttered, "I forgive you" (or something equivalent), and in the context we are in there is no room for doubt about whether, in the relevant speech-act-focused sense, you have forgiven me. The development of an account of standingless speech acts of forgiving is important in itself. Perhaps certain aspects of forgiveness are specific to communicative forgiveness. But it is also possible that the account will cast light on standingless emotion-centered forgiveness.[9]

Before proceeding, let me speak specifically to each of Conditions (1)–(4). (1) implies that when you inform someone who appears to have wronged

---

[7] In the relevant terminology, my definition focuses on declarative speech acts of forgiving.

[8] Without insincerity, one can perform a speech act of forgiving while still resenting the wrongdoer; thus, I might say, "I forgive you, but I still blame you in my heart." In such cases, the forgiver is typically also committing themselves to an effort to overcome their resentment and perhaps even thinks that publicly forgiving the wrongdoer is one way of effectively managing their own feelings about the matter, because (say) it pressurizes them to somehow get their feelings to conform with their publicly announced commitments.

[9] As we have seen, some argue that blame is "incipiently" communicative (Darwall 2006, 120; Fricker 2016, 177–180; McKenna 2012, 176; Smith 2013, 39; Section 1.2.1; cf. Driver 2016; Macnamara 2013a, 151–156). If so, I see no reason why the same should not be true of forgiveness (see also Warmke 2016, 691, on communicative forgiveness and Dougherty 2015, esp. 228–232, on whether consent is a mental state or a communicative act).

you that what they did was not wrong, or was excusable, you are not forgiving them, but doing something else. You are denying that blame was merited in the first place—in which case, there is no room for forgiving either.

Of course, those who forgive will often have previously (emotionally or communicatively) blamed. However, in some other cases they may never have gotten quite as far as blaming. They may have felt, merely, that they were ready to blame, or would be blaming at some point. On my analysis neither of these sequences identifies a necessary precursor of forgiveness. (1) requires the forgiver to express a belief to the effect that the wrongdoer has acted in a blame*worthy* way and, thus, that they are *entitled* to blame the wrongdoer, not that they necessarily do blame the wrongdoer.[10] This makes sense, because, on the present account, what one does when one forgives is renounce the *right to* blame (see (2)).[11]

Is (1) too strong? Suppose my partner did something damaging to me in the past. I have never blamed her for it. I might even think that it is not blameworthy, though I do not rule out the possibility that I am wrong about this, and I accept that if I were to reflect more on the incident, I would come to see why the act was in fact blameworthy. In these circumstances I can intelligibly say: "I don't think what you did was blameworthy. But if it is, I hereby forgive you." In my view, utterances like this are not acts of forgiving. Rather, they are *promises*, or undertakings, to forgive should forgiveness turn out to be relevant despite one's expectation that it is not. Promising to forgive and actually forgiving are as different as promising to go skiing and actually skiing.[12]

(2) implies that, in forgiving, one must convey to the person one forgives that one believes they did something blameworthy, and convey that one believes one has the standing to blame them (cf. Calhoun 1992, 95; Novitz 1998, 309–311). One must communicate that, in the absence of forgiveness, one is entitled to continue or to start to blame.[13] If I utter "I forgive" while

---

[10] Admittedly, there is more point in forgiving when one thinks that there is some probability that one will feel the pull of blaming in the future. However, even if one thinks the probability of that happening is near zero, there can still be some point in releasing the wrongdoer from their obligations.

[11] Suppose that I have never blamed my partner for a certain wrong she committed against me, and that I realize she feels bad about what she did. Surely, I can forgive her despite my never having thus far blamed her. In doing this I forgo any right to blame her at a later point in time. On the other hand, if I think I had no right to blame her, I am prevented from thinking that I can renounce such a right.

[12] To promise to forgive, where forgiveness is a feeling, might make little sense, because one does not directly control what one feels (Macnamara 2013, 156). However, this point is irrelevant given our focus on the communicative sense of forgiveness.

[13] Hence, in my sense I can forgive even if I *believe* there is nothing to forgive, and even if I think that there is, but also that I do not have the standing to do so (e.g., because my own relevantly similar wrongs committed against the recipient of the forgiveness are much greater: see Section 5.4). Additionally, the blamer's entitlement to continue blaming does not entail that the recipient deserves,

communicating that there is nothing to forgive, or that there is but I have no standing to forgive it, I am not really forgiving—perhaps I am best described as unsuccessfully trying to do so.[14] Condition (2) also ensures that forgiving is not merely ceasing to blame (see Allais 2014, 43–44; Brunning and Milam 2018, 146; Hieronymy 2001, 530; Milam 2019, 243; Milam 2022; Murphy 1982, 506; Pettigrove 2012, 4, 97).[15] Forgiving is something one does, not something that merely happens to the forgiver,[16] e.g., because they forget all about the wrong in question or simply stop caring about it.[17] This is trivially true of communicative forgiving, because to forgive in this sense involves performing a speech *act*.[18]

Finally, according to (2) forgiveness admits of degrees.[19] This corresponds well with the way in which people forgive. In many cases, of course, forgiveness is total, and the forgiver renounces any conversational rights in relation to the wrongdoer on account of their blameworthy action. However, forgiveness can be less than total. Thus, it may be that I renounce the right to bring

---

morally speaking, to be blamed. Generally, one can be entitled to do something to someone that that person does not deserve, morally speaking (cf. Kolnai 1973, 99, on the alleged paradox of forgiveness; cf. Twambley 1976, 88).

[14] This may sound similar to the infelicity account discussed in Section 1.4. Note, however, that here the act of forgiving misfires not simply because of the forgiver not having the standing to forgive, but by virtue of what the forgiver says in addition to "I forgive."

[15] Similarly, to refuse to forgive is essentially to continue to insist on the right to blame, and on the duty of the blameworthy party to respond to the blame (Radzik 2011, 583).

[16] In cases where one forgets about the wrong and someone else reminds one of it, suggesting that, apparently, one has forgiven the wrongdoer, one can correctly say: "I haven't forgiven them—I've just stopped thinking about it. But now that you bring it up . . ." While forgiveness, whether as a speech act or mental act, requires activity by the forgiver, the activity need not take the form of a conscious decision to forgive. I might discover that I have forgiven someone for their past wrong against me—e.g., I realize that whenever I interact with them, I try to give them the benefit of the doubt and attempt not to see their conduct in light of their past wrongdoing. In such cases, I can say: "Don't worry, I have forgiven you." In doing this I might not be performing an act of forgiving. I might simply be describing my mental states to the wrongdoer.

[17] "In order to forgive one must: i) overcome one's negative attitude toward an offender, ii) about their offense, iii) for the right reasons" (Brunning and Milam 2018, 147; see also 150–154). My account has no condition like iii), though, ultimately, 3) might come down to a concern about the sorts of reasons why the forgiver forgives. However, insofar as I perform a communicative act of the relevant kind, and in the right setting, I do forgive, whatever my reason for performing this action (e.g., whether that is to save myself the frustration of blaming my partner, to lower my blood pressure, or to better position myself for the purpose of being promoted).

[18] But this is also true of forgiving understood as an emotion. As Pamela Hieronymy (2001, 530) points out: to swallow a pill that erases blame (as an emotion) is not to forgive in an emotion-focused sense. Swallowing a pill that makes one perform an act meeting Conditions (1)–(4)—assuming that (3) does not rule out this possibility on the ground that swallowing a pill means that the setting is not right—counts as forgiving.

[19] Forgiving one's wrongdoer in my communicative sense *and* being willing to completely restore one's—say, loving—relationship to the wrongdoer and succeeding in doing so might in some sense constitute a more complete form of forgiveness than sheer communicative forgiveness.

up your wrong as a conversational matter and to start blaming you at will, but do not renounce the right to blame you again should you start blaming me for a similar wrong that I commit against a third party.

According to (3), the setting of the communicative act must be of the right sort. Quite what that means is a complex issue, which for present purposes we can ignore. However, to see the need for this qualification, suppose that I utter, "I forgive you" to my wrongdoer while they point a gun to my head threateningly, leaving me in no doubt as to what will happen if I do not "forgive" them. Certainly, I have performed the locutionary act of uttering a string of words people often utter when they forgive, but given the coercion my utterance does not have the illocutionary force of forgiveness.

(4) places a limit on who can perform an act of forgiving. Third parties can blame someone for their wrongdoing. Wrongdoers can blame themselves for their own wrongdoing.[20] However, only the *victims* of the wrongdoing—or, as my definition allows, those suitably related to the victims of the wrongdoing (Chaplin 2019)—can forgive a wrongdoer.[21] If you wrongfully insult one of my PhD students, I cannot forgive you for that.[22] In addition to that being demeaning—I would be treating my student as if they were some kind of private property of mine—my act would be infelicitous, considered as an act of forgiving. As Linda Radzik puts it:

> The ability to grant or withhold forgiveness requires a special kind of standing. Some argue that only the victims of the wrong, and perhaps their close loved ones, have such standing. For example, an employee who has been cheated by the boss can forgive, but the other co-workers are in no position to do so. Others grant that some non-victims can also have the standing to forgive or refuse to forgive, but only in virtue of a special need

[20] "I may forgive you for embezzling my funds; but it would be ludicrous for me, for example, to claim that I had decided to forgive Hitler for what he did to the Jews. I lack the proper standing for this" (Murphy 1982, 506). Some people distinguish between resentment and indignation, contending that it is only the victim of a wrongful action who can resent the wrongdoer for it, while anyone can be indignant over the wrong. On this view, forgiving is tied not to blame in general, but specifically to the sort of blame involved in resentment.

[21] One could add: only wrongdoers, or people relevantly related to them, can be the recipients of forgiveness. If one can wrong oneself, then one can forgive oneself in the same ways that one can forgive others. This is not to deny that one can forgive oneself for wronging others, but when one does so, one does it in a sense different from that in which one forgives others for wronging oneself. Self-forgiveness, like self-blame, raises interesting and complex issues of its own, and I shall largely set it aside here.

[22] If by insulting my PhD student qua PhD student you also insult me—the supervisor—I can forgive you for *that* insult; but that insult differs from the one to which you subjected my PhD student.

for support on behalf of the victim or a special obligation or relationship that the third party holds to either the victim or the wrongdoer. (Radzik 2011, 582; see also Griswold 2007, 117; but see Pettigrove 2009, esp. 593–595; Walker 2013, 495)

6.3. Dismissing Forgiveness as Standingless

Applying the notion of communicative forgiveness introduced in the previous section, I propose the following account of what it is to indirectly dismiss forgiveness as something the forgiver lacks standing to give:

The disjunctive view of indirectly dismissing forgiveness: W indirectly dismisses F's forgiveness for W's ϕ-ing on grounds of lack of standing if, and only if

(5) W denies that they have any duties to F, as a result of ϕ-ing, to respond to F's blaming of them for ϕ-ing, that F can free them from;

(6) or W denies that F has acquired any of the liberty rights against W to blame W for ϕ-ing that F can renounce (see Sections 1.3 and 5.3).[23]

On the disjunctive view, then, to indirectly dismiss forgiveness is to repudiate a claim that the communicative act of forgiving presupposes by virtue of (2). This is the claim that the recipient of the forgiveness has a duty, to the forgiver, to provide uptake of the forgiver's acts of blaming should they engage in such acts, or that the forgiver holds a liberty right against the recipient to blame them.

The disjunctive view has two important implications. First, it implies that when one dismisses forgiveness indirectly, one brackets—or, at least, might simply bracket—the question of whether the act for which one is being offered forgiveness was blameworthy and simply denies that the forgiver has the standing to blame in the way that their forgiveness presupposes. Second, in principle at least (though in practice often not), indirectly dismissing forgiveness can be a rather unemotional activity. Specifically, in indirect

---

[23] The rights and duties in question are conversational. Such rights and duties are different from, because less stringent than, say, the right to life and liberty and duties not to kill or enslave. Thus, while they can permissibly be enforced by silencing, or ignoring, others' utterances, they cannot be enforced with lethal force. However, this—unlike the normative structure that rights discourse imposes—is not important for present purposes.

dismissals, the potential recipient of the forgiveness need not be implying that the forgiver morally ought not, all things considered, to forgive. Indeed, consistently with the disjunctive view, the standingless forgiver might be morally required to offer (standingless) forgiveness, because the offer of forgiveness will turn the forgiver into an apparent moral exemplar capable of serving as an inspiration to many others. Likewise, consistently with the disjunctive account, there could be situations in which someone ought to accept forgiveness even though there is no wrong needing to be forgiven.[24] Similarly, there may be situations in which a wrongdoer should accept (what appears to be) forgiveness even though the forgiver is not the victim of wrongdoing and thus not the person with standing to forgive. This might be the case, for example, because the wrongdoer's self-blame is driving them toward suicide; only forgiveness from the person they falsely believe to be the victim of their wrong will prevent them from going down that route.

6.4. Hypocritical Forgiving

Against this conceptual background, I will now ask: Can forgiveness be hypocritical? If it can, can the hypocritical forgiveness be appropriately dismissed, indirectly, as standingless? There is a natural way of understanding these questions. When someone mentions "hypocritical forgiveness," the sort of case likely to spring to mind is one where someone, Tartuffe-style, pretends to forgive, conscious that, at heart, they will continue to nurse a grudge while aiming to appear magnanimous (Crisp and Cowton 1994, 343–344; see also Section 5.3). This is *not* the sort of hypocritical forgiveness I have in mind. Rather, the sort of hypocritical forgiveness I shall examine is the following:

F hypocritically forgives W for ϕ-ing if, and only if
(7) F forgives (in the communicative sense defined in Section 5.2) W for ϕ-ing;

---

[24] One such situation is where the recipient of forgiveness correctly believes they have done no wrong for which they can be forgiven. Cases like this are best described by saying that the recipient communicates acceptance of forgiveness even if, privately—or as we might say, at heart—the recipient does not really accept the forgiveness offered. To do that, the recipient would have to believe that what they are being forgiven for is something to be forgiven. This is symmetrical with the situation where someone communicates forgiveness for something they do not believe to be wrongful—i.e., in such a case the forgiver engages in what I have called communicative forgiveness but does not forgive in their heart (see footnote 13). Doing this requires them to believe that the recipient has done something to be forgiven.

(8) F believes, or should believe, that there are others to whom they themselves have done (or would have done) things that are both relevantly similar to φ-ing and contextually relevant;[25]

(9) Noncoincidentally, F does not suitably make themself, or accept themself being made, the target of forgiveness from others for *their* own conduct
that is relevantly similar to φ-ing;[26]

(10) (a) F does not believe there are morally relevant differences between
W's conduct and their own putatively similar φ-ing of the kind that justify
their forgiving W while not making themself, or accepting themself being
made, the target of others' forgiveness; (b) nor does F have a belief to this effect for reasons they can, or should be able to, see are not sufficient reasons
(see Section 1.2 and Section 5.2).

This definition successfully captures a range of cases in which we would
naturally consider the forgiveness hypocritical, but for reasons other than
the deception involved in the Tartuffe case. Indeed, given the definition,
Tartuffe-style forgiveness may qualify as nonhypocritical forgiveness if the
Tartuffe-style forgiver publicly and proportionately blames themself for their
greater wrong while publicly forgiving the lesser wrongdoer, though at heart
they have no regrets about their own greater wrong whatsoever and continue
to resent the lesser wrongdoer.

Condition (7) reflects the fact that, trivially, to forgive hypocritically one
must forgive.

---

[25] (8) implies that, in cases of hypocritical forgiveness, F need not believe that they have φ-ied in a
way that wronged W. It suffices that F believes that F has done similar wrongs to someone, and that
they do not think they have any reason to hope for forgiveness from others for these wrongs, and
does not even see them as wrongs. Note also that, according to (8), F must believe that they have
performed a certain action, and that, whether they believe this or not, the action is both relevantly
similar to φ-ing and contextually relevant. F need not believe that they have performed an action
under that description. Note, finally, that nonhypocrisy is not an Austinian felicity condition on the
view sketched here, though it affects the normative implications of forgiveness. I thank Jakob Elster
for clarification of this point.

[26] Suppose that, in my opening example, you forgive your partner for their many affairs, and
then ask your partner for forgiveness for your past neglectful behavior. In this case, if your unfaithful partner forgives your minor wrong, it would seem odd to consider that forgiveness hypocritical. I agree, but—so I conjecture—this is because we assume that the forgiveness is accepted,
in which case (9) is not satisfied—the forgiver does accept themself being a target of forgiveness
for their greater wrong. Suppose your forgiveness is not accepted—your partner denies that they
stand in need of forgiveness—but nevertheless your partner proceeds to forgive you for your having
been somewhat neglectful. Here I think it is very plausible to dismiss your partner's forgiveness on
grounds of lack of standing. I thank Patrick Todd and Alexander Velichkov for helpful discussion of
this point.

Conditions (8) and (9) provide the meat of the explanation of why F's forgiveness is hypocritical. Their satisfaction means that F fails to recognize that W has a right to blame F, and hence a right to renounce blaming F that has a foundation no less solid than F's own putative right to blame W. The "would have done" in Condition (8) allows for counterfactual hypocrisy. Thus, I might blame someone for something I have not done myself while also knowing that I would have done the same thing myself had I been in that person's situation (Piovarchy 2023). Roughly speaking, (8) is informed by this thought: the fact that F has done (or would have done under relevant hypothetical circumstances) something relevantly like W undermines F's right to blame W and demand uptake of that blame by W.

Condition (9) is designed to distinguish cases where F is simply incoherent: they might have as readily ended up blaming themself for φ-ing while not blaming W for doing similar things to them. While such a forgiver might display certain vices—incoherence, for a start—hypocrisy is not among them (see Fritz and Miller 2018, 122).

The purpose of (10) is to exclude foreseeable defeaters of hypocrisy. It says that F is warranted in believing that there is a morally relevant difference (located in the differential effects of forgiveness, for example) between their own forgiving of W and W's forgiving of them that morally justifies their act of forgiving and justifies them, again morally, in not accepting forgiveness from W. Suppose that F forgives W because W is psychologically fragile and consumed by guilt, whereas F is robust enough to live with a powerful sense of guilt. If *that* is F's sole reason for forgiving W while not considering themself an appropriate recipient of forgiveness, clearly F is not manifesting the vice of hypocrisy.

In my view, hypocritical forgiving, as I have defined it, can be rightly dismissed as standingless. In support of this view I offer, first, a case of political hypocrisy, in addition to the example involving forgiveness for infidelity offered in Section 6.1. My hope is that at least one of these scenarios, if not both, will convince readers of my position's plausibility:

Dresden: suppose that, in contrast to what happened, in the years after World War II the German state never apologized for Nazi atrocities but simply ignored the horrors inflicted on hundreds of millions by Hitler's regime. Suppose, with this as the background, that at a prominently staged fiftieth anniversary ceremony in Dresden town hall, counting the Israeli ambassador among its invitees, the German state through its representatives officially forgave the Allies for the militarily largely pointless terror bombing of Dresden in the final months of the war—bombing that resulted in the deaths of tens of thousands of innocent German civilians.[27]

Plausibly, the Allies, as the intended recipients of this forgiveness, are in a position to dismiss it as hypocritical even if they concede that the terror bombing of Dresden was blameworthy. Conditions (7)–(10) seem to be satisfied, (7) trivially so. Condition (8) is satisfied because the German state and its representatives know, or should know, that if the terror bombing in question was wrong, the Holocaust was a much greater wrong, and a relevant one, too, given the overall context of the Dresden attack and the invitees. (9) is satisfied in the Dresden case on account of the systematic failure to address the wrongs of the Holocaust. And (10) we can assume to be satisfied, because the reason for the discrepancy between what the German state is forgiving and what it seeks forgiveness for is wholly explained by its own reluctance to face up to its own wrongdoing.[28]

Having brought out the intuitive plausibility of the view that hypocritical forgiveness is standingless, I want now to offer a separate argument for the view:

(11) If F has standing to forgive W for φ-ing, then F has standing to renounce a liberty right against W to blame W for φ-ing or standing to renounce a claim right against W that W provides uptake to F's blaming W for φ-ing.

(12) If F has either standing to renounce a liberty right against W to blame W for φ-ing or standing to renounce a claim right against W that W provides uptake to F's blaming W for φ-ing, then F either has a liberty right against W to blame W for φ-ing or a claim right against W that W provides uptake to F's blaming W for φ-ing.

---

[27] My example presupposes (inter alia) that the German state is suitably related both to the perpetrators of Holocaust etc. and to the victims of the terror bombing of Dresden, so that it can both be subject to blame for the former and offer forgiveness for the latter. Most, I think, will not object to this presupposition. However, readers who do are invited to consider a suitably revised example not involving collective agents like states, but individual perpetrators and victims.

[28] If the German state did not seek, nor would accept, forgiveness for the Holocaust because its official view is that it ought not to be forgiven, then the forgiveness would not be hypocritical. However, then (10) would not be satisfied; i.e., the German state believes there is a morally relevant difference between terror bombing of German cities and the Holocaust such that the former should, or could, be forgiven, while the latter should and could not.

(13) If F has either a liberty right against W to blame W for φ-ing or a claim right against W that W provides an uptake to F's blaming W for φ-ing, then F has the standing to blame W for φ-ing.

(14) So, if F has standing to forgive W for φ-ing, then F has standing to blame W for φ-ing.

This argument is clearly valid, since (11)–(13) are three linked conditionals and its conclusion is a conditional with the antecedent of (11) as its antecedent and the consequent of (13) as its consequent. Hence, the crucial question is whether the premises are true. Arguably, (11) follows relatively straightforwardly from (2) in my definition setting out what communicative forgiveness is, i.e., the claim that F communicates to W that, henceforth, F *either* releases W from some or all of the duties to F that W has acquired, by φ-ing, to respond to the blame for φ-ing from F . . .; *or* renounces whatever liberty rights F has acquired against W to blame W for W's φ-ing. . . . And (12) strikes me as a conceptual truth. One cannot have the standing to renounce a right unless one has that right. Finally, (13) is a plausible account of what it is for F to have standing to blame W (in a communicative sense) for φ-ing: surely here, *either* F has a liberty right against W to blame W for φ-ing *or* W has a duty to F to provide an uptake to F's blaming W for φ-ing.[29] One reason why this account of standing to blame is attractive is that when people dismiss someone as not having the standing to blame they need not be claiming that the person should not (morally) engage in blaming. After all, standingless blame (like standingless forgiveness) may be morally justified by virtue of its good consequences.

These, then, are my arguments for the claim that forgiveness can be standingless. While the first, intuitive argument, appealing to the Dresden case (or for that matter, though I have not spelled it out, a similar argument appealing to the opening example of the cheating forgiver), carries greater weight for me, I think the second definition-based argument is also forceful.

---

[29] As already noted, not everyone accepts that there is something like standing to blame (Section 2.6). Skeptics about standing to blame are invited to assess the argument above as one that shows what would follow, as regards standing to forgive, if there were such a thing as standing to blame.

6.5. What Undermines Standing to Forgive?

If hypocritical forgiveness is standingless, what is it about the hypocrite that undermines their standing to forgive? I think the answer to this question is the following:

> *The commitment account of lack of standing to forgive*: what deprives the hypocrite of their standing to forgive others is the fact that they are not genuinely committed to the norm that their forgiveness presupposes (see Section 2.7 for the parallel commitment account of lacking standing to blame).

This account explicates the two examples of hypocritical forgiveness I have offered in a satisfying way. Through their unwillingness to address their own infidelity—and even more so through their affair itself—the cheating partner manifests lack of commitment to the norm on which their forgiveness is based—the norm that spouses should not deceive each other and ought to support one another emotionally. Similarly, the imagined German state in the Dresden case shows a lack of principled commitment to the norm of not killing civilians. It fails to apply the norm in a case where this would reflect badly on Germany (or the German state at least).

In other cases, however, the commitment account seems to deliver the wrong answers. In passing—lightheartedly, but not hypocritically—I might forgive someone. It is fairly obvious that I care little about the wrong committed against me, and that I think of the forgiveness in a rather businesslike way. Possibly, I forgive in a way manifesting no greater commitment to the norm at issue than a hypocritical forgiver does, with the difference that the latter is seriously upset about another's violation of the norm. Yet it would seem odd to say that my standing to forgive is undermined. A case such as this seems to be a counterexample to the commitment account.

I believe this challenge can be met through a more precise specification of the sort of lack of commitment that undermines standing to forgive. Perhaps only lack of commitment biased in one's own favor, or in favor of those with whom one somehow sympathizes, undermines standing. However, here the focus of my response to the present challenge is different. I wish to stress two things. First, if the present counterexample works against the commitment account, it also works against an analogous commitment account of standing to blame, thus supporting the standinglessness claim.

Second, clearly, if counterexamples of the kind I sketched above success-fully defeat the commitment account, we will need an alternative account of what it is about the hypocrite that undermines their standing to forgive. The literature on standing to blame suggests that a widely supported candidate would be this:

The moral equality account of lack of standing to forgive: what deprives the hypocrite of their standing to forgive others is the fact that, by virtue of the faults from which their hypocritical forgiveness results, the hypocrite's forgiving the recipient involves relating as people with une-qual moral status, e.g., by implicitly denying the recipient's equal moral status (see Section 2.7 for the parallel moral-equality-based account of lack of standing to blame).

The animating idea here is that hypocritical forgivers deny the moral equality of persons because they see themselves as being in a position to blame others for minor wrongs even though they themselves have committed greater wrongs against others and fail to acknowledge those greater wrongs.

Unfortunately, this account is defeated by the case of the *hyper*critical for-giver (cf. the discussion in Section 2.7 of hypercrisy). The hypercritical for-giver finds it very difficult to forgive themselves, but very easy to forgive others. If this person treats anyone as an inferior, thereby implicitly denying moral equality, presumably it is themself (cf. Murphy 1982, 505). Yet, when they forgive others, these others cannot dismiss the hypercrite's forgiveness as standingless in light of their failure to treat themself as an equal in relation to their acts of forgiveness.

The obvious response to this objection is to embrace something like the following modification of the moral equality account:

The antisuperiority account of lack of standing to forgive: what deprives the forgiver of their standing to forgive others is the fact that, by virtue of their hypocritical forgiveness, they affirm their moral superiority over other persons.

On this account, plainly, the hypercritical forgiver retains their standing to forgive. They do not affirm their moral superiority over others—far from it. Ultimately, however, the antisuperiority account is flawed for reasons similar to those presented in Section 2.7, and this drives us back to the commitment account (assuming we started there). Consider two aristocrats, both of whom think that, in a wide range of cases, aristocrats should forgive wrongs done to them by other aristocrats but almost never forgive wrongs committed against them by commoners. Both, then, affirm superiority over commoners. Suppose now that both aristocrats forgive a commoner who has committed the same minor wrong against each of them. And assume that the first aristocrat has not committed any wrongs against the commoner they are forgiving, while the second has committed much greater wrongs against the commoner than those they are forgiving. On the antisuperiority account, both commoners can indirectly dismiss the forgiveness they are being offered, since both aristocrats affirm their superior moral status relative to the commoners.[30] However, in addition to this, the second commoner can legitimately claim that, because the aristocrat has wronged them to a much greater degree, they are in no position to allocate the blame in the first place, and thus in no position to forgive. Hence, what undermines the second aristocrat's position to forgive is not their denial of moral equality, but the fact that they have committed greater wrongs against the recipient of their forgiveness.

I accept that some will take issue with this objection to the antisuperiority account, and, for that matter, with my previous objection to the moral equality account. Even they, however, should accept that what undermines the standing to blame—be that a denial of moral equality or an affirmation of one's own superiority—can be present in the case of forgiveness as well. Once this is accepted, it is hard to see how friends of the moral equality, or the antisuperiority, account of standing to blame could deny that there is such a thing as lacking the standing to forgive. If this is granted—always assuming that there is such a thing as lacking standing to blame—we have strong support for the standinglessness claim (see Section 6.1). This claim, it seems, is true whichever of the three accounts of standing to blame I have discussed in this section is correct.

---

[30] It might be objected that while both aristocrats affirm their own superiority explicitly, only one of them does so implicitly through their pattern of forgiveness. In reply, I must say that I fail to see how what one affirms, or denies, implicitly can undermine one's standing to perform certain acts if, when one says that very same thing explicitly (perhaps at the very moment one forgives), that does not undermine one's standing.

6.6. The Wrongfulness of Hypocritical Forgiveness

Let me now turn to the question of what makes hypocritical forgiveness wrongful. I want to defend two claims: that if hypocritical blame is pro tanto wrongful, then so is hypocritical forgiveness, and that hypocritical forgiveness is pro tanto wrongful. I defend these two claims by scrutinizing four accounts of why hypocritical blame is pro tanto wrongful.

In the previous section I considered the moral equality account of standing to forgive and to blame. On my conception of standing, the mere fact that your forgiveness is standingless does not in itself show that it is pro tanto wrongful. However, Fritz and Miller (2018, 122) and Wallace (2010, 332) all seem to take their accounts of why hypocritical blame is standingless to also be accounts of why hypocritical blame is pro tanto wrongful:

> *The moral equality account of the wrongfulness of hypocritical blame(/for-giveness)*: hypocritical blaming(/forgiving) is pro tanto wrongful because it involves the blamer(/forgiver) relating to the addressee(/recipient) as (if the addressee/recipient were) inferior (see Sections 3.9 and 5.5).[31]

On this account, hypocritical blame is pro tanto wrongful because it involves the blamer relating to the blamee as inferior, e.g., by either (implicitly) denying or acting in ways that are incompatible with the moral equality of persons. If this is the correct account of hypocritical blame, the analogous, parenthesized account of the pro tanto wrongfulness of hypocritical forgiveness is also correct. After all, on my account a hypocritical forgiver is involved in hypocritical blame (or, at least, must believe themselves to be entitled to blame—and, thus, forgive—where, as a matter of fact, such blame—and, thus, the corresponding forgiveness—would be hypocritical).[32] As we saw in Section 2.7, the moral equality account of the wrongfulness of hypocritical forgiveness captures a crucial element of what is intuitively objectionable about hypocritical forgiveness. For, intuitively, what is objectionable about the deceitful partner's forgiveness is the way in which they relate to their partner as someone whose entitlements, in relation to holding each other

---

[31] The formulation of the account here accommodates the intuition that the hypercritical blamer(/forgiver) does not act in a pro tanto wrongful way because they do not relate to others as a superior.

[32] I need the parenthesized qualification because, on my account, one might forgive someone for a wrong that one believes one would be entitled to blame them for even if, as of yet, one does not blame them (see Section 6.2).

accountable, are lesser than their own, and that way of relating to others is built into hypocritical forgiveness by definition.[33]

Not everyone accepts the moral equality account of the wrongfulness of hypocritical blame, so let us consider three other accounts and ask how they apply to hypocritical forgiveness. Return to

The desert account of the wrongfulness of hypocritical blame(/forgiving): hypocritical blaming(/forgiving) is pro tanto wrongful because it involves trying to acquire (or actually acquiring) more esteem in the eyes of others than one deserves (Sections 3.2 and 5.5).

If the desert account explains the wrongfulness of hypocritical blaming, the equivalent explanation of hypocritical forgiveness is also correct. After all, the hypocritical forgiver neglects to address their own faults in a way that seems to involve trying to acquire, or acquiring, more esteem than they merit: that acquisition is the upshot of their avoidance of deserved blame. Additionally, by conveying a false impression of magnanimity the hypocritical claimer lays claim to underserved esteem.[34]

As discussed in Section 3.2, it might be objected that in *some* cases avoiding having one's esteem lowered in deserved ways, or having one's esteem boosted in undeserved ways, will move one closer to possession of the amount of esteem that one deserves. It will do so, for example, if, for other reasons, one's level of actual esteem diverges from one's level of deserved esteem. In my view, this objection might well defeat the desert account. However, in the present context I need only note that assessments of the objection will be symmetrical across the desert account of moral wrongfulness of hypocritical blame and the desert account of moral wrongfulness of hypocritical forgiveness—they will apply as powerfully, or feebly, to both.

It can also be objected that, implausibly, the desert account seems to imply that forgiveness is pro tanto wrongful. After all, part of what one does when one forgives is wipe the slate clean—e.g., by renouncing one's right to blame the wrongdoer in a way that this person deserves. Hence, if the forgiver acts in accordance with this renouncement, the wrongdoer receives less blame

---

[33] I also think that this is part of what makes the forgiveness in the imagined Dresden case intuitively objectionable, though other factors might be at play here as well.

[34] Recall that on my view you can forgive even if you never experience any resentment against the recipient of forgiveness. Hence, by forgiving you need not invite the thought that you were too judgmental in the past, something that might reduce your esteem.

than they deserve, and therefore probably more esteem than they deserve. In response, I note that my account of what forgiveness involves does not speak to the issue of esteem. It is compatible with it that someone who is forgiven for their wrongs should have the esteem they have in the eyes of others lowered in proportion to the wrong despite the forgiveness. Hence, even if the empirical conjecture involved in the present challenge is correct, it would not challenge the desert account.

Third, consider again:

The reciprocity account of hypocritical blame(/forgiveness): hypocritical blaming (forgiving) is pro tanto wrongful because it involves a failure to reciprocate to the recipient of blame(/forgiveness) on part of the blamer(/forgiver); i.e., the blamer(/forgiver) demands something from the recipient while rejecting a relevantly similar demand from them (see Sections 3.6 and 5.5).[35]

Hypocritically forgiving someone who has wronged you while displaying disproportionately little attention to your own similar, or greater, wrongs against the recipient of your forgiveness amounts to a failure of reciprocity relevantly like that involved in hypocritical blame. One expects others to take one's own complaints against their wrongful actions seriously by accepting one's forgiveness (thereby acknowledging one's entitlement to blame), yet one does not honor the expectation that one will take the similar or greater complaints of others seriously, e.g., by apologizing and asking for forgiveness. Hence, from the perspective of reciprocity, hypocritical forgiveness and blame are wrongful on the same grounds.[36]

---

[35] Some might ask how, exactly, the moral equality and the reciprocity accounts of the wrongness of hypocritical forgiveness are related—e.g., whether they are distinct accounts or the reciprocity account is a subspecies of the moral equality account (in which case my argument above in relation to the moral equality argument applies here as well). In my view, the accounts are distinct because norms of reciprocity can govern relations between unequals in some domains (the superior and the inferior do have reciprocal expectations; it is just that the superior expects more in return than the inferior—"I protect you against other lords and you work for me on my instructions all your life in return," says the lord to the peasant in medieval Europe), and because sometimes the relations between equals may justifiably not be governed by norms of reciprocity (e.g., because one party to the relation consents to a deviation from those norms in the other party's favor). For present purposes—i.e., to show that the main accounts on offer of why hypocritical blame is wrong apply to hypocritical forgiveness as well—I can sidestep questions about the precise relationship between the moral equality and reciprocity accounts (see Sections 3.6 and 3.9).

[36] Some might challenge this, arguing that forgiveness is supererogatory and, thus, that forgiving one's wrongdoer does not result in any moral requirement that the wrongdoer reciprocate by forgiving the forgiver for the forgiver's wrongings committed against the forgiver. Against this view, I would suggest that a norm of reciprocity can apply to supererogatory acts (assuming acts of forgiveness to be such acts) even if it does not manifest itself in moral requirements; e.g., in an extended

Consider, finally:

The falsehood account of hypocritical blaming: hypocritical blaming is pro tanto wrongful because it involves the suggestion of a false claim; i.e., the claim that the blamer's and blamee's moral relationship is impaired as a result of the blamee's, not the blamer's, faults (see Sections 3.8 and 5.5).

This account can readily be generalized to cover hypocritical forgiveness:

The falsehood account of hypocritical forgiving: hypocritical forgiving is pro tanto wrongful because it involves the suggestion of a false claim, i.e., the claim that the forgiver's and the recipient of forgiveness's moral relationship is impaired as a result of the recipient's, not the forgiver's, faults, and is now partly, or fully, repaired as a result of the forgiver's (hypocritical) forgiveness.

Again, I am not championing falsehood accounts of the wrongfulness of hypocritical blame or forgiveness. I am simply contending that the suggestion of a false claim about what modifies the relation between the involved parties is as involved, or implicit, in cases of hypocritical forgiveness as it is in cases of hypocritical blame. For example, the deceitful partner's forgiveness suggests that they are the party with legitimate cause to withhold goodwill and trust from their deceived partner, and therefore the one with discretion to either restore or not restore their relationship. So, if the false suggestion is wrongful in the case of hypocritical blame, the same seems true when hypocritical forgiveness is at issue.

I have now supported the wrongness claim—the claim that hypocritical forgiving is pro tanto wrongful. Such forgiving is wrongful, I have argued, because it amounts to relating to the recipient as an inferior. I have also supported the conditional claim that if hypocritical blame is pro tanto wrongful, then so is hypocritical forgiveness. I have pointed out that several familiar accounts of the wrongfulness of hypocritical blame imply that, likewise, hypocritical forgiveness is also wrongful. Admittedly, this does not show that no account of the wrongfulness of hypocritical blame could imply

relationship one party who always forgives the other, who in turn never forgives, can complain on grounds of nonreciprocity even if the forgiving party has no right to be forgiven as a result of their own generous acts.

that while hypocritical blame is pro tanto wrongful, hypocritical forgiving is not, but it does confer a degree of robustness on my conditional claim about the wrongness claim.

6.7. Other Ways in Which Forgiving Can Be Standingless

Thus far I have focused on the case of standingless (because) hypocritical forgiveness. However, as we saw in Chapter 4, blame can be standingless for reasons other than hypocrisy. In this section I argue that forgiveness, too, can be standingless for these additional reasons, thus defending the plurality claim (see Section 5.1; Chapter 4 and Section 5.6).

First, blame can be standingless because the blamer has done something similar or worse than what the blamee is being blamed for (Section 4.2). I argued that, often, this will amount to hypocrisy, but in some cases—e.g., where the blamer is innocently unaware that they have done something similar or worse—it will not, and these are the cases I want to discuss here. In cases like this the recipient of blame can still indirectly dismiss it, exclaiming, "Tu quoque!" (Cohen 2013, 118–125). Something similar can happen in relation to forgiveness. Consider a variant of the opening example where—amazingly—the cheating partner has nonculpably forgotten about the affair. Having done so, they forgive their (actually, deceived) partner, absolving them of their earlier wrongful neglect. This forgiveness is not hypocritical, because *ex hypothesi* the deceiver is innocently unaware of their worse wrong. Even so, the recipient of the forgiveness can surely indirectly dismiss it: if they can do that in the original case, they must be able to do so in this variant of that case. Of course, once the forgiver has been made aware of their past infidelity, they can no longer persist in forgiving nonhypocritically unless they engage properly with their own relevantly similar past wrongdoing, thereby regaining their standing to blame, as it were. However, this does not affect my point that just before the forgiver has their attention directed to their own past infidelity, the recipient of forgiveness can dismiss the forgiveness as standingless even if, at that point in time, the reason for the standinglessness cannot be hypocrisy on part of the forgiver. It must simply be the fact that the forgiver has done something similar or worse than the conduct they are forgiving the recipient for.

Second, in Section 4.3 I argued that blame is standingless when the putative blamer is complicit in the wrong for which they are blaming another.

If I knowingly assist a bank robber's criminal plans, I lack the standing to blame them (Cohen 2013, 125–131; cf. Todd 2019, 354). In my view, complicitous forgiveness is similarly standingless. If we assume that it is only the victims of wrongs, as opposed to wrongdoers and third parties, who have standing to forgive, then, to test this view, we will need to assume that the complicit blamer is also the victim of the wrong for which they are offering forgiveness. Suppose someone assists me in smashing up a car whose owner, so it turns out to our shared surprise, is my complicitous partner. My partner provides me with a sledgehammer after urging me to smash up the car, not recognizing that it is theirs. If this person grandly declares that they forgive me, I can indirectly dismiss their forgiveness as standingless, pointing to their complicity.[37] From that moment they would be hypocritical if they were to persist in forgiving, and their forgiveness could be dismissed on that ground; but, as with the tu quoque reply discussed in the previous paragraph, just before that, the ground offered by the intended recipient for dismissing forgiveness must be different; it must be complicity, not hypocrisy.

Third, as I argued in Section 4.4, when someone blames another for something that (though blameworthy) is none of the blamer's business, the blamee can indirectly dismiss the blame (by the person whose business it is not) as standingless. Again, on the assumption that only victims of wrongs have the standing to forgive, it is difficult to test this view, as it requires a case where the wrong is none of the victim's business and, obviously, such a case is difficult to imagine—but not impossible. Suppose I solemnly relinquish my right to blame you if you embezzle my savings, and even my right to bring up this issue with you should you do that. I have not relinquished the right not to have my savings embezzled by you, and therefore it remains true that your embezzlement would wrong me. You do embezzle the savings, and discovering this I remonstrate, blaming you for taking them, but after a while I forgive you. In this peculiar circumstance, it seems correct to conclude that you can indirectly dismiss my forgiveness on the basis that it is none of my business to blame you given my promise.[38] This concludes my defense of the plurality claim.[39]

---

[37] This case complements nicely Murphy's (1982, 505) observation that sometimes eagerness to forgive reflects a lack of self-respect by showing that eagerness to accept forgiveness can reflect the very same thing.

[38] If this intuition is correct, we must revise the relation and interest principle proposed in Section 4.4 such that it accommodates cases where someone relinquishes the right to blame.

[39] I have not discussed whether forgiveness can be standingless because the forgiver fails to grasp the wrongdoer's situation or because the forgiveness rest on a principle that the forgiver does not accept themself. Intuitively, the latter form of standinglessness clearly seems possible. The former is

6.8. Fromtaking

In this section, I briefly generalize my claims about forgiving to what I suggest is the negative, unnamed analogue of forgiving: I baptize this "fromtaking."[40] In forgiving, I exercise a discretionary power regarding blaming: I have the right to blame, but I choose not to exercise it. Indeed, on the account I have given I *relinquish* it. Thus—to put it in Hohfeldian terms—I exercise my normative power to make it the case that I no longer have such a right. Fromtaking involves a comparable discretionary exercise of one's normative power regarding praising (taking praising as the positive equivalent of blaming). In cases of it, I have the liberty right to praise (in a way that I will explain presently, but, for example, by expressing my sincere gratitude) and I choose not to exercise that right.[41] Indeed I relinquish my right to praise.[42] Like forgiving, fromtaking can take the form of a mental state or a speech act. It is the latter, the communicative notion of fromtaking, that I am interested in here.[43]

As we have seen, "praising," as that term is often used in ordinary language, is not an exact positive equivalent to "blame" and refers simply to the expression of a positive evaluation (Section 5.2). However, this does not prevent us from identifying a subspecies of praise that, like blame, involves more than the mere expression of an evaluation—i.e., a subspecies involving features similar to those that distinguish blame from a mere negative evaluation of actions and the character that they reflect—and which, at least in an important range of cases, captures what people do when they praise (cf. Watson 1996, 242). This is the sort of praising I will be occupied with here. More specifically, I am interested in praise in the sense introduced in Section 5.2:

more dubious, but on reflection also possible. If the forgiver's lack of comprehension concerns the wrongdoer's perspective when they acted wrongly, it seems the wrongdoer can dismiss the forgiveness as manifesting a lack of comprehension of the nature of the object of forgiveness.

[40] There is also a neutral equivalent of forgiving and fromtaking, but I will not go into this here.

[41] The claim applies to the claim right to an uptake to one's blame. However, to keep things simple I set that aside here.

[42] There is no English word for taking back one's praise. However, the phenomenon is certainly recognizable for English speakers (and others) once described. I call this analogue "fromtaking" because, unlike forgiving, it is not a matter of giving something to someone.

[43] Here is a case that illustrates fromtaking as a mental state: one decides to stop feeling gratitude toward another for past help considering the bad character that they have acquired since then, while thinking that one would be entitled to feel gratitude toward them without ever expressing one's change of mind (or heart).

P (the praiser) praises R (the recipient) for φ-ing to A (the addressee) if, and only if

(15) P communicates to A their positive evaluation of A based on R's φ-ing;[44]

(16) P communicates to A that in doing (16) they demand suitable uptake from A in response.

With this definition in place, we can now ask whether fromtaking is capable of being hypocritical in a way that undermines the fromtaker's standing. The following case shows it can:

> *Disappointment*: some time ago, Britta helped Charlotte greatly in a su- pererogatory way. Charlotte has praised Britta for her help ever since. However, Britta has gradually turned more self-centered and egoistic since then. Charlotte's frustration with Britta has grown. At some point in time Charlotte decides that she has had enough, and she promises Britta she will never again praise her for the assistance she once gave her.[45] What Charlotte prefers to ignore is that she has helped Britta in a rather minor way compared with the ways in which Britta has helped Charlotte on sev- eral previous occasions; that Britta has always praised Charlotte for her comparatively small good deed; that Charlotte's character has worsened even more seriously than Britta's; and that when, a couple of months ago, Britta decided that she had had enough and renounced her liberty right to praise Charlotte for her minor good deed, Charlotte protested in the strongest terms.

My view is that Charlotte fromtakes Britta in a hypocritical way, and that Britta can indirectly dismiss Charlotte's fromtaking as standingless in the same way that she might, in different circumstances, dismiss hypocritical forgiveness as standingless. That is, Britta might agree that she has indeed changed in such a way that, given the considerable praise she has received in the past for her good deed, she is no longer praiseworthy on account of her past good deed. What she denies is simply that *Charlotte* has the standing to

---

[44] "P" and "R" might refer to the same person (self-praise), as might "A" and "R" (second-person praise).

[45] Praise and blame seem different in that, unlike what I suggested in Section 4.7, repeated instances of praise do not undermine one's standing to praise, whereas repeated instances of blame do.

fromtake her given Britta's own insistence that she fromtakes Charlotte for her own lesser good deed.

Quite a lot of ink has been spilled on forgiving. To the best of my knowledge, no philosopher has analyzed the concept of fromtaking even though, once it is described, it appears to be the clear negative equivalent of that discretionary exercise of our normative powers that amounts to forgiveness.[46] I think much more can, and should, be said about fromtaking. Specifically, more needs to be said about standing to fromtake, and what, for example, undermines one's standing to fromtake. Is hypocritical fromtaking pro tanto wrongful, and, if so, what makes it so? Again, can fromtaking be standingless for reasons other than hypocrisy, such as meddlesomeness or complicity (see Section 5.7)? I am strongly inclined to think that these questions should be argued along the same lines as those along which I have answered similar questions about forgiveness and standing to forgive. However, my main aim in this section, other than enlarging our normative vocabulary in a way that I hope enables us to better understand our practice of holding people responsible, is to suggest that, ultimately, we should think of standing to forgive within the wider setting of the discretionary exercise of rights to blame and praise, and our power to renounce such rights.

6.9. Conclusion

If the arguments in this chapter are sound, one can lack the standing to forgive; one can do so if, as many philosophers—myself included, obviously— think, one can lack the standing to blame. Moreover, this standing can be eradicated for reasons like those annulling standing to blame, hypocrisy being the most fully discussed of those. Hypocritical forgiveness is pro tanto wrongful because, like hypocritical blame, it involves relating to the recipient of forgiveness as a superior.[47] At any rate, if hypocritical blame is pro

---

[46] While people are typically pleased to accept forgiveness, they will not usually wish to accept fromtaking. This may explain this differential focus. However, conceptually speaking, fromtaking can be accepted by the person being fromtaken. In some situations, it will make good psychological sense to accept fromtakenness. For example, perhaps that is a way of (resentfully) holding the fromtakers to their own past declarations in a way that one thinks they will then regret ("Don't you dare come and praise me now"), and thus a way of making them think twice about the way in which they hold one responsible.

[47] Recall that I have discussed two antisuperiority accounts: one of what undermines the standing of the hypocrite to forgive (Section 6.5), and one of the pro tanto moral wrongness of hypocritical forgiveness (Section 6.6). As I explained earlier in connection with the hypocritical aristocratic forgiver, I reject the former account. However, I am sympathetic to the latter.

tanto wrongful for that reason, then so is hypocritical forgiveness. Finally, I have introduced the concept of fromtaking, thereby pointing to the wider setting in which standing to exercise rights and normative powers with respect to holding agents responsible should be comprehensively assessed. It seems natural to conjecture based on the first six chapters that the idea of standing applies to ways of holding people responsible other than just by way of blaming them. In Chapter 7 we will consider whether these ideas apply even more broadly than that, e.g., in the sphere of morality that does not pertain to holding each other responsible and even outside the sphere of morality altogether.

6.10. Appendix: Forgiving and Standing to Apologize

It is an interesting question how apologizing relates to forgiveness and whether there is such a thing as having the standing to apologize. In response to the former question, I think there are strong connections, even if one can apologize without thereby asking for forgiveness and even given that one can forgive without an apology from the wrongdoer. As noted, apologizing is the wrongdoer side of a wrong, while forgiving is the victim side of a wrong, as it were. In one sense of "apologizing," by apologizing the apologizer acknowledges, or publicly affirms, the existence of certain rights that the recipient of the apology has. Apologizing in this sense is not "normative transformative action" and involves no exercise of discretionary normative authority. However, in another sense of "apologizing," by apologizing one exercises a discretionary normative authority; i.e., one thereby changes the rights the recipient of the apology now has. For instance, apologizing in this sense might confer on the recipient of the apology a normative power to determine (within reasonable constraints) the conditions for an acceptance of the apology in a way that the recipient of the apology did not have prior to the apology being offered. "Apologizing" in this sense is like promising, permitting, consenting, and forgiving (cf. Pallikkathayil 2011).

In response to the second question, I think one can lack the standing to apologize for reasons like those that I have explored in relation to blame. Here is a case of a hypocritical apology: while torturing their victim, a torturer apologizes for having slapped the victim's face yesterday. The standards to which the torturer appeals in identifying the slapping as a wrong condemns torturing much more strongly, and yet the torturer does not apologize for torturing (or, even better, apologize for that *and* stop torturing). In this case, the victim can indirectly dismiss the torturer's apology as standingless—it is one that they have every right to simply ignore (though that might be unwise).[48] We can also imagine someone apologizing to a person whose face they slapped in the presence of someone else whom they tortured and to whom they do not apologize. In this case the recipient might dismiss the apology as standingless in solidarity with the victim of torture. One conjecture is that the moral equality account of wrongfulness of hypocritical blame applies to such apologies as well. I also believe, though for reasons of space I cannot go into it here, that apologies can be standingless for the reasons other than hypocrisy that blame can be standingless (see Chapter 4); e.g., in my example in Section 5.7 I am in no position to apologize to the car owner who is complicit in the wrong for which I apologize (smashing up their car) and the car owner can dismiss my apology as standingless (though, of course, they might accept it nevertheless and can accept my apology in a more minimal sense than the one I have in mind here, i.e., they can accept my apology as an expression of the absence of ill will on my part against them).

---

[48] Presumably, the torturer's apology can also be dismissed as insincere. But this need not be the case—the torturer might weirdly be truly sorry about the slapping yesterday. In any case, like blame, apologies can sometimes be dismissed on several grounds.

7

Morality, Normativity, and Standing

7.1. Introduction

In the six preceding chapters, I have focused on the nature of standing to
hold morally responsible.[1] I took my point of departure from hypocritical
blame and analyzed how one might lack standing to blame and how it can be
wrongful to blame despite lack of standing (Chapters 1–3). In the sense that
I have been focusing on, to blame is to perform a particular communicative,
illocutionary act. That is, in, say, uttering the sentence that one employs to
express one's blame, one does something. Specifically, I suggested that one
does something such that, in cases where the blamer has standing to blame
the blamee, the recipient of the speech act is under an obligation to provide
an uptake to the blamee. In later chapters I extended my analysis to communicative praising and forgiving, inter alia (Chapters 5 and 6).

Assuming that these lines of argument are correct, two questions impose
themselves upon us. The first question is whether there are illocutionary acts
other than those discussed in previous chapters, and that are not narrowly
tied to acts of holding morally accountable, that likewise can be performed
with or without standing.[2] I address this question in Section 7.2. Focusing on
encouraging people to act in certain ways, I argue that there are indeed such
illocutionary acts. The second question is whether the notion of standing is
specific to moral illocutionary acts or whether it applies to illocutionary acts
that pertain to norms other than moral norms. Section 7.3 addresses this
question.[3] Section 7.3 shows that the notion of standing applies to epistemic
blame as well. You can dismiss my epistemic blame of you for your sloppy

---

[1] This is not quite true of Chapter 5 on praising. I can praise someone without implying anything
about the moral qualities of that for which I praise them. However, this does not indicate any deeper
asymmetry between praise and blame (Section 7.3).

[2] Indeed, one might ask whether it is true of all illocutionary acts—which are such that if
performed under favorable conditions, the addressee is now under certain obligations—that they
can be performed with or without standing.

[3] Implicitly, Section 7.2 does that as well, because one might encourage someone to do something
because it is the epistemically, aesthetically, prudentially, or rationally right thing to do, or simply the
thing the encourager wants to happen, and not because it is the morally right thing to do.

The Beam and the Mote. Kasper Lippert-Rasmussen, Oxford University Press. © Oxford University Press 2024.
DOI: 10.1093/oso/9780197544594.003.0008

reasoning, when, say, I am a much sloppier reasoner than you are in much the same way that one can dismiss hypocritical moral blame.[4]

Section 7.4 addresses the significance of the present discussion for some basic questions in normative theory. Specifically, I argue that norms of standing embody a particular kind of interpersonality—namely, the relation between pairs of persons where one holds a claim right against the other that they can relinquish. This interpersonality not only applies more broadly than simply to norms regulating holding people accountable in a narrow sense. It also renders many discussions of consequentialism and nonconsequentialist alternatives misleading. Generally, discussions of the distinction between consequentialist and nonconsequentialist moral theories focus on two elements of nonconsequentialist moral theories: moral constraints and moral options. The relevant interpersonality that characterizes our normative life, whether moral or not, is not best thought of as exhausted by these two elements. Hence, the wider upshot of the present inquiry is that there is an important component in our common-sense (and nonconsequentialist) moral thinking that is neither compatible with consequentialism nor captured by some of the standard descriptions of the alternatives to consequentialism. Section 7.4 also notes that norms pertaining to holding accountable embody a certain conditionality. This conditionality is recognizable from first-order moral norms, e.g., norms pertaining to self-defense.

Section 7.5 explores what this conditionality implies in relation to the issue of moral encroachment. Recently, several theorists have argued that one can wrong others by virtue of holding certain beliefs about them. One way of doing so is by holding beliefs about them that are in a certain sense discriminatory, e.g., racist or sexist, or in other ways demeaning. This one can do even if one has evidence for the relevant belief, e.g., that a black or female diner will tip less generously than a white male diner, such that one would be justified in believing claims about nonpersons, say, based on evidence of the same quality. For instance, in cases involving racial profiling there is the risk of wrongfully inferring some demeaning fact about some individual member of a group from statistical facts about that group and that, theorists of moral encroachment argue, implies that more evidence is needed

---

[4] If there is such a thing as epistemic standing, then that gives rise to the question of what this possibility implies for my previous analyses of what undermines standing to blame; e.g., does the lack of commitment account apply to standing to engage in nonmoral blame? Also, if one accepts my analysis of standing in relation to nonmoral blame, the question arises whether nonmoral blame is pro tanto wrong and, if so, whether it is pro tanto wrong for the same reason as standingless moral blame.

before one is epistemically justified in holding the relevant belief about the individual in question.

While I am sympathetic to central tenets in the theories of moral encroachment, I extend the claims about the conditionality of first-order moral norms mentioned in Section 7.4 and of norms of standing to the kind of moral concerns at stake in moral encroachment. I argue that in cases where people stereotype others such that they would be hypocritical if they were to complain about their being stereotyped themselves, they are not wronged by being stereotyped.[5] Hence, some influential theories of moral encroachment are compatible with certain forms of cognitive statistical discrimination not wronging the discriminatees for reasons that have so far been overlooked. To avoid misunderstanding: I think this is an important point for the purpose of moral theory. However, I am not suggesting that, on account of my arguments in Section 7.5, we should worry much less about statistical discrimination or moral encroachment than several authors suggest. The conclusion briefly sums up the main claims of this book.

7.2. Encouraging

In the chapters on blame and forgiving, I have primarily analyzed standing in relation to holding people morally responsible in a narrow sense—"narrow" because, first, my focus has been on acts of holding responsible whose focus is backward-looking and, second, setting aside praising, acts that involve making demands on the recipient. However, there is a broader sense of holding responsible that is not backward-looking and that does not involve making demands; e.g., if I encourage someone to act in a particular way in the future, I am neither focusing on what they have already done nor making any demands on them.[6] Still, I am holding them responsible in the broader sense that I am encouraging them to let certain considerations determine their actions.[7]

---

[5] This applies not only when the stereotyped stereotype the stereotypers, but also when the stereotyped stereotype, not their stereotyper, but others.

[6] Urging, which I mentioned above as an example of a directive that, however, does not involve the issuing of a demand, is a particularly strong form of encouraging others to perform a certain act. You can encourage someone to do something (in this perhaps partly stipulative sense) without urging them to do it, but not the other way around.

[7] Similarly, if I make a moral demand on someone pertaining to their future acts or the terms of our future interaction, I am not blaming them, since my action does not refer to anything that they have done (nor, necessarily, to anything that I think they will do). In my view, there are illocutionary acts that involve holding people responsible in a broader sense.

In this section I limit myself to exploring the notion of standing in relation to encouraging.[8]

Encouraging someone to do something in the sense I am interested in here is a public, communicative act. Perhaps there is a sense of "encouraging" such that one can encourage someone to do something without verbally communicating with them—say, by secretly manipulating or nudging them in the direction of doing whatever one "encourages" them to do, e.g., by putting the shelves with the candy right next to the checkout counter—but that is not the sense of encouraging under discussion here.[9] However, here I set such cases aside. Accordingly, for present purposes I adopt the following definition (parallel to my definition of blaming$_p$ offered in Section 1.2.1):[10]

X encourages$_p$ Y to ϕ if, and only if
(1) X communicates to Y that X believes that Y's ϕ-ing is desirable;
(2) X communicates to Y that X demands a suitable uptake from Y in response to their communicative act; and
(3) X is different from Y.

This definition implies that encouraging someone to do something involves more than just communicating to them that one believes that the action one encourages them to do is desirable in some way. It also involves demanding a certain response from them—not necessarily that one expresses an intention to do what one is encouraged to do, but at least some kind of recognition of the encouragement.[11] The definition also implies that in encouraging the other person to do something one is putting oneself behind the act that one is encouraging the other person to do.

One aspect of putting oneself behind the act one encourages someone to do is that one relinquishes certain rights to hold the agent accountable for

---

[8] There are illocutionary actions other than actions involving holding accountable in a broad sense that involve standing. Some of these acts involve our exercise of discretionary normative authority, e.g., permitting and consenting. I have no standing to consent to something if I have no moral authority over that matter. There are other acts too, e.g., giving reasons, that involve issues of standing; e.g., I have no standing to give p as a reason for q if, in all our previous discussions where you have offered p as a reason for q, I have denied that p is a reason for q.

[9] However, unlike blaming, there are no purely private acts of encouraging others.

[10] "Encouraging" in its ordinary language sense is probably an impure performative in the same way as "blaming" and "forgiving" (see Section 6.2).

[11] Exceptions exist, though. If I say: "It would be so good of you to extinguish the fire in my room! Don't respond in any way, just do it, please!" surely, I am encouraging the recipient to extinguish the fire, even if I am not demanding any kind of uptake—at least, other than extinguishing the fire.

that action ex post; e.g., if I encourage you to act in a certain way, I thereby relinquish my right to blame you for doing what I encourage you to do (cf. Section 4.3)—at least, if I neglect to blame myself for my encouragement.[12] By encouraging you to act in a certain way I also acquire certain duties that I did not have before; e.g., if somebody thinks that the act that I encouraged you to do is blameworthy, I might now be under a stronger obligation to provide an uptake to that person if they hold me accountable for what you did than I would have been had I not encouraged you to act in this way.

I can encourage someone to do something that I find morally desirable. However, I might find what I encourage someone else to do to be desirable in other ways; e.g., I might simply think that what I encourage the other person to do is desirable because it makes me better off. However, whichever form of desirability is at stake, if I encourage someone to do something, I relinquish my standing to then blame them, morally speaking, for doing what I encouraged them to do—e.g., if I blame you for doing what I encouraged and you dismiss my blame on that ground, I cannot retort: "Oh yes, I did encourage you to ϕ, because it would have been a good thing for me if you did it. But I never said it would be morally permissible for you to ϕ, so, surely, I can blame you, morally speaking, for ϕ-ing." I could have blamed you for the act in question if I had simply publicly registered the fact that it would be good for me if you performed the action in question. But then I would not have encouraged you to perform the action; i.e., I would not have put myself behind your performing the action in question.[13]

This definition also implies that encouraging is different from demanding.[14] If an encourager demands that their encouragee ϕ-ies, then

---

[12] This qualification is like how the greater sinner might be in a position to criticize the lesser sinner provided they blame themselves for their greater faults.

[13] This is not to deny that in many situations, communicating to someone else that it would be good for oneself if the other person ϕ-ies is a way of encouraging them—perhaps demanding of them—that they ϕ. If the Mafia boss invites someone to a meeting and informs the person that it would be good for the Mafia boss if the invitee ceases doing something, the context might be such that the Mafia boss is ordering that person to cease the activity in question and is not simply conveying an interesting observation that the Mafia boss has made in the interest of expanding the recipient's store of true beliefs. Note also that warnings—perhaps unlike threats—need not involve encouragement in my sense (though they clearly involve encouragement in a different sense). If a coercer holds a gun to a coercee's head, informing the coercee that if and only if the coercee refuses to hand over their money, the coercer will shoot them, there is a sense of "encouraging" where the coercer might deny encouraging the coercee to hand over their money: "I'm not encouraging you to do anything. I am simply issuing a warning to the effect that if you don't hand over your money, I'll shoot you. You might see this bit of information as an encouragement, but I am not encouraging you to do anything."

[14] Similarly, it is different from commanding. Commanding is a form of demanding where the demand is backed up by some special kind of position of authority, which one does not have over another simply by virtue of, say, being a moral agent or a friend of the person being commandeered.

ipso facto the encourager encourages the encouragee to φ. However, the encourager might encourage the encouragee to φ, even if the encourager does not thereby demand that the encouragee φ-ies. On this assumption—that demands are a subspecies of encouragements—the analysis in this section applies to demands too. Moral demands can be positionless in the same way as blame and as encouragements; e.g., my neighbor to the left, who always does their fair share, might be in a position to encourage me—even in the form of demanding—to do my part in keeping the neighborhood tidy, whereas my neighbor to the right, who is notoriously messy and always shirks joint efforts to clean up the neighborhood, has no position to encourage—even not in a nondemanding way—that I do my fair share (for a helpful discussion of the relation between standing and moral demands, see Pallikathayil 2011).

A natural starting point for an investigation into whether one can lack standing to encourage others in the indicated sense is to see whether the very same sort of hypocrisy that I argued in Chapter 1 undercuts the standing to blame can undercut the standing to encourage. Return to the case of Jack, i.e., the carbon-dioxide-emitting philosopher, who occupied the opening pages of Section 1.1. By slightly tweaking the story, we can use it to show that just as the story in its original version lends intuitive support to the claim that blame can be hypocritical and for that reason standingless, its tweaked version lends support to the claim that encouragements can be hypocritical and for that reason standingless. Recall that Jack travels quite a lot on airplanes. He has two siblings, Al and Greta. One day Jack has a phone conversation with Al. Jack says:

> Al, you really shouldn't fly so much. We all have a moral duty to do our share to reduce global warming, but you are very far indeed from doing your part. I simply fail to understand how your political career can be so important that you can ignore what you ought to do. I strongly encourage you to significantly reduce the number of miles you travel on planes in the interest of not contributing to future flooding and droughts across the world.

Amazingly, Jack encourages his sister, Greta, in the same way ad verbatim when, half an hour later, he talks to her. As the reader will recall, Greta flies

I can make certain demands on my friend, but I cannot command my friend to act in certain ways simply by virtue of being that person's friend.

much less than Jack because of her convictions regarding climate change and our obligations in relation to climate change, and Al flies much more than Jack does.

If you think of this case like I do, you will think that Al and Greta can appropriately respond quite differently to Jack's encouragement. Greta might respond to Jack:

> Perhaps even I fly too much. Still, a strongly worded encouragement directed at *me* to fly less is a bit rich when coming from *you*. You travel to conferences around the world all the time. You even choose to enjoy your holidays in ways involving transoceanic flights. True, in the future I might occasionally travel by air, e.g., when I speak at an important climate event, potentially resulting in the promotion of climate-friendly policies, and when traveling there by other means takes weeks. Perhaps there are reasons why I should not do even that. However, there are much stronger reasons why *you* should travel less by plane and yet you have the audacity to encourage me to travel less without even considering whether you yourself should reduce the number of miles that *you* travel by plane. While I will consider whether there are facts that suggest that I should revise my plans regarding future air travel, the fact that you encourage me to do so is not one of them.

Whether or not Al might also bring to the table for scrutiny Jack's own flying habits, unlike Greta, Al cannot dismiss Jack's encouragement in the same way Greta does—he does owe Jack a response to his encouragement.

What goes on in this case is structurally similar to what goes on in the case of hypocritical blame that I discussed in Section 1.1. Encouragements can be dismissed directly as well as indirectly (Section 1.3). Direct dismissals involve a denial of there being the sort of reasons motivating the action in question that the encourager takes there to be; e.g., Al might directly dismiss Jack's encouragement by denying that it would make any positive difference to anything if he flies less; or he might concede that it would, but assert that there are countervailing and weightier reasons in favor of his traveling as well; or he might concede that there are not, but submit that he is excused for not reducing the number of miles he travels by air. Alternatively, one might bracket all these questions and instead focus on whether the encourager has the standing to encourage a person to ϕ. This indirect dismissal is what is at stake here. While it would be hypocritical of Jack to encourage Greta to reduce the number of miles that she travels by plane, it would not be hypo-critical (or least it would be less hypocritical) of Jack to encourage Al to do so.[15] Moreover, just as blame can be indirectly dismissed when it is hypocrit-ical, encouragements can be indirectly dismissed when they are hypocritical:

> The appropriate encouragement dismissal claim: if X hypocritically encourages Y to ϕ, then, by virtue thereof, Y has a reason to dismiss X's encouragement.

What does it mean to indirectly dismiss an encouragement? Precisely be-cause the dismissal here is indirect, it is not to deny that the action one is encouraged to do is desirable (not even desirable all things considered). Rather, I understand dismissal of encouragement here in parallel to what I called the disjunctive view in relation to indirect dismissal of blame in Section 1.3:

> The disjunctive view: X dismisses Y's encouraging$_p$ X's ϕ-ing if, and only if, X denies that Y has a liberty right against X to encourage$_p$ X to ϕ or X denies that X has a duty to respond to Y's encouraging$_p$ X to ϕ.[16]

Perhaps it is more common to dismiss hypocritical encouragements in the latter way, but the dismissal in the way set out by the former disjunct is com-monplace as well. The response "How dare you encourage me to ϕ, when you yourself . . ." certainly indicates that the speaker thinks they are under no conversational duty to respond to the encourager's act, but it is particularly forceful because it suggests that the speaker thinks the encourager violates a conversational duty owed to them by encouraging them to ϕ even though the

---

[15] One reason one might think it would only be less hypocritical is that the reasons that he would give for why it is desirable for Al to reduce the number of miles he flies would also motivate the desir-ability of Jack himself reducing the number of miles that he flies (see the complications discussed in Section 2.5 regarding degrees of wrongdoing and how the lesser sinner's blame of the greater sinner might be hypocritical).

[16] Dismissing an encourager's encouragement on grounds of hypocrisy typically involve both a denial of any duty to provide any communicative uptake and a denial that the encourager's encouragements have the normative force of adding to the recipient's reasons to do as encouraged to do. One can imagine accounts of what it is to dismiss encouragements that are like the infelicity, the moral wrongness, and the incoherence accounts of what it is to dismiss moral blame (see Section 1.4). Such accounts of what it is to dismiss encouragements are subject to weaknesses parallel to those weaknesses suffered by the relevant accounts of what it is to dismiss blame; e.g., if I hypocritically en-courage someone to do something, it is not the case that I merely tried to perform an illocutionary act of encouraging but failed to do so.

reasons that motivate them not φ-ing apply with even greater force in rela-tion to the encourager's own actions.

When are encouragements hypocritical? We can answer this question by offering the slightly modified version of the definition of hypocritical blame offered in Chapter 1:

X hypocritically encourages Y to φ if, and only if
(1) X encourages Y to φ;
(2) X themself believes or should believe that the facts that make Y's φ-ing something to be encouraged also apply to their own φ-ing or some other similar action being something to be encouraged;
(3) in a way that does not reflect a sheer coincidence, X is not to a suitable degree or in a suitable way committed to their own φ-ing or committed to doing that which is both relevantly similar to φ-ing and also contextually relevant;
(4) it is neither (a) the case that X believes there are morally relevant differences between their own φ-ing or their doing what is both relevantly similar to φ-ing and also contextually relevant, on the one hand, and Y's φ-ing, on the other hand, that justify their encouraging Y to φ and not being committed to their φ-ing or committed to their doing what is relevantly similar to φ-ing, nor (b) the case that X has a belief to this effect but that X has so for reasons which they can, or should be able to, see are not sufficient reasons.

I have already said something about what I mean by encouraging, i.e., (1), so let me comment on these conditions starting with (2). (2) accommodates the fact that encouragements can be hypocritical even if the encourager is committed to doing what they encourage others to do if there are other rele-vantly similar things that they are also committed to doing that, for the same reasons that bear on the action they encourage others to do, speak against that relevantly similar thing. Jack's encouraging Greta to fly less would be hypocritical even if he himself did not fly but was instead, say, funding a large shale oil extraction project.

(3) reflects that it is at least unusual, perhaps impossible, for an agent to encourage themself to perform a certain action. One reason why it might be outright impossible is that, as I defined encouraging, if an encourager encourages an encouragee to φ, then the encourager thereby relinquishes their right to blame the encouragee if they φ. However, one cannot relinquish

one's own entitlement to self-blame. Hence, if it is a definitional property of encouraging that one does so, one cannot encourage oneself in the relevant sense. This is not to say that one cannot do so in other senses of "encouraging"; e.g., one can form the intention of rewarding oneself with a nice vacation should one succeed in mustering the will required for pursuing some desirable, but difficult, project.

Consider finally (4). Suppose that Jack accepts that the same reasons that render it desirable for Al to fly less render it desirable that he himself fly less. However, he thinks—correctly, let us suppose—that he is an extremely fragile person and that he would break down if his ego were not regularly boosted by ego-boosting performances at prestigious conferences and VIP treatment at exotic retreats. Suppose Jack has a third sibling, Gina, who flies even more than Al and has the same fragile psychological constitution as Jack and that Jack would never even consider encouraging Gina to fly less. In this case, whatever others flaws Jack's stance might manifest, arguably, hypocrisy is not among them. This motivates (4a).

(4b)'s motivation can be seen from the following sort of case. Suppose Jack believes, say, that his fragile constitution justifies his not downscaling his commitment to activities involving flying, but he should be able to see that these are insufficient reasons, e.g., because he knows that Al has an even more fragile constitution than he himself has, which should alert him to the fact that his appeal to his own constitution really is just a matter of a self-serving rationalization. In this case, his encouragement would be hypocritical, despite belief that his differential blame is justified.

Having defined hypocritical encouragements, I want to show that the commitment account of what defeats standing to blame and the moral equality account of the wrongfulness of hypocritical blame can be extended to apply to hypocritical encouragements as well. Consider:

> *The commitment account*: what deprives the hypocrite of their standing to encourage others to φ is the fact that by virtue of their own lack of commitment to φ-ing (or to their lack of commitment to doing something relevantly similar to φ-ing), they show themself to lack commitment to the desirability of φ-ing.

The commitment account fits well with the adapted version of my vignette involving Jack. The fact that he is in no way committed to cutting down on his own number of flights shows that his commitment to the desirability of reducing the amount of flying that takes place is deficient (or at any rate weaker than his encouragements would suggest).[17]

Is it wrong to hypocritically encourage others to do certain desirable things? Essentially, one can wrong others by doing so. Hypocritical encouragements can be wrongful for the same reason as hypocritical blame, i.e., for the reasons captured by the following:

> *The moral equality account*: what deprives the hypocrite of their standing to encourage others is the fact that by virtue of the facts about them that render their encouragement hypocritical, the hypocrite's encouraging the encouragee involves relating as people with unequal moral status, e.g., by implicitly denying the encouragee's equal moral status.[18]

The moral equality account captures well the intuitive sense of the wrong one is being subjected to when encouraged to do something by someone who has even stronger reasons themself to be committed to doing otherwise in some relevant respect and yet has no intention whatsoever to act otherwise, and would simply ignore encouragements to do otherwise.

As we saw in Chapter 4, blame can be standingless for reasons other than hypocrisy. The same is true of encouragement. More specifically, all five sources of standinglessness surveyed in Chapter 4 apply to encouraging people to act in certain ways as well. If Jack has honestly forgotten about his own traveling patterns, Greta might dismiss his encouragement by reminding him thereof (tu quoque). If Jack promotes Al's extensive flying schedule by funding his flights—perhaps in almost the same breath as encouraging Al to travel less—Al might dismiss the encouragement on grounds of complicity.[19] If Jack really lacks a basic understanding of what it is like to be in the shoes

---

[17] Some might challenge my use of this example on the ground that in principle Jack might be strongly committed to the principle—it is just that he is not very committed to doing his part. Indeed, it is precisely his being so strongly committed to the principle that makes his failure to act on it so despicable. However, this challenge applies, mutatis mutandis, to the commitment account of standing to blame and, accordingly, it is one that does not undermine my symmetry view regarding standing, on the one hand, and blame and encouragement, on the other hand. Additionally, and in response to both challenges, it might be said that being willing to "do one's part" in relation to a principle or concern to which one appeals is a constitutive part—though not the only part—of what it is to be committed to that principle or concern and, accordingly, that commitment and doing one's part are internally connected in a way that, perhaps, the present challenge presupposes they are not.

[18] The comparison of a pair of aristocratic encouragers analogous to the pair introduced in Section 1.4 defeats the moral equality account of that by virtue of which one lacks standing to encourage.

[19] Jack might be able to offer a justification for his complicity that outweighs the reasons speaking against his funding Al's flights and against Al flying in the first place and, if so, he retains standing to encourage, despite his complicity in Al's doing what he encourages Al not to do.

of an ambitious politician with a great need for getting elected and thus to get around frequently and quickly for campaigning purposes, Al might dismiss the encouragement as one that manifests Jack's lack of understanding of his situation, even if he agrees that, really, he ought to do as Jack encourages him to do.[20] If Greta knows that Jack himself does not really think that it is desirable to reduce greenhouse gas emissions and, thus, to reduce flying, she might ignore his encouragement. Finally, if the bus driver uninvitedly encourages Al to do his fair share of the household chores, Al might dismiss the encouragement on the ground that it is none of the bus driver's business, though Al could not say that to his wife, sibling, or friend etc.

This completes my treatment of standing and encouragement. I have argued that moral blame and encouragement are structurally similar when it comes to standing.[21] This is an important conclusion, because it strengthens the claim that issues of standing are not tied specifically to the nature of moral blame or, more broadly, moral accountability. One can encourage without holding morally accountable. Nevertheless, one can lack standing to encourage.

7.3. Epistemic Blame

With some exceptions, e.g., the previous section on encouraging, thus far my focus has been on standing in relation to illocutionary acts that involve appeal to *moral* norms. But it is commonly thought that there is a plurality of norms, e.g., that in addition to moral norms there are prudential norms, epistemic norms, aesthetic norms, and norms of rationality. These norms are generally believed to be related in certain ways—e.g., what norms of rationality prescribe is somehow a function of what the other norms prescribe—and they

[20] If you think that there are reasons why (Jack thinks) Al ought to fly less that have nothing to do with, nor can be defeated by reasons generated by, how the world looks from Al's perspective, you will be skeptical of this example. If so, think of a sort of case where you would accept that there is such a thing as not having the standing to blame, e.g., a just war theorist blaming a combatant for a certain minor wrong on the battlefield, where the theorist is completely ignorant of what it is like to be on a battlefield and where what it is like is relevant for how one should assess the situation. Suppose then that instead of blaming ex post, the theorist is encouraging ex ante, speaking to the combatant on their cell phone and from a safe distance encouraging them not to commit the minor wrong. In some such cases, I suspect encouragement might be standingless. (Not in all such cases, because being on the battlefield with a just war theorist on the phone is a different experience. I suppose.)

[21] Since I have argued in Chapters 5 and 6 that blame, on the one hand, and praise and forgiveness, on the other hand, are also structurally similar, it follows that they too are structurally like encouraging.

are believed not to be reducible to each other. Call this the *plurality assumption*.[22] I shall not defend the plurality assumption here, but simply take it for granted. Monists about norms and people who think that norms of rationality are not somehow a function of moral norms etc. can read this section as charting what follows regarding epistemic standing if nonmonism is true.

Given the plurality assumption and given that there is such a thing as having standing to engage in moral blame, it is natural to ask whether there is such a thing as standing in relation to other norms as well. Can I reject prudential blame for an instance of relatively harmless shortsightedness on my part as standingless, when it comes from someone who is notoriously myopic? Can I dismiss aesthetic criticisms of my shirt as being slightly tasteless, when it comes from someone whose entire wardrobe is revolting? Can I indirectly dismiss epistemic criticism for being slightly superstitious when it comes from someone who believes in the (many) miracle(s) of Lourdes? Do I have the standing to subject others to rational blame, when I persistently act in ways that I have no reason to act?

What the correct answers are to questions such as these is important. First, if our standing to engage in nonmoral blame can be undermined too, then it is natural to suppose that this will have important implications for what undermines the standing to blame, or for that matter some of the other standing-involving illocutionary acts that I have analyzed. Specifically, it might be natural to think that what undermines standing is not the putative fact that standingless moral blame is pro tanto wrongful in a particular way, but instead perhaps lack of commitment to the norm in question (see Piovarchy 2022; Rossi 2018, 560–561). Or, at least, this is plausible provided that, say, standingless hypocritical aesthetic blame is not pro tanto morally wrongful (see Sections 1.4 and 2.8).

Second, if our standing to engage in nonmoral blame can be undermined too, then, plausibly, this has implications for what makes, say, hypocritical blaming morally wrong, when it is. Offhand, it seems that hypocritical aesthetic blame need not involve any denial of equal moral standing of persons; e.g., there is not any obvious sense in which hypocritical aesthetic blame per

---

[22] For an excellent discussion of normative pluralism, see Sagdahl (2022). Sidgwick's "dualism of practical reason," i.e., the view that prudence and morality are two distinct normative perspectives and that often an act is required from one perspective but not from the other, and performing this act is thus rational from one perspective but not from the other, is an influential example of a normative pluralist theory (Parfit 2017a, 130–149; 2017b, 335–338). Whether pluralists or not, some philosophers argue that epistemic blame is reducible to moral or prudential blame or to blame based on social norms (Dougherty 2012; Goldberg 2018; for counterargument, see Cassam 2019, 18).

se implies the denial of the claim that the interests or will of the person being subjected to hypocritical aesthetic blame somehow counts for less, morally speaking, than that of the blamer or of third parties, for that matter.[23] Given that the content of the blame does not bear on moral matters, including is- sues about moral standing, why should hypocritical aesthetic blame clash with persons having equal moral status? Or so it may seem.

Finally, if nonmoral blame can be standingless too, if standingless non- moral blame is not always morally wrongful, and if standingless moral blame is pro tanto wrong, then that would lend support to my view that what undermines standing to blame (morally) is different from what makes standingless blame morally wrong.

In what follows and mainly for reasons of space, I will adopt a narrower focus than the one suggested in the first three paragraphs of this section. This narrowness relates to two different dimensions. First, I will discuss standing to hold responsible only in relation to epistemic norms—only occasion- ally will I say something about possible extrapolations of my arguments to, say, prudential norms. Second, I will focus on the kind of holding respon- sible constituted by blaming as opposed to some of the other illocutionary acts that I have been addressing—only occasionally will I hint at parallel extensions to some of the other illocutionary acts that I have analyzed in re- lation to standing, e.g., epistemic (self-)praise and epistemic forgiveness.[24]

While I will not offer any argument in defense of this claim, I shall assume that many of the points I make about epistemic blame generalize to other ways of holding responsible—also in relation to other nonmoral norms. Essentially, this assumption is warranted because what I have been exploring in the previous chapters are the norms regulating holding people *morally* re- sponsible, and these norms really are similar when it comes to holding people responsible *in other ways* as well, I shall argue. In other words, the present brief exploration of epistemic blame serves as a case study aimed at casting light on a broader set of issues.[25] In any case, for many of the conclusions I defend in this section, the core issue is not whether similar points that apply

---

[23] To the extent that we have an interest in avoiding aesthetic blame, Wallace's account might apply equally well to aesthetic blame as to moral blame. Things are different, it seems, with Fritz and Kyle's moral equality account.

[24] Epistemic forgiveness makes sense on some of the accounts of epistemic blame that I discuss below on the assumption that to forgive, epistemically speaking, is to relinquish the right to epistemi- cally blame someone (see also note 375).

[25] For an overview of recent work on epistemic blame, see Boult (2021c).

to standing and moral blame apply to all other forms of blame, but whether there is a nonmoral form of blame to which these points apply as well.

The first thing to address is the question of what epistemic blame is. Indeed, since some people deny that there is such a thing as distinctively epistemic blame, it is particularly urgent to start by carving out the present territory of exploration. Given our starting point, it is natural to think about paradigmatic epistemic blame in parallel with what I defined as paradigmatic moral blame in Section 1.2.1:

X epistemically blames$_p$ Y for ϕ-ing if, and only if
(1) X communicates to Y that X believes that Y's ϕ-ing was blameworthy in relation to particular epistemic norms and[26]
(2) X communicates to Y that X demands a suitable uptake from Y in response to their communicative act.

Essentially, epistemic blame is parallel to moral blame, but the norms in question are epistemic norms as opposed to moral norms; e.g., the norm in question that the blamee is blamed for violating is not a norm to the effect that one should respect other people or promote their interests, when doing so is not very costly for oneself, but a norm to the effect that one should hold the beliefs that are supported by the evidence available to one.[27]

So construed, epistemic blame raises many of the same issues as moral blame. First, epistemic blame is different from, and something that goes beyond, simply informing someone that they violate a certain epistemic norm in a way for which there is no excuse (assuming that there are such a thing as epistemic excuses [Littlejohn, forthcoming]), just as morally blaming someone is doing more than saying that what they have done is morally wrongful. As Cameron Boult (2021b, 11359) puts it: epistemic blame is a fitting response "that goes beyond mere negative [epistemic] evaluation or grading."[28]

[26] The paradigm case of "ϕ-ing" in relation to epistemic blame is believing, but an individual can also be the proper target of epistemic blaming on account of other (mental) acts, e.g., asserting, inquiring, or inferring (Boult 2021c, 2), and on account of character traits, e.g., being gullible or careless.
[27] Some virtue epistemologists might say that epistemic norms are simply a subset of moral norms (Zagzebski 1996, xiv, 6). I can remain neutral on this matter. But if they are right and epistemic blame in the way I construe it really is a subset of moral blame and moral blame in general is characterized by involving standing conditions, then my present point about epistemic blame goes through for reasons other than the ones I offer here.
[28] Similarly, merely expressing the view that someone has acted imprudently is not to engage in prudential blame of that person. Something else is required, e.g., some uptake to the blamer's

Second, paradigmatic epistemic blame is communicative. Hence, just as my focus in previous chapters was on communicative acts of holding responsible, my focus here is on communicative acts of epistemic blame (Section 1.2.1). This is not to deny that there is such a thing as engaging in private epistemic blame. I can privately blame someone—myself in some cases—for being gullible even if I never display, let alone communicate, this blame to the blamee. As with private moral blame, I have no need to deny that there is such a thing as private epistemic blame. All I need to claim is that there is (also) such a thing as communicative epistemic blame and that understanding this species of blame is an important endeavor. Similarly, communicative blame is directed at someone other than the blamer. However, just as one can engage in moral self-blame, one can engage in epistemic self-blame. I accept this, but my present focus is elsewhere.

In Section 1.2.1, I reviewed three different accounts of what moral blame is, i.e., conative, emotion-focused, and functional accounts. Something similar is true of epistemic blame, and, strikingly, the alternatives to the communicative account of epistemic blame are similar to the alternatives to the communicative account of moral blame (cf. Brown 2020, 3612 n. 8).[29] First, we might subscribe to a conative account of epistemic blame. Take, for instance, the parallel to the Scanlonian relational account of moral blame. On this account, to epistemically blame someone is to negatively modify one's relation to the blamee in response to that person's perceived epistemic failings. As Cameron Boult (forthcoming, 11) puts it: "[O]ne's modification of [the expectation that others will be epistemically trustworthy] and corresponding intentions—for example, revising one's intention to epistemically trust the word of another person on a subject matter they seem to be prone to think dogmatically about—in a way made fitting by the judgment that one's

---

criticism of the blamee's foolish behavior. Possibly, not all responses that are relevant in the case of moral blame are relevant in the case of prudential blame; e.g., if I act foolishly in a way that is harmful to myself, I do not need to apologize to anyone else. Still, I can engage in collective deliberation, e.g., with my paternalistic blamer, about how to avoid similar imprudent behavior in the future. Additionally, one might ask whether one's prudential faults per se are anyone else's business. Paternalizers, of course, think they are.

[29] Brown (2018) defends an account of epistemic blame that is analogous to Sher's account of moral blame, i.e., "epistemic blame as consisting in a characteristic set of emotional and behavioural dispositions unified by a certain belief-desire pair" (Brown 2020, 3612 n. 8).

epistemic relationship has been impaired, just is what it means to epistemically blame that person for their epistemic failing."[30]

Second, on emotion-focused accounts of epistemic blame, to engage in epistemic blame involves certain negative reactive emotions to epistemically blameworthy failings such as wishful thinking or intellectual laziness (Nottelman 2007, 3; Rettler 2018, 2208). In narrow parallel with the, broadly speaking, Strawsonian account of moral blame, central to such negative reactions are epistemic resentment and indignation. Broader accounts might focus on other negative reactive emotions. Some might be skeptical about epistemic blame precisely because they think that epistemic blame would have to involve something like epistemic resentment and indignation, and they think that such emotions make no sense; or even if they do, we never have them; or if we do, these would not be fitting reactions.[31] Unlike moral blame, epistemic blame is "cool."

For what it is worth, I think epistemic blame can involve strong emotions. Suppose you're having a discussion with someone about some matter that is morally and prudentially nonsignificant, e.g., when the Jurassic period started. Surely, one can epistemically resent someone for being intellectually lazy, and sometimes people can even experience indignation about the way in which people are biased or sloppy in their cognition. Obviously, in many such cases the relevant epistemic failings go hand in hand with moral failings; e.g., it is not just that the employer has negatively biased beliefs about the qualifications of female applicants but also that this harms them or is morally disrespectful of them.[32] However, even when we set aside these morally relevant correlated facts, we can get quite worked up simply by learning about someone's epistemic failings; e.g., we can feel indignation about how someone happily accepts claims simply because they confirm this person's

---

[30] Incidentally, this account makes it clear that there is such a thing as epistemic forgiveness. To forgive in this sense is simply to undo the relevant intention to cease epistemically not trusting the word of another person on a subject matter they seem to be prone to thinking dogmatically about.

[31] One reason why one might think that such responses are never fitting is that our doxastic beliefs are not under our control, and that it makes sense to blame us only for that which is under our control. For convincing responses to this view, see Boult (forthcoming, 19); Brown (2020, 3597); Nottelman (2007); and Peels (2017). Also note that in the literature on moral reactive attitudes, resentment is experienced by the victims and is directed at their wrongdoers, whereas indignation is the third-party analogue to resentment. Similarly, one might say that epistemic resentment is directed against violators of epistemic norms who reason about matters pertaining to the holder of resentment, while epistemic indignation is a third-party analogue to epistemic resentment.

[32] Even in cases where epistemic and moral blame go hand in hand, we can establish that epistemic failings are an independent source of blameworthiness, e.g., by comparing cases that involve both epistemic and moral failings with cases involving only comparable moral failings. My conjecture is that the former involves greater blameworthiness, or additional forms of blameworthiness.

ideological views, even in the absence of any beliefs about whether their doing so is harmful or even beneficial to others.

Finally, one can provide a functional account of epistemic blame. According to an epistemic authority account of blame parallel to the moral authority account of moral blame, to blame an epistemic agent in that capacity is to issue a certain demand on that agent in addition to stating that the agent has violated a relevant epistemic norm. As with moral blame, issuing this demand involves positing an epistemic authority on behalf of the blamer over the blamee, i.e., the blamer can make a certain demand on the blamee, e.g., to account for their reasoning behind a certain claim, that results in the blamee now having some reason to comply with that demand.

As I did in my parallel survey of different accounts of moral blame, I submit that, for the central purpose of this section, I can set aside the differences between these accounts of epistemic blame. What is central for present purposes is that there is a distinction between merely judging someone to be blameworthy in relation to some epistemic standing and epistemically blaming that person. However, I do need this assumption, since, plausibly, epistemic hypocrisy does not undermine one's standing to engage in the former; e.g., if I merely point out that someone has failed to comply with a certain epistemic standard without demanding any uptake, my utterance cannot be dismissed on the ground that I too have failed to comply with that standard. Additionally, while I shall employ the authority view of epistemic blame, I do not need, or want to, deny that other views of epistemic blame capture important dimensions of epistemic blame that the epistemic authority account does not elucidate. Like moral blame, epistemic blame is complex—most likely because blame in general is complex.

This concludes my delimitation of what epistemic blame is and my defense of the claim that there is such a thing as epistemic blame. I now turn to the questions of whether there is such a thing as hypocritical epistemic blame and whether such blame is standingless. Here is a case—an adaption of my opening example of the carbon-dioxide-emitting philosopher in Section 1.1—that hopefully will persuade the reader that epistemic blame can be standingless in much the same way as moral blame: Jack is skeptical about whether climate change is anthropogenic. He realizes that virtually all climate scientists think scientific evidence speaks in favor of the latter hypothesis. He also knows that many who subscribe to the former hypothesis have vested interests in its being true (or, at any rate, believed). Jack has two siblings, Al and Greta. One day he has a phone conversation with Al, and then an hour later a conversation with Greta. During the first conversation, Al starts subjecting Jack to epistemic blame:

> Jack, you really should not be skeptical about whether climate change is the result of human activities. All the available scientific evidence clearly supports this view, and there are debunking stories to tell about many of the few so-called scientific studies that imply that climate change might be a purely natural phenomenon. Moreover, you do not even have or know of a credible causal account of natural changes in climate over the last fifty years. Alas, your skeptical stance is silly.

Amazingly, Greta makes the same complaint ad verbatim to and about Jack an hour later, when they have their conversation. Suppose Jack replies in the same way to both of his siblings:

> Perhaps I should accept that climate change is anthropogenic. However, I refuse to accept being held accountable for believing what I do by you. If you like, we can in impersonal terms discuss what the scientific evidence regarding the etiology of climate change suggests, but I refuse to address your blaming me for failing to comply with the relevant epistemic standards in question. I am simply going to ignore your epistemic blame.

If you think like me, you think that the following piece of information is relevant to how we should think (differently) of the appropriateness of Jack's replies to his siblings: while Al has sensible views on climate change as a general matter, he is extremely inclined to believe all sorts of conspiracy theories that somehow save his favored beliefs from obvious refutation. All in all, the mismatch between what evidence is available to him and what he believes is much greater than is the case with Jack. Greta, however, is a conscientiously critical and consistent thinker. On virtually no matter is there any glaring (self-serving or otherwise) gap between what she believes and what the evidence available to her implies she should believe. If we share an outlook in the relevant way, we agree that Jack's reply to Al might be appropriate (because he lacks standing to give it), while his reply to Greta is not. This is so even though the content of the blame that Al and Greta direct at Jack is identical. Greta has earned her epistemic right to blame Jack, whereas Al has done just the opposite, as it were.[33] While Greta has the standing to blame Jack for his excessive flying habits, Al has not. More generally, I accept the following claim:

> *The appropriate dismissal claim of hypocritical epistemic blame*: if X epistemically blames Y hypocritically for φ-ing, then, by virtue thereof, Y has a reason to dismiss X's blame.[34]

Just as dismissing hypocritical moral blame does not imply that the dismisser denies having done something morally blameworthy—the dismisser simply dismisses being held accountable by the blamer in question and might think that many others are well positioned to hold them accountable—dismissing hypocritical epistemic blame does not imply that the dismisser denies having failed to comply with epistemic norms. Whether or not they have done that is a question that is simply bracketed, and the dismisser's dismissal targets epistemic blame coming from the blamer in question and is consistent with the dismisser thinking that other individuals are well placed to hold them responsible for their intellectual laziness etc.

This concludes my brief defense of the claim that epistemic nonmoral blame can be hypocritical and that when it is, it can be indirectly dismissed as standingless. I now want to consider whether some of the other points I made about standingless blame apply to epistemic blame as well, e.g., whether epistemic blame is morally wrongful for reasons similar to why standingless moral blame is, and whether epistemic blame can be standingless for some of the same reasons other than hypocrisy that moral blame can be standingless.

The first question to ask about epistemic blame is whether hypocritical epistemic blame is *epistemically* wrongful, i.e., whether one violates any epistemic norms by engaging in hypocritical epistemic blame. I do not have a settled view on this matter. I believe that at least some cases of hypocritical epistemic blame might be epistemically wrongful, e.g., if it involves harmfully misleading other agents about the comparative quality of one's own

---

[33] Piovarchy (2022) argues that what undermines the standing of a hypocrite to engage in epistemic blame is the same as what undermines the standing of a hypocrite to engage in moral blame, i.e., lack of commitment to norms to which the blame appeals.

[34] As with hypocritical moral blame, this does not mean that the blamer has no standing to blame as such. The blamer has standing to blame provided they address their own relevantly similar faults in a manner proportionate to the way in which they address the faults of their blamee. Moreover, epistemic blame and standing to engage in epistemic blame most plausibly are thought of as a scalar matter (as is the case with moral blame—see Section 2.5—but here I ignore this complication).

testimony. However, I am not certain that all cases of epistemic hypocritical blame involve violations of epistemic standards; e.g., it is quite plausible that people known to be epistemic hypocrites will not mislead other people about the quality, comparatively speaking, of their testimony.[35] However, for present purposes I need not take any stand on this matter.

We might think that hypocritical epistemic blame is either always or typically morally wrongful in addition to being epistemically wrongful. I am persuaded by Jessica Brown's (2020) arguments for why not all cases of epistemic blameworthiness involve moral blameworthiness. Essentially, Brown zooms in on issues that are morally insignificant, e.g., whether the president is in New York, and where an individual has epistemically blameworthy beliefs about the matter, e.g., based on clairvoyance (Brown 2020, 3598). Plausibly, the individual is epistemically blameworthy even if the person is not blameworthy in any other way; e.g., the individual does not risk harming or disrespecting anyone by holding the relevant belief (Brown 2020, 3611–3612). However, that does not imply that hypocritical communicative epistemic blame is not morally wrongful—hypocritical epistemic blame in relation to beliefs about morally nonsignificant matters could be morally wrongful despite the moral nonsignificance of the substantive matter in question. The moral equality account that I discussed in Section 3.9 explains well why cases of hypocritical epistemic blame intuitively involve a moral wrong. The reason for this is that while we care about the basic equality of individuals with regard to the moral significance of their interests, e.g., in well-being, and the significance of their will, e.g., the moral significance of their consenting to being treated in a certain way, we also care morally about our basic equality as knowers, e.g., that, setting aside issues of differential expertise, my testimony counts for as much as yours does. Typically, if not always, hypocritical epistemic blame involves the hypocritical blamer subordinating the epistemic credentials of the blamee relative to their own, and this involves a denial of epistemic equality in a way that is disrespectful of the blamee.

It is true that usually discussions of equality of standing focus on our capacity as people with interests (in a prudential, nonepistemic sense) or will.

---

[35] It might be instructive at this point to compare Isserow and Klein's (2017; see Section 3.2) esteem-based account of the wrongfulness of hypocritical moral blame with a similar epistemic esteem-based account of the wrongfulness of hypocritical epistemic blame. Just as one can engage in hypocritical moral blame to boost one's moral esteem in the eyes of others, so can one engage in hypocritical epistemic blame to boost one's epistemic esteem in the eyes of others.

However, we also care about our standing as knowers, and this has come out clearly in the last 15 years' expanding body of literature on epistemic injustice.[36] To my mind, hypocritical epistemic blame is a central, so far not much explored form of epistemic injustice—one that often goes hand in hand with the moral wrongfulness of disrespecting someone's equal standing as a knower and, more broadly, as a rational being.

I now turn to the issue of non-hypocrisy-related sources of standingless epistemic blame. In Sections 4.2–4.6, I surveyed five ways other than hypocrisy in which a blamer's standing can be undermined, i.e., because the blamer has the same fault as the blamee (tu quoque—Section 7.2); the blamer is complicit in that which they blame the blamee for (Section 7.3); that which the blamee is blamed for is none of the blamer's business (Section 7.4); the blamer lacks understanding of the action for which they blame the blamee (Section 7.5); and, finally, the blamer does not accept the principle to which they appeal (Section 7.6). While I think epistemic blame can be standingless in all these ways, I am not sure that epistemic blame that is standingless in any of these ways is necessarily epistemically—or, for that matter, morally— wrongful. However, my present main concern is simply to examine whether standingless epistemic blame has the same sources as standingless moral blame.

Clearly, epistemic blame can be dismissed as standingless on grounds of the tu quoque, the no-understanding, and the no-acceptance conditions; e.g., if someone blames me for violating an epistemic norm that they themself reject, I am entitled to simply ignore their blame. I am entitled to do so in view of the fact that, by the lights of my blamer, I have violated no epistemic norm and, thus, have not acted in a blameworthy way, even if I myself accept the norm and thus must provide an uptake to the epistemic blame of others, who, like me, share the norm.[37] In the interest of brevity, however, I will focus on the two sources where it is less clear that there is an epistemic analogue to the source of lack of standing to engage in moral blame, i.e., the complicity and the no-business replies. I will argue briefly that while there is something like having no standing to blame epistemically because of one's epistemic complicity, there is no such thing as having no standing to blame

---

[36] Arguably, the starting point here was Fricker (2007).

[37] In this case, the blamer might have the standing to blame me for not reasoning in accordance with the epistemic norms that I accept, but as I noted in Section 4.6, this is a different criticism from the one that concerns us here.

epistemically due to the object of belief being none of one's business, epistemically speaking.

In many cases, people reason together. Suppose you and I reason together about the risks involved in vaccines. In defense of the claim that HPV vaccines are very risky, I describe a couple of cases of people who received HPV vaccines and then became ill—cases that have received much attention from vaccination skeptics. Initially, I question what one can infer from such cases and point to a double-blind, large-scale experimental study published in *Science* concluding that HPV vaccines involve no serious risk of side effects and are highly effective in significantly reducing the risk of cervical cancer. You dismiss my doubts, offering various unfounded conspiracy theories in response and eventually, we end up concurring that HPV vaccination is dangerous. Later you come back to me, having reached a more defensible view on the matter, and blame me for the shaky grounds of my vaccine skepticism. You are right, of course, that my beliefs on the matter are based on culpably, epistemically speaking, shaky grounds. However, that is not the issue—just as the moral wrongfulness of that for which one is being blamed by one's complicit partner is not at issue when one dismisses blame coming from the complicit partner. The issue is that, by virtue of your complicity in my believing as I do on insufficient grounds, I can dismiss your blame.

This leaves us with the none-of-your-business indirect dismissal of blame. If there is a similar source of lack of epistemic standing to blame, this would be because there are matters about which one ought not, epistemically (not morally) speaking, to form beliefs. I do not believe there are such matters. In short, I think that, unlike its moral analogue discussed in Chapter 4, the following view is true:

The universalist view: for any epistemic failing, any person is in a position to epistemically blame the agent of that act for this failing.[38]

---

[38] Boult (forthcoming, 3) takes a different view. He thinks that the none-of-your-business condition applies to epistemic blame as well and that "one person's epistemic failing can be another's business in virtue of the way it impairs their epistemic relationship," where he understands "impairment of epistemic relationship" along the line suggested by Scanlon's account of moral blame. Central to Boult's account is the idea of an epistemic division of labor. If Boult's view is taken to imply that one does not have the standing to subject others to epistemic blame when the parties have no epistemic relationship, then I would contend that people always stand in an epistemic relationship qua knowers (cf. Chuard and Southwood 2009, 623). This is consistent with saying that some matters are more of one's business than others, e.g., because one is cooperating to establish the truth about some matter. However, while we have an epistemic interest (however weak) in knowing any fact, we do not have a morally relevant interest in any matter. In support of Boult's view, one might note that often the epistemic faults of others have no impact on how I can achieve my epistemic aims and that in those cases, their epistemic faults are none of my business. I take the conspiracy example above to

This is not to deny that there are epistemic failings such that there are moral reasons why one should not subject the agent to epistemic blame in response to their epistemic failings; e.g., it might be the case that there are moral reasons why I should not subject a friend of mine to epistemic blame for being gullible in response to their beliefs about their partner's fidelity. However, I do not think that there are any matters that are none of one's business from an epistemic point of view.

Why should morality and epistemology be different regarding this potential source of lack of standing to blame? In Chapter 4, I noted that the no-business source of lack of standing to blame is different from some of the other sources. Specifically, I submitted that while the other sources of lack of standing that I have discussed all involve a certain feature by virtue of which one has lost the standing to blame that one had initially, e.g., one having acted in similar blameworthy ways, the no-business condition is different in that it points to the putative fact that one never had the relevant standing to begin with. There are moral norms, e.g., privacy norms, that imply that, in relation to certain matters, some persons have no entitlement to responses to their moral blame of others. I do not think that there are epistemic norms to this effect. Central epistemic norms of the sort that come up in the literature on epistemic blame, e.g., that one ought not to believe p if the evidence supports not-p, seem to permit any knower to form beliefs about anything and to epistemically blame others for whatever epistemic failings they may have.

This concludes my treatment of standingless epistemic blame. I have argued that there is such a thing as not having the standing to subject others to epistemic blame; that hypocritical epistemic blame is standingless and typically is morally wrong for the same reason as hypocritical moral blame; and that, setting aside the no-business condition, epistemic blame is undermined by the same sources as standing to engage in moral blame. The main takeaway point from this section is this symmetry between standing in epistemic and in moral blame. Specifically, this symmetry implies that any account of what undermines standing to subject to moral blame must be generalizable in the sense that it can also explain what undermines standing to subject others to epistemic or—generalizing further—simply nonmoral blame.

---

speak against this view. In my view, it makes perfect sense to blame conspiracy theorists epistemically even if we in no way rely on them for achieving our epistemic aims, and conspiracy theorists cannot dismiss the epistemic blame from others saying: "None of your business! You do not rely on us for achieving your epistemic aims" (cf. Boult 2021b, 11366—Boult admirably explicitly acknowledges a bit of bullet-biting on his part here).

The commitment account of lack of standing to blame has this feature. The standing-undermining feature it points to pertains not to the content of the relevant norms in question, but to how the blamer relates to those norms.

7.4. Consequentialism, Deontology, and the Interpersonal Nature of Holding Accountable

Suppose that the analysis that I have offered of the wrongfulness of holding accountable is correct. This has implications for wider issues in moral theory. More specifically, it shows that an important part of common-sense morality—that which pertains to our holding each other accountable— has a nature such that it is at odds with standard ways of drawing the distinction between consequentialist and nonconsequentialist—or, more specifically, deontological—moral theories and, thus, that, on the assumption that it is prima facie evidence against a moral theory if it fits considered moral intuitions badly, the present inquiry provides prima facie evidence against consequentialism *and* nonconsequentialism—at least as it is often characterized.[39] Obviously, it is not the first time a theorist points to the counterintuitiveness of consequentialism.[40] However, the specific dimension that I explore in this book has received far less attention than it deserves. Indeed, much moral theorizing has been conducted on the assumption that a crucial theoretical choice in moral theory is whether to accept consequentialism or deontology (or, more broadly, nonconsequentialism) as normally characterized. If I am right, this is a false choice.

In this section, I first set out the standard way of distinguishing consequentialist from nonconsequentialist moral theories. While doing so, I will explain why the normativity of standing is not only hard to capture in consequentialist terms, but also hard to capture in terms of two core elements of anticonsequentialist ethics, i.e., agent-relative constraints and agent-relative options. Next, I characterize the distinctive features of the interpersonal

---

[39] This methodological injunction follows from the idea of reflective equilibrium in some broad sense. Classical formulations of reflective equilibrium are found in Rawls (2000, 42–45, 507–508) and Daniels (1979).

[40] For prominent characterizations of the distinction between consequentialism and deontology, see Kagan (1989, 19–32; 1998, 70–78, 161–170); Kamm (2007, 14); Nagel (1986); and Scheffler (1982). Consequentialists have certain standard argumentative strategies that they employ in response, e.g., the distinction between criteria of rightness and decision rules (Railton 1984) and the related idea of a two-level moral theory (Hare 1981, 44–64), some of which I shall briefly touch upon.

normativity involved in the second-order norms pertaining to holding people accountable and discuss whether similar normativity can be found in first-order normativity. Let us start with a definition of consequentialism:

> An act is morally right (or morally permissible) if, and only if, it produces the best consequences. (Kagan 1998, 61; compare Parfit 1984, 24; Parfit 2017a, 374)

On this view, it is generally true that, in any given choice situation, one and only one act is morally permissible. It is not universally true, however, since there are choice situations where an agent has two or more choices available that are equally good and better than all other available choices. However, given a reasonable fine-grained ranking of the goodness of different outcomes, according to consequentialism it will very rarely be the case that more than one morally permissible choice will be available to a moral agent.[41] Moreover, those cases where an agent will have a choice between different courses of action that are morally permissible according to consequentialism will not overlap nicely with the much larger set of cases that exists according to common-sense morality. Some cases that belong to the former do not belong to the latter, e.g., cases where the same good and optimal results come from killing or not killing an innocent person. A much greater number of cases belong to the latter set, e.g., most cases of forgiveness where, intuitively, we think that it is both permissible for the victim of wrongdoing to forgive and permissible not to forgive despite the fact that one of these two options has better consequences than the other.

Which consequences are best, then? On a simple and perhaps the most common view among consequentialists, there is one and only one thing that is good and the more the better, and that thing is well-being, whether the well-being of persons or nonpersons. Among consequentialists who accept this view are utilitarians.[42] However, nothing in the definition of consequentialism rules out that factors other than well-being determine the goodness of consequences. Some consequentialists have argued that the degree to which people's well-being matches their level of moral desert determines the goodness of outcomes as well (Feldman 1997). The way in which desert influences

---

[41] However, there will always be at least one such option.
[42] Not all are, because consequentialists who accept an objective list account of well-being—at least if there are other elements on that list than, say, pleasurable mental states—are generally not seen as utilitarians.

goodness of outcomes need not be a simple additive way—essentially, you determine how much goodness an outcome contains regarding well-being and how much goodness it contains regarding desert and then you add the two numbers. It could instead interact—possibly in complicated ways—with other goodness-of-outcome-affecting factors such as well-being. And there are countless other factors that consequentialists might think determine the goodness of outcome.[43]

However, whichever substantive view consequentialists take on which factors determine the goodness of outcomes, there is a formal constraint on what such ranking must respect for the ranking to be part of a consequentialist theory of rightness: impersonality. The impersonality constraint says that the relevant sort of ranking of consequences does not vary across persons, i.e., the ranking is such that if Jack and John both correctly use the relevant theory of goodness to rank outcomes from worst to best, their rankings will be identical. In this way, consequentialism differs from

> *Ethical egoism*: an act is morally right (or morally permissible) if, and only if, it produces the best consequences *for the agent* (cf. Kagan 1998, 63).

Since often the consequences that are best for Jack are different from those that are best for John, when applying the relevant theory of goodness to rank states of affairs, they will rank them differently. This means that even if ethical egoism is identical to consequentialism, when it comes to the requirement to do what has the best consequences, its theory of goodness is a personal theory, not an impersonal theory. It is a theory of what is best for each and every individual, not a theory of what is impersonally best.

Essentially, nonconsequentialists reject consequentialism because they affirm either

> *Agent-relative constraints*: there are acts that are morally wrong (or morally impermissible) even if they produce the best consequences from an impersonal perspective (cf. Scheffler 1982, 80–114)

or (typically: in addition to)

---

[43] As a definitional matter, it is open to them to think that neither well-being nor desert determines the goodness of outcomes.

Agent-relative options: there are acts that are morally right (or morally permissible) even if they do not produce the best consequences from an impersonal perspective (Scheffler 1982, 22–24).

To use a standard example (Kagan 1998, 71): if we could save five innocent
patients from death by killing a sixth innocent patient and using her organs
to save the five others, the consequences would be better than if the sixth
patient survives and the five others die. Yet doing so is morally impermissible. It violates an agent-relative constraint against killing innocent people.
Similarly, if the sixth patient somehow killed herself through transplanting
her vital organs to the five other patients suffering vital organ failure, thus
saving their lives while ending her own, she would be bringing about the
best consequences. However, she would also be acting supererogatorily in
the sense that while she would be acting permissibly and admirably in doing
what she did, it would also have been permissible for her not to sacrifice her
own life to save a greater number of other people. Not doing so is permitted
by the agent-relative option.

The definition I have offered of agent-relative options above is formal
and does not say anything about which actions are permissible even if they
produce worse consequences than alternative actions. There are various
constraints on agent-relative options. First, most believe that while agent-
relative prerogatives apply to allowing harm to others, they do not apply to
doing harm to others; e.g., while the sixth patient is morally permitted to
refrain from sacrificing her life and thus allowing the five other patients to
die, she is not morally permitted to kill them to save herself (Kagan 1984;
1989, 186–194; Kamm 1985; Scheffler 1992). Second, there are limits to
how suboptimal the consequences can be for actions to still be permissible;
e.g., I cannot permissibly let someone die because saving them would cause
me slight discomfort (Kagan 1998, 78–84). Third, and most relevantly for
present purposes, what grounds the agent-relative prerogative is that the
consequences of not doing what is impersonally best are better from the
agent's perspective (Kagan 1989, 16). While the sixth patient might refrain
from sacrificing her life to save five others, because from her perspective it
is better that she survives and the five other patients die than that she dies
and the five others survive, it is not the case that the sixth patient can permissibly save a parrot instead of the five patients if she can save either the five or
the parrot. Thus basically, when nonconsequentialists defend agent-relative
prerogatives, what they defend is:

Agent-relative, agent-interest-based options: there are acts that are morally right (or morally permissible) even if they do not produce the best consequences from an impersonal perspective and produce better consequences from the agent's personal perspective.

These paragraphs provide a standard, thumbnail sketch of consequentialism and nonconsequentialism. It leaves out a huge number of details and complications, but it suffices for our purpose, which is to ask whether the normativity this study has found in relation to considerations about standing fits well with these understandings of consequentialism and nonconsequentialism.

I start with consequentialism. Here I can be quite brief, since, setting aside the standard consequentialist responses to its counterintuitiveness, clearly and unsurprisingly consequentialism is hard to reconcile with considerations about the morality of standing. First, recall that one way of dismissing blame, praise, forgiveness, etc. is by denying that the blamer etc. has a liberty right to blame (Section 1.3). In some cases, of course, blaming etc. would produce suboptimal consequences, but since what undermines standing to blame etc. is not the fact that blaming will produce suboptimal consequences, many cases of standingless blame etc. are cases where blaming etc. would produce better consequences than not blaming. Similarly, in dismissing blame etc. by denying that one has no duty to the blamer to respond, it is not the fact that responding to the blamer will produce suboptimal consequences that renders the blame such that the blamer has no standing to engage in it.

In response, some might say that consequentialism is not a theory about standing, but about the moral rightness (or permissibility) of actions, so the present fact simply shows that it has a different focus from that of an account of standing to blame etc. This takes me to my second point, which is that on my account of why standingless blame is wrong, the wrong-making feature that I have focused on is that central cases of standingless blame etc. involve relating to the victim of standingless blame as if they were an inferior, and that feature is very different from the feature of not producing the optimal consequences, which in a certain sense is the only wrong-making feature that exists according to consequentialism.

In response, some might say that, in a way, consequentialists could consider the fact that blame etc. is standingless to be a wrong-making feature. They could say that it is bad in itself if someone is subjected to standingless blame and, thus, that it is a pro tanto wrong-making feature of blame that

it is standingless. However, saying that would imply that one should min-
imize the number of cases of standingless blame etc., other things being
equal, e.g., by hypocritically blaming someone when that would result in
fewer instances hypocritical blaming overall.[44] However, this is not the way
in which we think about the morality of standing.

Another standard consequentialist reply would be to try to explain our
intuitions regarding standingless blame and our practice of dismissing it as
somehow better from a consequentalist perspective than our having different
intuitions and different ways of responding to standingless blame. I am skeptical of this reply. First and foremost, I am not sure how it really amounts to a
response to, say, the view that there is something wrongful about standingless
blame to argue that it is a good thing, consequentialistically speaking, that we
have this view. Of course, if part of the argument is an error theory of the view
in question, then that does amount to a reply. But then the claim about our
having this view being optimal from a consequentialist point of view seems
irrelevant. This takes me to my second reason for skepticism, which is that
while one can no doubt point to features of our present practice of dismissing
standingless blame that might improve outcomes from a consequentialist
point of view, e.g., that people become more inclined to attend to their own
faults than they would be if standingless blame were generally considered
no more dismissible than standingful blame, the number of factors and
alternatives that an argument for the optimality of our present practices must
take into account is daunting. Nothing remotely resembling an argument to
this effect has been offered and, thus, confidence that such an argument can
be offered cannot be based on an assessment of the strength of any known
argument. Partly for that reason, an error theory of the belief that our views
on standingless blame etc. are in some way optimal is more plausible—this
belief satisfies the theory holder's desire that their favorite moral theory can
avoid an objection—than an error theory of our views in question.

The discussion so far might be taken to show that the morality of standing
simply falls within nonconsequentialist theories as I defined them above.
Essentially, the morality of standing can be seen as giving rise to certain
agent-relative constraints against standingless blame etc. However, that
is inadequate. One reason why is that nothing in the morality of standing
implies that it is wrong or impermissible for someone who is subjected to

---

[44] At this point, I am skirting over some complicated issues about whether agent-relative
constraints can be consequentialized, as it were (Brown 2011; Portmore 2009).

standingless blame to provide an uptake to standingless blame. This might suggest that, in addition to certain agent-relative constraints, we should also include agent-relative options to provide an uptake to standingless blame etc. However, this suggestion is misleading for two reasons.

First, what grounds the permission to respond to standingless blame has nothing to do with the fact that from the blamee's personal perspective blaming is somehow better than not responding to standingless blame, something that happens to produce the optimal consequences. In some cases, responding to standingless blame is suboptimal not only impersonally, but also from the blamee's personal perspective. Yet the blamee is permitted to respond to the standingless blame to which they are subjected. Hence, the permission to respond to standingless blame must be grounded in something other than what grounds the agent-relative permission, e.g., the blamee's normative authority over a certain matter. True, that permission is a moral permission, but it is grounded in a way very different from the moral permission to save one's own life instead of that of five strangers.

Second, the crucial thing about many of the standingless acts that we have discussed, however, is not so much whether what the agent does is wrong or impermissible, all things considered, but the fact that they affect what it is wrong for other agents to do. In an obvious sense, consequentialists can agree that this is a possibility, since often what one agent does affects the consequences of the acts available to other agents and, thus, affects what they are morally required to do. However, the idea in relation to standing is that what an agent does, e.g., forgives the other agent for a wrong, can affect the moral rights and duties of the other agent, within certain constraints, irrespective of how the act of forgiveness changes the consequences of the acts available to other agents ("within certain constraints" because such changes affect moral permissibility too). If the victim forgives the wrongdoer, the wrongdoer might thereby be released from, say, the duty to apologize. And even where this is not the case, because the consequences of not apologizing are sufficiently bad, the duty to offer apologies is no longer owed to the victim, but either to those who would suffer the bad consequences or simply to no one at all. Hence, the following claim captures a way in which common-sense morality is nonconsequentialist and which is captured by neither agent-relative constraints nor agent-relative options:

Normative-authority-exercising acts: there are acts that affect what is morally wrong (or morally impermissible) for other agents to do independently of how they affect the consequences of what other agents do.

This claim contradicts consequentialism because consequentialism entails the following:

Any act that affects what it is morally wrong (or morally impermissible) for other agents to do affects which are the consequences of what these agents do.

This is entailed by consequentialism because if it were not true, then it would have to be the case that factors other than the goodness of consequences determine the wrongness of actions, and that proposition contradicts the definition of consequentialism. The existence of normative-authority-exercising acts is not entailed by the existence of agent-relative constraints and options. Moreover, since normative-authority-exercising acts are central to common-sense morality, this implies that many standard discussions of the distinction between consequentialism and nonconsequentialism omit a central aspect of common-sense morality.[45]

Not only is the morality of standing one that ascribes us normative authority of a kind like that involved in promising, consenting, etc. It also brings to attention how parts of morality are interpersonal in a way that is captured by neither agent-relative constraints nor by agent-relative permissions. By this I mean the relevant conversational rights and duties that characterize the normative relations between specific persons, i.e., the normative authority the victim of wrongdoing has to release the wrongdoer from the duty to apologize, but that third parties do not have, just as the victim of wrongdoing cannot forgive others' wrongdoers and thereby release them from their duties to apologize. The idea that agents can affect what is morally wrong (or morally impermissible) for other agents to do irrespective of *how* they affect which are the consequences of what other agents do, e.g., by blaming or forgiving, is absent from both consequentialism and from the two nonconsequentialist components of agent-relative constraints and agent-relative options. This is not to deny that morality does not partly consist of impersonal reasons as well and that these will sometimes, perhaps often, outweigh whatever moral

---

[45] Nagel (1986) can serve as an example.

reasons interpersonal relations involve. Indeed, from the very beginning of this book I emphasized that to say that blame is standingless is not to imply that it is not morally permissible, all things considered.

One specific issue where this comes up in relation to cases where blame is standingless due to hypocrisy etc. is the conditionality of moral norms. One central claim here is that one's liberty right to blame others for a certain wrong is conditional on one's moral conduct. Specifically, one might forfeit one's liberty right to blame if one is blameworthy oneself in a relevantly similar way. This sort of conditionality is, I have argued, quite central when it comes to our moral practice of holding people accountable. However, it is a sort of conditionality that applies not only to second-order moral norms, but also to first-order ones. Take the ethics of self-defense. Most believe that the right not to be subjected to harmful defensive force is conditional on not being blameworthy, causally responsible, or morally responsible for posing a threat to the potential imposer of harmful defensive force (Frowe and Parry 2021). Some people hold the view that while certain rights are conditional in this sense, not all are; e.g., the right not to be tortured is not conditional on not torturing others, one's own torturer included.[46] Second-order interpersonal morality of holding accountable is conditional in this sense through and through. Possibly, the same is true of first-order interpersonal morality, though I will not defend this claim here. My main concern here is to note that the sort of conditionality that we have encountered in relation to holding accountable is known from (part of) first-order morality as well.

7.5. Standing and Moral Encroachment

In closing, I want to illustrate the importance of the interpersonal dimension of morality embodied in the conditionality of norms by briefly discussing the issue of moral encroachment. Moral encroachment nicely connects issues of standing in general and standing in relation to epistemic norms (Section 7.3). Consider the following case by Rima Basu:

> *Conference*: The conference has ended, and the organizers have had the forethought to book a number of tables at a nearby restaurant so that conversation can continue over dinner. You're having a good time at dinner

[46] As we have seen (footnote 53, Chapter 3), Scanlon (2008) takes a view of this kind.

and, after a few drinks, you get up to use the restroom. As you return to your table, one of the diners, Jim, attempts to get your attention and says, "Where's my water? I asked for a refill fifteen minutes ago." For a moment you're confused, then it dawns on both of you what mistake has been made. Most philosophers don't look like you. With regard to melanin levels, you share more in common with the wait staff than your fellow diners. Given your skin color, the likelihood that you are a member of the staff rather than a fellow diner was high enough to seemingly make it rational for Jim to assume that you were a waiter, not a fellow diner. (Basu 2019a, 915–916; see also Gendler 2011)[47]

As Basu submits, Jim wrongs the conferencegoer (also) by virtue of his belief that the conferencegoer is a waiter (and not just by virtue of what he does, i.e., asking for the requested water) (see also Schroeder 2018, 116). Moreover, there seems to be something morally problematic about Jim's belief, even if he has good statistical evidence supporting it, e.g., evidence of such a strength that had he instead believed on equally epistemically strong grounds that the conferencegoer had an Ivy League university degree (or simply was not a waiter), then he would have been epistemically justified in doing so.[48] Moreover, nothing in the example hangs on Jim's belief being false. Even if the dark-skinned conferencegoer had in fact been a waiter, Jim would still have wronged the person.

One initial response to Basu's analysis of Conference is to say that it is odd how Jim could wrong his fellow conferencegoer if one cannot wrong someone by forming a belief about them that one is epistemically justified in forming and if the strength of evidence available to Jim was such that he would have been justified in forming many other beliefs about his fellow conferencegoer, e.g., that the person had an Ivy League university degree or was not a waiter.[49]

---

[47] To the extent that the reason why the conferencegoer feels wronged is that they somehow think—as many people do—that being a waiter is a less worthy profession than being a philosopher etc., this complicates moral assessment of the case.

[48] While *more* evidence is needed to be epistemically justified in believing that the person is not a conferencegoer, Basu does not rule out that, in principle, other conferencegoers could have *sufficient* evidence to believe it despite the risk of its wronging the person. Eliminating any risk of wrongful false beliefs in effect seems to imply a requirement never to hold demeaning beliefs.

[49] Another line of reply would be to claim that one can wrong by φ-ing only if one controls whether one φ-ies (cf. previous arguments regarding control, on the one hand, and forgiveness and epistemic blame, on the other). Since one does not control what one believes, one cannot, so the present argument goes, wrong anyone by believing something about them. Essentially, there are two ways of responding to this challenge (cf. Basu 2019b, 2508, 2513–2514). First, one can deny that "wronging"

In response, the moral encroachment theorist might accept that one cannot wrong someone by believing something about them that one is epistemically justified in believing, but deny that Jim is epistemically justified in believing that his fellow conferencegoer is a waiter. In defense of the latter claim, note that whether one is epistemically justified in believing a proposition depends on what is at stake in relation to whether it is true; e.g., to know that one can get to the hospital in less than ten minutes requires better evidence if one wants to go there because one has been bitten by a poisonous snake than if one wants to go there because there is a nice coffee shop nearby where one wants to enjoy a cortado. Similarly, given that dark-skinned conferencegoers are likely to feel demeaned if they are assumed to be waiters, more evidence is required for it to be epistemically justified for Jim to believe that a dark-skinned person present at the conference is not a conferencegoer than, say, that his typically white, male fellow conferencegoers hold PhDs from Ivy League universities on otherwise equally good evidential grounds. As Basu (2019a, 924) puts it: "The difference depends on the way in which members of marginalized groups are dispositionally vulnerable with respect to their self-descriptions while members of dominantly-situated groups are not. There is something more that is epistemically owed when it comes to our attitudes and beliefs towards members of nondominantly situated groups."[50] In failing to be sensitive to the vulnerability of minority people such as the dark-skinned conferencegoer, Jim adopts a diagnostic perspective on them—observes them as an object "to be studied, predicted, and managed," where in fact he owes it to them to adopt a participant stance toward them, where one thing that this involves is "according a certain importance to others' attitudes and intentions towards ourselves and being cognizant of those demands with regard to our treatment of others" (Basu 2019a, 920, 923).[51] In most

---

implies "can avoid." Second, one can deny that one does not exercise the relevant sort of control, e.g., indirect control, over what one believes (cf. Munch 2022).

[50] "Underrepresented groups are more often mistaken for employees because of the color of their skin and the racist institutions that make their skin color such a determining factor of their inability to gain access to more prestigious employment opportunities. Being mistaken in this context, namely one in which you've historically been excluded, is a moral wrong that is absent in spaces where that historical disadvantage is lacking" (Basu 2019c, 13).

[51] This takes on additional urgency when many others are likely to rely on the same generalizations. As Bolinger (2020, 2424) puts it: "The evidence used as grounds for accepting p can partially shape the pattern, disproportionately exposing an individual or group to repeated risks of the harms of that type of error."

situations, we owe it to others to adopt a participant stance toward them, also when it comes to our beliefs about them.[52]

While the general thrust of Basu's arguments is forceful, many of the details in her account could be disputed.[53] However, my aim here is to diagnose what makes Conference and similar situations ones that involve morally problematic doxastic attitudes that wrong the objects of those attitudes. Consider:

> *Mutual Mistake*: As in Conference, except this time Jim is Jill—a white woman—and the other conferencegoer—Jerome—is a dark-skinned man. They both asked for more water 15 minutes ago and are getting impatient. As they see each other they both address the other, saying simultaneously: "Where's my water? I asked for a refill fifteen minutes ago." As before, it may seem like a reasonable thing for Jill to assume that Jerome is a waiter, since few conferencegoers are dark-skinned and many waiters are. Similarly, it may seem like a reasonable thing for Jerome to assume that Jill is a waiter, since few conferencegoers are women and many waiters are.

The reason this case is interesting is that, on the one hand, there is something morally disturbing about this situation—it would have been in one way better, morally speaking, if only one of them or if neither of them had formed their relevant beliefs. If I could have made both Jerome and Jill avoid making their mistakes, I would have had some moral reason to do so. On the other hand, it does not seem that either of them wrongs the other; e.g., if both understand retrospectively what happened in the situation, it would be weird for either to complain about, as Basu puts it, the other's failing to adopt a participant attitude toward them.[54] Similarly, if two people hypocritically

---

[52] I find Basu's concrete analysis more persuasive than the appeal to an underlying distinction between diagnostic and participant stances. Plausibly, one can adopt a participant stance toward someone and still fail in various significant ways, as Jim does, to be sensitive to their interests and intentions.

[53] Some might think that the fault in question is merely moral—i.e., Jim is not epistemically blameworthy for forming the belief he forms even though he is morally blameworthy for acting on the belief given the risk of hurting the fellow conferencegoer—while others might think that the fault in question is purely epistemic—i.e., Jim is not epistemically entitled to form a full belief of the sort he forms solely on the basis of the statistical information available to him and this has nothing to do with the moral stakes in play (Gardiner 2018).

[54] Why not say that they both wrong each other? Jill commits a racist wrong against Jerome and Jerome commits a sexist wrong against Jill. In response, I could amend the example such that both make the same wrong against each other—suppose Jill is brown-skinned as well and Jerome for that reason too, and that reason only, infers that she is a waiter. (I am not suggesting that this is the right way to go, for reasons similar to those that came out in Section 2.6. I am just saying that this example might establish my main point without relying on the feature appealed to in this critical reply.)

blame each other, it would be weird for them to think that the other person wronged them and that, say, they can rightfully resent their fellow hypocrite or hold their fellow hypocrite accountable.

However, we can make sense of this somewhat ambiguous assessment of the situation. We can say that there are personal moral reasons to avoid harm to others, including the sort of relational harm that Basu plausibly submits is at stake in cases like the ones that we have discussed here, even when victims are not wronged by the person who harms them.[55] There might also be impersonal moral reasons to reduce the degree to which our social environment is one in which people form racist and sexist beliefs. This impersonal reason applies independently of whether the one who is subjected to relational harm relationally harms others, and its existence is why the situation is morally problematic. Moreover, while Jill and Jerome normally would have a complaint against the sort of belief being formed about them that is formed in Mutual Mistake, they have no standing to make that complaint in light of how they themselves form beliefs about others.[56] Accordingly, they do not wrong each other, morally speaking, just as two aggressors who culpably aggress against each other do not wrong each other.[57]

Second, suppose that you can either prevent Jill and Jerome from making their mistake or that you can instead prevent Joan and John, who never stereotype others in ways that are objectionable on moral encroachment theories, from being the objects of sexist (in Joan's case) and racist (in John's case) stereotypes. In this case, you should prevent the latter stereotyping, and the best explanation of that is that, unlike Joan and John, Jill and Jerome are not being wronged in my example. I thank Anne-Sofie Greisen Højlund and Lauritz Munch for pressing me on this point.

[55] In cases of self-defense, there is reason not to use more harmful means than necessary for a successful self-defense even if the employment of such means would be morally justified were they necessary for this purpose.

[56] Moss (2018, 197) focuses on the harms that individuals might suffer as the result of being confronted with "false statistical opinions about individual members of" their "racial group" without making any claims about whether racial profilers wrong those being subjected to racial profiling. Bolinger (2020, 2422) mentions both harms and wrongs, but makes it clear that at least one reason not to accept p when one cannot rule out not-p is that, "[m]orally, in doing so S fails to give adequate weight to A's moral claims, and recklessly imposes a risk of the error costs on A." Bolinger (2020, 2423) also stresses that accepting p without due epistemic care wrongs A, even if p is true: "She wrongs A if she accepts p without adequate justification. She's closed inquiry too early, recklessly exposing A to unjustified risk of suffering the harms involved in p-based mistakes."

[57] Basu (2019c, 15) writes that "there exists a neglected demand for extra care and diligence when believing things of others" as opposed to when believing something about non-(potential)persons. What I am suggesting is that while such a demand might typically exist in the sort of cases she has in mind, in some cases it is not a personal demand; i.e., it does not reflect a duty owed to the person about whom the belief is formed, and in some cases perhaps not more—perhaps even less (see next footnote)—care is impersonally demanded. (Basu [2019c, 18] might accept the second point; e.g., it might take less evidence to be justified in believing that a friend is trustworthy than to believe that a watch is trustworthy.) While these two claims are related, one could accept one without accepting the other.

My crucial claim here, however, is not about whether Jill and Jerome wrong each other. My central concern here is whether they are epistemically justified in believing what they believe about each other, and my claim is that the sort of conditionality involved in the norms that I have described in relation to second-order norms of holding accountable—whether in relation to moral or nonmoral norms, e.g., Section 7.4—applies to epistemic norms as well. We owe it to others to adopt a participant perspective when forming beliefs about them and, among other things, this involves "being more careful in our belief formation when it comes to members of nondominantly situated groups."[58] However, perhaps we (minority- or majority-identifying people) do not owe this—not even to members of nondominantly situated groups—if they themselves are careless in their belief formation when it comes to other members of nondominantly situated groups (cf. Bolinger 2020, 2428).[59] Or at least, people who themselves are members of nondominantly situated groups do not owe it to careless fellow belief-formers of similarly situated groups to be careful in their belief formation. As I have stressed, this is not to say that there are no moral reasons not to be careful—and, definitely, more careful than when forming beliefs about entities that cannot experience any relational harms—when forming beliefs about careless nondominantly situated agents. However, insofar as there are such moral reasons, these are not owed to these people—they have no claim rights against us that we form our beliefs about them in the relevantly careful way such that we wrong them if we do not; but this is due to there being impersonal moral reasons for not forming beliefs about persons in this way. If we fail to act on these reasons, bystanders and the relevant careless belief-forming agent are no differently located when it comes to holding us responsible. In a way, the present point is consistent with much of Basu's analysis. However, it amounts to an important clarification of the different moral concerns from which moral encroachment results and, thus, clarifies the different sources of epistemic wrongs and casts light on the

---

[58] It is an interesting question, then, whether Basu's view implies that in some cases less care is required for statistical beliefs about subjects to be true; e.g., suppose that the character of a certain majority member who tends to wrong others in their formation of beliefs about them would benefit significantly from being in the shoes of someone about whom others form negative, statistically based beliefs, e.g., that a certain type of person is dangerous. Perhaps in such cases one could know that this person is dangerous on the basis of less evidence than one could know that a pit bull terrier is dangerous (cf. Schroeder [2018, 126], who thinks that "the morality of belief, just like the moral encroachment on knowledge and epistemic rationality, works solely by making it harder to justify some beliefs—not by making it easier to justify others").

[59] Carelessness, if that is the right term, in relation to dominated and dominantly situated groups imposes relevantly different derivative requirements.

different ways in which moral considerations might interact with what is required for epistemic justification. Issues of standing arise also in connection with epistemic wrongs.

7.6. Conclusion

We have come a long way since we encountered Jack's hypocritical blame of Greta in Section 1.1. Hypocritical blame was this book's starting point and took center stage in the first three chapters. There I defended and clarified what I take to be a central feature of common-sense morality, i.e., that one can dismiss hypocritical blame even if one is blameworthy. I also argued that hypocritical blame is, as it is generally taken to be, morally deficient. Specifically, I have argued that it involves failing to relate to one's blamee as an equal. In the last four chapters I extrapolated some of the lessons from the first three chapters.

I argued that hypocrisy is not the only factor that undermines standing to blame and that blame is not the only illocutionary action that can be standing(less)—inter alia praise and forgiveness can be too. In this concluding chapter I have further expanded the scope of the analysis to look at encouraging people to act in certain ways—something that does not naturally seem to qualify as an act of holding responsible and need not involve any appeal to moral considerations—and I have looked at how standing influences non-moral norms regulating epistemic blame and norms regulating belief. I have argued that the notion of standing points to a central feature of our common morality that is hard to capture in consequentialist terms and that is typically ignored in standard discussions of central elements in nonconsequentialist theory. Specifically, I have argued that standing involves a particular kind of interpersonality and normative authority, which exists not only in relation to second-order moral norms pertaining to holding people accountable, but also in relation to first-order norms and might even be of relevance to wrongs involved in negative, statistically based beliefs about others. While hypocritical blame is an important topic in its own right, I hope that my attempt to show that standing applies to many other normative acts renders it more plausible to skeptics about the notion of standing to blame. I hope also to have highlighted a particular aspect of nonconsequentialist morality that deserves greater attention in future work.

Bibliography

Adams, Marilyn McCord. 1991. "Forgiveness: A Christian Model." *Faith and Philosophy* 8.3: 277–304.

Aikin, Scott F. 2008. "*Tu Quoque* Arguments and the Significance of Hypocrisy." *Informal Logic* 28.2: 155–169.

Aikin, Scott F. and Talisse, Robert. 2008. "The Truth about Hypocrisy." *Scientific American*, 1 December. https://www.scientificamerican.com/article/the-truth-about-hypocrisy/.

Allais, Lucy. 2008. "Wiping the Slate Clean: The Heart of Forgiveness." *Philosophy & Public Affairs* 36.1: 33–68.

Allais, Lucy. 2014. "Freedom and Forgiveness." *Oxford Studies in Agency and Responsibility* 2: 33–61.

Alterman, Eric. 2004. "The Hollywood Campaign." *Atlantic Monthly* 294 (September): 73–88.

Anonymous. Forthcoming. "Conversational Hypocrisy." *Philosophers' Imprint*.

Aspeitia, Axel Arturo Barceló. 2020. "Whataboutisms and Inconsistency." *Argumentation* 34: 433–447.

Austin, J. L. 1962. *How to Do Things with Words*. Oxford: Clarendon Press.

Bartel, Christopher. 2019. "Hypocrisy As Either Deception or Akrasia." *Philosophical Forum* 50.2: 269–281.

Basu, Rima. 2019a. "What We Epistemically Owe to Each Other." *Philosophical Studies* 176: 915–931.

Basu, Rima. 2019b. "The Wrongs of Racist Beliefs." *Philosophical Studies* 176: 2497–2515.

Basu, Rima. 2019c. "Radical Moral Encroachment: The Moral Stakes of Racist Beliefs." *Philosophical Issues* 29: 9–23.

Beardsley, Elizabeth Lane. 1970. "Moral Disapproval and Moral Indignation." *Philosophy and Phenomenological Research* 31.2: 161–176.

Beardsley, Elizabeth Lane. 1979. "Blaming." *Philosophia* 8: 573–583.

Bell, Macalaster. 2013. "The Standing to Blame: A Critique." In Coates, D. Justin and Tognazzini, Neal A., eds., *Blame: Its Nature and Norms*. New York: Oxford University Press: 263–281.

Bennett, Christopher. 2018. "The Alteration Thesis." *Philosophy & Public Affairs* 46: 207–233.

Bolinger, Renee Jorgensen. 2020. "The Rational Impermissibility of Accepting (Some) Racial Generalizations." *Synthese* 197: 2415–2431.

Boult, Cameron. 2021a. "There Is a Distinctively Epistemic Kind of Blame." *Philosophy & Phenomenological Research* 103.3: 518–534.

Boult, Cameron. 2021b. "Standing to Epistemically Blame." *Synthese* 199: 11355–11375.

Boult, Cameron. 2021c. "Epistemic Blame." *Philosophy Compass* 16.8: e12762. https://doi.org/10.1111/phc3.12762.

Boult, Cameron. Forthcoming. "The Significance of Epistemic Blame." *Erkenntnis* 88: 807–828. https://doi.org/10.1007/s10670-021-00382-0.

Brown, Campbell. 2011. "Consequentialize This!" *Ethics* 121.4: 749–771.

Brown, Jessica. 2018. "What Is Epistemic Blame?" *Noûs* 54: 389–407.

Brown, Jessica. 2020. "Epistemically Blameworthy Belief." *Philosophical Studies* 177: 3595–3614.

Brunning, Luke and Milam, Per-Erik. 2018. "Oppression, Forgiveness, and Ceasing to Blame." *Journal of Ethics and Social Philosophy* 14.2: 143–178.

Calhoun, Cheshire. 1989. "Responsibility and Reproach." *Ethics* 99.2: 389–406.

Calhoun, Cheshire. 1992. "Changing One's Heart." *Ethics* 103: 76–96.

Cassam, Quassim. 2019. *Vices of the Mind*. Oxford: Oxford University Press.

Cervantes Saavedra, Miguel de. 2008 [1605/1615]. *Don Quixote*. Hertfordshire: Wordsworth.

Chaplin, Rosalind. 2019. "Taking It Personally: Third-Party Forgiveness, Close Relationships, and the Standing to Forgive." In Mark Timmons, ed., *Oxford Studies in Normative Ethics*, vol. 9. Oxford: Oxford University Press: 73–94.

Chuard, Philippe and Southwood, Nicholas. 2009. "Epistemic Norms without Voluntary Control." *Noûs* 43.4: 599–632.

Coates, D. Justin. 2016. "The Epistemic Norm of Blame." *Ethical Theory and Moral Practice* 19: 457–473.

Coates, D. Justin and Tognazzini, Neal A., eds. 2013. *Blame: Its Nature and Norms*. New York: Oxford University Press.

Cohen, G. A. 2008. *Rescuing Justice and Equality*. Cambridge, MA: Harvard University Press.

Cohen, G. A. 2013. *Finding Oneself in the Other*. Princeton, NJ: Princeton University Press.

Crisp, Roger and Cowton, Christopher. 1994. "Hypocrisy and Moral Seriousness." *American Philosophical Quarterly* 31.4: 343–349.

Daniels, Norman. 1979. "Wide Reflective Equilibrium and Theory Acceptance in Ethics." *Journal of Philosophy* 76.5: 256–282.

Darwall, Stephen. 2001. "Normativity." In *Routledge Encyclopaedia of Philosophy*. https:// doi.org.10.4324/9780415249126-L135-1.

Darwall, Stephen. 2006. *The Second-Person Standpoint: Morality, Respect, and Accountability*. Cambridge, MA: Harvard University Press.

Dougherty, Tom. 2012. "Reducing Responsibility: An Evidentialist Account of Epistemic Blame." *European Journal of Philosophy* 20.4: 534–547.

Dougherty, Tom. 2015. "*Yes Means Yes*: Consent as Communication." *Philosophy & Public Affairs* 43.3: 224–253.

Dover, Daniela. 2019. "The Walk and the Talk." *Philosophical Review* 128.4: 387–422.

Driver, Julia. 1992. "The Suberogatory." *Australasian Journal of Philosophy* 70.3: 286–295.

Driver, Julia. 2016. "Private Blame." *Criminal Law and Philosophy* 10: 215–220.

Duff, R. A. 2003. *Punishment, Communication, and Community*. Oxford: Oxford University Press.

Duff, R. A. 2010. "Blame, Moral Standing, and the Legitimacy of the Criminal Trial." *Ratio* 23: 123–140.

Duus-Otterström, Göran and Kelly, Erin I. 2019. "Injustice and the Right to Punish." *Philosophy Compass* 14.2: 1–10.

Dworkin, Gerald. 2000. "Morally Speaking." In Ullmann-Margalit, Edna, ed., *Reasoning Practically*. New York: Oxford University Press: 182–188.

Elster, Jakob. Forthcoming. "You Don't Know What It Is Like!" on file with author.

Elster, Jon. 1998. "Deliberation and Constitution-Making." In Elster, Jon, ed., *Deliberative Democracy*. Cambridge: Cambridge University Press: 97–122.

Enoch, David. 2011. "Reason-Giving and the Law." *Oxford Studies in the Philosophy of Law* 1: 1–38.

Feldman, Fred. 1997. *Utilitarianism, Hedonism, and Desert*. Cambridge: Cambridge University Press.

Fragnière, Augustin. 2016. "Climate Change and Individual Duties." *WIREs Climate Change* 7: 798–814.

Frankfurt, Harry G. 1999. *Necessity, Volition, and Love*. Cambridge: Cambridge University Press.

Frick, Johann. 2016. "What We Owe to Hypocrites: Contractualism and the Speaker-Relativity of Justification." *Philosophy and Public Affairs* 44.4: 223–265.

Fricker, Miranda. 2007. *Epistemic Injustice*. Oxford: Oxford University Press.

Fricker, Miranda. 2016. "What Is the Point of Blame?" *Noûs* 50.1: 165–183.

Friedman, Marilyn. 2013. "How to Blame People Responsibly." *Journal of Value Inquiry* 47: 271–284.

Fritz, G. Kyle. 2018. "Hypocrisy, Inconsistency, and the Moral Standing of the State." *Criminal Law and Philosophy* 13: 309–327.

Fritz, G. Kyle and Miller, Daniel. 2018. "Hypocrisy and the Standing to Blame." *Pacific Philosophical Quarterly* 99: 118–139.

Fritz, G. Kyle and Miller, Daniel. 2019a. "When Hypocrisy Undermines Standing to Blame: A Response to Rossi." *Ethical Theory and Moral Practice* 22: 379–384.

Fritz, G. Kyle and Miller, Daniel. 2019b. "The Unique Badness of Hypocritical Blame." *Ergo* 6.19: 545–569.

Fritz, G. Kyle and Miller, Daniel. 2021. "Two Problems of Self-Blame for Accounts of Moral Standing." *Ergo* 8.54: 833–856.

Fritz, G. Kyle and Miller, Daniel. 2022. "A Standing Asymmetry between Blame and Forgiveness." *Ethics* 132.4: 559–586.

Frowe, Helen and Jonathan Parry. 2021. "Self-Defense." In Zalta, Edward N., ed. *Stanford Encyclopedia of Philosophy*. https://plato.stanford.edu/entries/self-defense/#GrouLiab.

Gardiner, Georgi. 2018. "Evidentialism and Moral Encroachment." In McCain, Kevin, ed., *Believing in Accordance with the Evidence: New Essays on Evidentialism*. Cham, Switzerland: Springer Verlag: 169–195.

Gendler, Tamar Szabó. 2011. "On the Epistemic Costs of Implicit Bias." *Philosophical Studies* 156.1: 33–63.

Goldberg, Sandy. 2018. *To the Best of Our Knowledge*. Oxford: Oxford University Press.

Govier, Trudy. 1983. "Ad Hominem." *Teaching Philosophy* 6.1: 13–24.

Griswold, Charles L. 2007. *Forgiveness: A Philosophical Exploration*. New York: Cambridge University Press.

Hare, Richard. 1981. *Moral Thinking*. Oxford: Oxford University Press.

Hellman, Deborah. 2008. *What Is Discrimination?* Cambridge, MA: Harvard University Press.

Herstein, Ori J. 2017. "Understanding Standing: Permission to Deflect Reasons." *Philosophical Studies* 174: 3109–3132.

Herstein, Ori J. 2020. "Justifying Standing to Give Reasons." *Philosophers' Imprint* 20.7: 1–18.

Hieronymi, Pamela. 2001. "Articulating an Uncompromising Forgiveness." *Philosophy and Phenomenological Research* 62.3: 529–555.

Holroyd, Jules. 2021. "Oppressive Praise." *Feminist Philosophy Quarterly* 7.4: 1–26.

Hughes, Paul M. and Warmke, Brandon. 2017. "Forgiveness." In Zalta, Edward N. (ed.) *Stanford Encyclopedia of Philosophy*. https://plato.stanford.edu/entries/forgiveness/#StanForg.

Isserow, Jessica and Klein, Colin. 2017. "Hypocrisy and Moral Authority." *Journal of Ethics and Social Philosophy* 12.2: 191–222.

Jeppsson, Sofia and Brandenburg, Daphne. 2022. "Patronizing Praise." *Journal of Ethics* 26.4: 663–682.

Jones, Karen. 1999. "Second-Hand Moral Knowledge." *Journal of Philosophy* 96.2: 55–78.

Kagan, Shelly. 1984. "Does Consequentialism Demand Too Much?" *Philosophy & Public Affairs* 13: 239–254.

Kagan, Shelly. 1989. *The Limits of Morality*. Oxford: Oxford University Press.

Kagan, Shelly. 1998. *Normative Ethics*. Boulder: Westview Press.

Kamm, Frances. 1985. "Supererogation and Obligation." *Journal of Philosophy* 82: 118–138.

Kamm, Frances. 2007. *Intricate Ethics*. Oxford: Oxford University Press.

Kelly, Erin I. 2018. *The Limits of Blame*. Cambridge, MA: Harvard University Press.

Khoury, Andrew C. 2022. "Forgiveness, Repentance, and Diachronic Blameworthiness." *Journal of the American Philosophical Association* 8.4: 700–720.

King, Matt. 2015. "Manipulation Arguments and the Moral Standing to Blame." *Journal of Ethics & Social Philosophy* 9.1: 1–20.

King, Matt. 2019. "Skepticism about the Standing to Blame." *Oxford Studies in Agency and Responsibility* 6: 265–288.

King, Matt. 2020. "Attending to Blame." *Philosophical Studies* 177.5: 1423–1439.

Kittay, Eva Maria. 1982. "On Hypocrisy." *Metaphilosophy* 13.3–4: 277–289.

Kolnai, Aurel. 1973. "Forgiveness." *Proceedings of Aristotelian Society* 74: 91–106.

Kukla, Rebecca and Lance, Mark. 2009. *"Yo!" and "Lo!"*. Cambridge, MA: Harvard University Press.

Laborde, Cécile. 2017. *Liberalism's Religions*. Cambridge, MA: Harvard University Press.

Lang, Gerald. Forthcoming. "Overrating Hypocrisy." On file with author.

Laurent, Sean M. and Clark, Brian A. M. 2019. "What Makes Hypocrisy? Folk Definitions, Attitude/Behavior Combinations, Attitude Strength, and Private/Public Distinctions." *Basic and Applied Social Psychology* 41.2: 104–121.

Lepore, Chiara and Goodin, Robert. 2015. *On Complicity and Compromise*. Oxford: Oxford University Press.

Liberto, Hallie. 2021. "Coercion, Consent, and the Mechanistic Question." *Ethics* 131.2: 210–245.

Lippert-Rasmussen, Kasper. 2013. "Who Can I Blame?" In Kühler, M. and Jelinek, N., eds., *Autonomy and the Self*. Dordrecht: Springer: 295–315.

Lippert-Rasmussen, Kasper. 2018. *Relational Egalitarianism*. Cambridge: Cambridge University Press.

Lippert-Rasmussen, Kasper. 2020. "Why the Moral Equality Account of the Hypocrite's Lack of Standing to Blame Fails." *Analysis* 80.4: 666–674.

Lippert-Rasmussen, Kasper. 2022. "Praising without Standing." *Journal of Ethics* 26: 229–246.

Lippert-Rasmussen, Kasper. Forthcoming. "A Duty Not to Remain Silent: Hypocrisy and the Lack of Standing Not to Blame." *Philosophical Quarterly*.

Littlejohn, Clayton. Forthcoming. "A Plea for Epistemic Excuses." In Dorsch, F. and Dutant, J., eds., *The New Evil Demon*. Oxford: Oxford University Press: 1–30. https://core.ac.uk/download/pdf/131198921.pdf.

Mackie, John L. 1967. "Fallacies." In Edwards, Paul, ed., *Encyclopedia of Philosophy* 3. London: Collier Macmillan Ltd.: 169–179.

Macnamara, Coleen. 2011. "Holding Others Responsible." *Philosophical Studies* 152: 81–102.

Macnamara, Coleen. 2013a. "Taking Demands Out of Blame." In Coates, D. Justin and Tognazzini, Neal, eds., *Blame: Its Nature and Norms*. New York: Oxford University Press: 141–161.

Macnamara, Coleen. 2013b. "'Screw You!' & 'Thank You.'" *Philosophical Studies* 165.3: 893–914.

Mason, Elinor. 2019. *Ways to Be Blameworthy*. Oxford: Oxford University Press.

McKenna, Michael. 2012. *Conversation and Responsibility*. Oxford: Oxford University Press.

McKenna, Michael. 2013. "Directed Blame and Conversation." In Coates, D. Justin and Tognazzini, Neal, eds., *Blame: Its Nature and Norms*. New York: Oxford University Press: 119–140.

McKiernan, Amy L. 2016. "Standing Conditions and Blame." *Southwest Philosophy Review* 32.1: 145–152.

McKinnon, Christine. 1991. "Hypocrisy, with a Note on Integrity." *American Philosophical Quarterly* 28.4: 321–330.

McKinnon, Christine. 2005. "Hypocrisy, Cheating and Character Possession." *Journal of Value Inquiry* 39: 399–414.

McNaughton, David. 1988. *Moral Vision*. Oxford: Basil Blackwell.

Milam, Per-Erik. 2019. "Reasons to Forgive." *Analysis* 79.2: 242–251.

Milam, Per-Erik. 2022. "Forgiving and Ceasing to Blame." In Satne, P. and Scheiter, K. M., eds., *Conflict and Resolution*. Cham, Switzerland: Springer: 143–164.

Misak, Cheryl. 2008. "Experience, Narrative, and Ethical Deliberation." *Ethics* 118.4: 614–632.

Moss, Sarah. 2018. "Moral Encroachment." *Proceedings of the Aristotelian Society* 118.2: 177–205.

Munch, Lauritz Aastrup. 2022. "How Privacy Rights Engender Direct Doxastic Duties." *Journal of Value Inquiry* 56: 547–562 .

Murphy, Jeffrie G. and Hampton, Jean. 1988. *Forgiveness and Mercy*. Cambridge: Cambridge University Press.

Murphy, Jeffrie. 1982. "Forgiveness and Resentment." *Midwest Studies in Philosophy* 7.1: 503–516.

Nagel, Thomas. 1979. *Moral Luck*. Cambridge: Cambridge University Press.

Nagel, Thomas. 1986. *The View from Nowhere*. Oxford: Oxford University Press.

Nagel, Thomas. 1998. "Concealment and Exposure." *Philosophy & Public Affairs* 27.1: 3–30.

Nelkin, Dana K. 2013. "Freedom and Forgiveness." In Haji, Ishtiyaque, and Caouette, Justin, eds., *Free Will and Moral Responsibility*. Newcastle: Cambridge Scholars Press: 165–188.

Nelkin, Dana K. 2022. "How Much to Blame? An Asymmetry between the Norms of Self-Blame and Other-Blame." In Carlsson, Andreas Brekke, ed., *Self-Blame and Moral Responsibility*. Cambridge: Cambridge University Press: 97–116.

Nottelman, Nikolaj. 2007. *Blameworthy Belief*. Dordrecht: Springer.

Novitz, David. 1998. "Forgiveness and Self-Respect." *Philosophy and Phenomenological Research* 58.2: 209–315.

O'Brien, Maggie. 2021. "Easy for You to Say." *Australasian Journal of Philosophy* 100.3: 429–442.

Pallikathayil, Japa. 2011. "The Possibility of Choice." *Philosophers' Imprint* 11.16: 1–20.

Parfit, Derek. 1984. *Reasons and Persons*. Oxford: Clarendon Press.

Parfit, Derek. 2017a. *On What Matters*. Vol. 1. Oxford: Oxford University Press.

Parfit, Derek. 2017b. *On What Matters*. Vol. 3. Oxford: Oxford University Press.

Peels, R. 2017. *Responsible Belief*. Oxford: Oxford University Press.

Pettigrove, Glen. 2009. "The Standing to Forgive." *The Monist* 92.4: 583–604.

Pettigrove, Glen. 2012. *Forgiveness and Love*. Oxford: Oxford University Press.

Pickard, Hannah. 2013. "Irrational Blame." *Analysis* 73: 613–626.

Piovarchy, Adam. 2020. "Hypocrisy, Standing to Blame and Second-Personal Authority." *Pacific Philosophical Quarterly* 101: 603–627.

Piovarchy, Adam. 2022. "Epistemic Hypocrisy and Standing to Blame." OSF Preprints. December 5. doi:10.31219/osf.io/xgd6e.

Piovarchy, Adam. 2023. "Situationism, Subjunctive Hypocrisy, and Standing to Blame." *Inquiry* 66.4: 514–538.

Portmore, Douglas W. 2009. "Consequentializing." *Philosophy Compass* 4.2: 329–347.

Quinn, Warren. 1993. *Morality and Action*. Cambridge: Cambridge University Press.

Rachels, James. 1975. "Why Privacy Is Important." *Philosophy & Public Affairs* 4.4: 323–333.

Radzik, Linda. 2011. "On Minding Your Own Business: Differentiating Accountability Relations within the Moral Community." *Social Theory and Practice* 37: 574–598.

Radzik, Linda. 2012. "On the Virtue of Minding Our Own Business." *Journal of Value Enquiry* 46: 173–182.

Railton, Peter. 1984. "Alienation, Consequentialism, and the Demands of Morality." *Philosophy & Public Affairs* 13: 134–171.

Rawls, John. 2000. *A Theory of Justice*. Rev. ed. Cambridge, MA: Harvard University Press.

Raz, Joseph. 1986. *The Morality of Freedom*. Oxford: Clarendon Press.

Rettler, L. 2018. "In Defense of Doxastic Blame." *Synthese* 195: 2205–2226.

Riedener, Stefan. 2019. "The Standing to Blame, or Why Moral Disapproval Is What It Is." *Dialectica* 73.1–2: 183–210.

Rivera-López, Eduardo. 2017. "The Fragility of Our Moral Standing to Blame." *Ethical Perspectives* 24.3: 333–361.

Roadevin, Cristina. 2018. "Hypocritical Blame, Fairness, and Standing." *Metaphilosophy* 49.2: 137–152.

Rossi, Benjamin. 2018. "The Commitment Account of Hypocrisy." *Ethical Theory and Moral Practice* 21: 553–567.

Rossi, Benjamin. 2020. "Feeling Badly Is Not Good Enough: A Reply to Fritz and Miller." *Ethical Theory and Moral Practice* 23.1: 101–105.

Rossi, Benjamin. 2021. "Hypocrisy Is Vicious, Value-Expressing Inconsistency." *Journal of Ethics* 25: 57–80.

Russell, Luke. 2019. "The Who, the What, and the How of Forgiveness." *Philosophy Compass* 15: 1–9.

Ryle, Gilbert. 1949. *The Concept of Mind*. Harmondsworth: Penguin Books.

Ryle, Gilbert. 1954. *Dilemmas*. Cambridge: Cambridge University Press.

Sagdahl, Matthea S. 2022. *Normative Pluralism*. Oxford: Oxford University Press.

Scanlon, Thomas. 2008. *Moral Dimensions*. Cambridge, MA: Harvard University Press.

Scanlon, Thomas. 2013. "Interpreting Blame." In Coates, D. Justin and Tognazzini, Neal A., eds., *Blame: Its Nature and Norms*. New York: Oxford University Press: 84–99.

Scheffler, Samuel. 1982. *The Rejection of Consequentialism*. Oxford: Oxford University Press.

Scheffler, Samuel. 1992. "Prerogatives without Restrictions." *Philosophical Perspectives* 6: 377–397.

Schemmel, Christian. 2021. *Justice and Egalitarian Relations*. Oxford: Oxford University Press.

Schroeder, Mark. 2018. "When Beliefs Wrong." *Philosophical Topics* 46.1: 115–128.

Searle, John and Vanderveken, Daniel. 1985. *Foundations of Illocutionary Logic*. Cambridge: Cambridge University Press.

Sher, George. 2006. *In Praise of Blame*. Oxford: Oxford University Press.

Sher, George. 2017. *Me, You, Us*. Oxford: Oxford University Press.

Sher, George. 2021. *A Wild West of the Mind*. Oxford: Oxford University Press.

Shoemaker, David. 2022. "The Trials and Tribulations of Tom Brady Self-Blame, Self-Talk, Self-Flagellation." In Carlsson, Andreas Brekke, ed., *Self-Blame and Moral Responsibility*. Cambridge: Cambridge University Press: 28–47.

Shoemaker, David and Vargas, Manuel. 2021. "Moral Torch Fishing: A Signaling Theory of Blame." *Noûs* 55.3: 581–602.

Sinnott-Armstrong, Walter. 2010. "It's Not *My* Fault." In Gardiner, S., Caney, S., Jamieson, D., and Shue, H., eds., *Climate Ethics: Essential Readings*. Oxford: Oxford University Press: 332–346.

Smilansky, Saul. 1994. "On Practicing What We Preach." *American Philosophical Quarterly* 31: 73–79.

Smith, A. M. 2007. "On Being Responsible and Holding Responsible." *Journal of Ethics* 11.4: 465–484.

Smith, A. M. 2013. "Moral Blame and Moral Protest." In Coates, D. Justin and Tognazzini, Neal, eds., *Blame: Its Nature and Norms*. New York: Oxford University Press: 27–48.

Statman, Daniel. 1997. "Hypocrisy and Self-Deception." *Philosophical Psychology* 10.1: 57–75.

Statman, Daniel. 2023. "Why Disregarding Hypothetical Blame Is Appropriate." *Ratio* 36.1: 32–40.

Statman, Daniel. Forthcoming. "The Moral Standing to Blame: An Attempt at Resolution."

Strawson, P. F. 1962. Freedom and Resentment. *Proceedings of the British Academy* 48: 1–25.

Szabados, Béla. 1979. "Hypocrisy." Canadian *Journal of Philosophy* 9.2: 195–210.

Tadros, Victor. 2011. "Poverty and Criminal Responsibility." *Journal of Value Inquiry* 43.3: 391–413.

Taylor, Gabrielle. 1981. "Integrity." *Proceedings of the Aristotelian Society* 55: 143–159.

Telech, Daniel, and Tierney, Hannah. 2019. "The Comparative Nonarbitrariness Norm of Blame." *Journal of Ethics and Social Philosophy* 16.1: 25–43.

Tierney, Hannah. 2021. "Hypocrisy and Standing to Self-Blame." *Analysis* 81.2: 262–269.

Todd, P. 2019. "A Unified Account of the Moral Standing to Blame." *Noûs* 53.2: 347–374.

Tognazzini, Neal A. Forthcoming. "On Losing One's Moral Voice." https://core.ac.uk/download/pdf/231877459.pdf: 1–20.

Tosi, Justin and Warmke, Brandon. 2016. "Moral Grandstanding." *Philosophy & Public Affairs* 44.3: 197–217.

Turner, Dan. 1990. "Hypocrisy." *Metaphilosophy* 21.3: 262–269.

Twambley, P. 1976. "Mercy and Forgiveness." *Analysis* 36.2: 84–90.

Upadhyaya, Kartik. 2020. "What Is Wrong with Hypocrisy." PhD dissertation, Warwick University.

Waldron, Jeremy. 1981. "A Right to Do Wrong." *Ethics* 92.1: 21–39.

Walker, Margaret Urban. 2013. "Third Parties and the Social Scaffolding of Forgiveness." *Journal of Religious Ethics* 41.3: 495–512.

Wallace, R. J. 1994. *Responsibility and the Moral Sentiments*. Cambridge, MA: Harvard University Press.

Wallace, R. J. 2010. "Hypocrisy, Moral Address, and the Equal Standing of Persons." *Philosophy & Public Affairs* 38: 307–341.

Warmke, Brandon. 2016. "The Normative Significance of Forgiveness." *Australian Journal of Philosophy* 94.4: 687–703.

Watson, Gary. 1996. "Two Faces of Responsibility." *Philosophical Topics* 24: 227–248.

Watson, Gary. 2004. *Agency and Answerability*. Oxford: Clarendon Press.

Watson, Gary. 2013. "Standing in Judgment." In Coates, D. Justin and Tognazzini, Neal A., eds., 2013. *Blame: Its Nature and Norms*. New York: Oxford University Press: 282–302.

Watson, Gary. 2015. "A Moral Predicament in the Criminal Law." *Inquiry* 58.2: 168–188.

Zagzebski, Linda. 1996. *Virtues of the Mind*. Cambridge: Cambridge University Press.

Zaragoza, Kevin. 2012. "Forgiveness and Standing." *Philosophy and Phenomenological Research* 84.3: 604–621.

Index

For the benefit of digital users, indexed terms that span two pages (e.g., 52–53) may, on occasion, appear on only one of those pages.